Coaching for Learning

Also available from Continuum

Coaching Solutions, Will Thomas and Alistair Smith
Coaching Solutions Resource Book, Will Thomas

Coaching for Learning

A Practical Guide for Encouraging Learning

Jacquie Turnbull

continuum

Continuum International Publishing Group

The Tower Building   80 Maiden Lane, Suite 704
11 York Road   New York, NY 10038
London
SE1 7NX

www.continuumbooks.com

British Library Cataloguing-in-Publication Data
A catalogue record for this book is available from the British Library.

ISBN: 9781847061065 (paperback)

Library of Congress Cataloging-in-Publication Data
Turnbull, Jacquie.
  Coaching for learning : a practical guide for encouraging learning / Jacquie Turnbull.
     p. cm.
  Includes bibliographical references.
  ISBN 1-84706-106-0 (pbk.)
1. Learning. 2. Motivation in education. 3. Reflective teaching. I. Title.

  LB1060.T87 2009
  370.15′23–dc22

                                     2008045241

Typeset by YHT Ltd, London
Printed and bound in Great Britain by CPI Antony Rowe, Chippenham, Wiltshire

Contents

Acknowledgements

At the beginning this book was mainly for my own benefit. I had been involved in the launch of the Learning Coach training for Welsh Assembly Government – following consultations with practitioners across Wales I was part of a team of academics and trainers who wrote the modules and delivered the training. As with many things, the training had been conceived and delivered at quite a pace to meet the requirements of government. Since I'm the sort of person who likes to reflect on what I'm doing, it was a process that left me mentally with some loose ends, some loops that needed closing for my own satisfaction.

Even though the book was to satisfy my own need for closure, it plainly needed contributions from many others for it to come into existence. My role has been to attempt to distil their ethos and practice into a framework for working with young people: a framework that would serve to clarify my own thinking processes, and at the same time a framework that will hopefully provide a guidebook for anyone else embarking upon a similar educational endeavour.

So the initial impetus was the Learning Coach training, and the whole project wouldn't have happened without the leadership of Danny Saunders at the University of Glamorgan and the managerial expertise of Aly Acreman. Danny Saunders has subsequently produced a comprehensive report on the whole operation, and I am grateful to him for allowing me to draw on the report for the final appendix of this book.

There was a team approach to the whole Learning Coach project, and I enjoyed the stimulus of working with colleagues from Cardiff University, UWIC in Cardiff and University of Wales, Newport. The first drafts of my ideas were firmed up in discussions with members of the training team: Steve Ferrugia, Anne Dawson, Ann George, Gwyneth Spadato-Dutturi, Richard Waller and Helen Williams. I am grateful to Anne, Ann, Richard and Helen for allowing me to use their insight and examples of their practice, and for reading and making constructive comments on first drafts. They have been a stimulus for creativity – and provided emotional support with the group hugs!

In a wider field, there are many people who have gone out of their way to respond to my research needs and I am indebted to them for their personal and practical support. Conversations with Gary Brace at the General Teaching Council for Wales evolved into one of the appendices, and Hayden Llewellyn has given invaluable practical support in my research. The Principal of Coleg Glan Hafren, Malcolm Charnley, has been unfailing in his personal encouragement, and I am grateful to

David Newman at the college for graciously allowing me to draw on his technical expertise for the diagrams. My research of course involved many pleasurable moments, and I particularly enjoyed the time I spent with Year 5/6 at Oakfield Primary School in Barry. Their teacher Michael Chapman readily shared his experience with me, and took time to make the necessary arrangements for me to feature the children's art work. I feel that the contributions from Rachel Dodge of St David's College and Rachel Mitchell of Hawthorn Primary School have clearly articulated the enthusiasm of enlightened teachers keen to progress their own learning and professional development.

You will see that I have used the appendices to describe the work of people who are making a difference in working with young people. Mandy Scanlon at the Sorted Project, Siriol Burford and Karen Marsh at Ysgol Plasmawr and Asha Ali at Fitzalan High School were all generous with their time. I am grateful to Melissa Buckwell and Angela Taylor for allowing me to quote from their reflections on their work as Learning Coaches. I hope the descriptions I have written provide a small tribute to the work they are all doing.

I am sure that those who have been responsible for my own training and continuing development in recent years will recognize that their influence resonates in these pages. Liz Burns and Ian Newton were patient and caring trainers when I followed their courses to become a Master Practitioner and Certified Trainer in Neuro-linguistic Programming. I appreciate their generosity in allowing me to reproduce their original material.

There are of course many others whose influence permeates the pages of this book: teachers and trainers I have worked with, the young people I have encountered over many years teaching in high school and in university and, latterly, people working in various roles in education in Wales who I met when they were taking the Learning Coach training. They have all played their part in the overall experience I have drawn on in constructing this text, and without them it would not have come into existence.

I do of course have a special word of thanks for those close to me who have given personal support. I have been buoyed throughout a lengthy endeavour by the unfailing enthusiasm and encouragement of friends. To my loyal family I offer my apologies if I have neglected them in my concentration on this project; they have been tolerant and patient with me, and always kept me grounded in reality.

So many people contributed to this book, whether they know it or not, though the final responsibility for what is written is very much my own.

Introduction

Half way through writing this book I decided to start again. It had become a bit like our modern world – so complex and busy that I was in danger of losing the plot. So I started again and concentrated on the questions I really wanted to address. The questions that really concerned me and that concern many other people: why, with all our material resources in the Western world, do we also have the most unhappy young people? Why have our systems of state schooling become so irrelevant for many young people that they vote with their feet? Not only that, why do thousands of professionals working in education either find it such a stressful occupation that they are unable to cope, or remain, going through the motions, marking time until their retirement?

Of course, not everything is doom and gloom, and in researching this book, I have been fortunate to experience the other side of the coin. I have sat in with a class of young people of diverse abilities – including serious behavioural issues and special education needs – where there was a buzz of excitement at the thrill of learning. I have got to know teachers who have such a passion for the well-being of young people that they enthuse everyone around them to higher efforts. I know counsellors and mentors who maintain unlimited patience in supporting young people through serious difficulties so that they are able to continue their pursuit of educational achievement.

So when I took a step back from where I was getting bogged down in too much detail I decided to focus on the most important elements. I needed to get a clearer sense, an overarching framework for working with young people that would incorporate the knowledge we now have about the optimum conditions for learning. It needed to be an approach that would not be circumscribed by the structures of systems of schooling, or by role descriptions; rather it would take the learner as the focus, and the realisation of learning potential as the outcome. I also wanted to be able to identify what it was about certain people that meant they were able to infuse young people with a joy of learning, keep them motivated and on track, and at the same time maintain their own enthusiasm and energy for educational endeavour.

One thing I remain convinced about is that we can't wait for the reform of systems of schooling. Despite all the different initiatives that have been introduced in the UK – including 20 different Education Acts over 20 years – the education system as a whole remains remarkably resistant to change. The basic format and 'script' for education have not changed for decades; the system clings to features even though the original purpose may be lost and forgotten. We have to develop individuals *within* the structure; we can't wait for reform of the structure to establish fundamentally different ways of working. The young people currently experiencing schooling can't afford to lose out while we wait for the optimum solutions to the organisation of state education.

So the focus of this book became: what can we do **now** to facilitate a better educational experience and solutions for the young people we come into contact with? What are the common factors that all of us can apply in our work – whatever our designated role – that will help young people to be more personally involved in their learning? And in the process, can we maintain our interest and enthusiasm in role-modelling the attitudes of active and self-motivated learners?

Of course it is essential that the answers to these questions are not based on personal preferences alone. 'Evidence-based practice' has been one of the buzz-words of the 21st century and policy makers have increasingly stressed that decisions in policy and practice need to be based upon evidence from research. As you will see from this book, some of the research that influenced educational practice no longer appears as relevant as it did in the past. Other theories and concepts have taken their place that appear more relevant in our modern world. But people working in education don't just base their practice on the results of research; their work also evolves from their own experience of what works; they will hone their skills and expertise into their own 'practice-based evidence''

Such professional expertise doesn't evolve from merely routinized actions. It evolves because successful people take the time to think about what they are doing, and why they are doing it. We all need to be reflective practitioners; reflection can stir us when practice may have become routine; we need to be able to question why we do things the way we do, we need to challenge why we keep doing the same things even when they may not be getting the results we desire. Most importantly, reflection means we take the time to examine our beliefs and values – about education, about young people, and about ourselves.

So this book is my own moment of reflection, written in the hope that it will encourage you to reflect on your own practice. It is not about presenting a clutch of techniques for working with young people, although there *are* very effective techniques featured. Techniques are rarely effective if practised in isolation from an examination of the theory and beliefs that underpin them. Rather this book is about reviewing the knowledge we have at the present time about how learning occurs, articulating a set of beliefs and values, and devising a framework for working with young people on their learning.

In coming back to this book, I have also drawn away from devising a model of coaching for learning for use with a particular age group, or for use by people with a particular job description. This is an important point for me because I believe we need to have a shared philosophy of learning across all professional practice. The main value in breaking things down into smaller and smaller sub-sets and classes, and allocating 'specified work' to particular groups of people, is that it aids the management of large institutions. For me, placing young people into categories does them a disservice if it distracts us from a holistic approach to their learning. An example has been in the way of thinking about learning styles; no sooner do we latch on to a useful metaphor for understanding someone's learning, than we create a 'box' to put them into. There's a comfort zone for us in being able to say 'Ah yes, of course, he/she's a visual / auditory / kinaesthetic learner, that's why they do things the way they do'. It can be a convenience, but unfortunately, it's a convenience that blinds us to the unique complexity of each individual.

So I would invite you to consider what is offered in this book in the context of your own work with young people – whatever their age group and whatever your particular professional occupation. You will find that, rather than providing definitive answers to a set of problems, this book suggests a framework that can be applied broadly for work with young people. The book has two main parts: Part I sets out the context in which we work in education, reviews our understanding of learning, and identifies the features of a model of coaching as it sits alongside teaching and mentoring. Part II follows through to deal with the practice as conceived in the CARE model. In the Appendices you will find examples of different people, working in different contexts, who are adapting their practices to support the learning of young people. They are just examples of the many people I have talked to about their work in trying to synthesize disparate elements of good practice into a model of coaching. The common factor that motivates them and underpins all their work is a desire to help young people realise their learning potential.

Most of all, I hope this book will throw down a series of challenges. A challenge to you to consider whether you access the latest research to inform your practice; a challenge to reflect on how your beliefs and values have been fostered, and whether they still serve you as a relevant and congruent basis for your work with young people; a challenge to consider whether you have kept up an enthusiasm for your own learning and development so that you provide an active and self-motivated role model for young people. If not, I hope this book will provide a stimulus for you to recapture and revitalize your joy in learning to motivate your students and stimulate your professional development.

PART I – THE CONTEXT

1 Why coaching for learning?

O! This learning, what a thing it is.
William Shakespeare[1]

> If you are the sort of person who likes to see an overview or the 'big picture' first, this first section of the book will draw your interest. You may also want to satisfy a 'Why?' question before you read any further, so this chapter will aim to answer that question.
>
> On the other hand, you may be a person who prefers to get a grasp of the details first. In which case you may be thinking that you'll skip this section in order to get to more detailed chapters.
>
> Self-awareness is a central part of learning – and also central to working with other learners. The special way you have become accustomed to thinking and learning will be personal to you, and will influence how you feel about this book, just as it influences everything you do. You may feel a need to gather the details first, or you may have found you understand better if you take a step back to get the whole picture. To use a favourite metaphor of mine, you may like to be down in the forest among the denseness of the undergrowth, or you may prefer hovering in the helicopter taking a panoramic view. The challenge in working with people – whether teaching, training or coaching – and of course in writing – is being able to respond to a range of unique and individual ways of thinking and learning.

We now live in an era of 'personalized learning'. The worlds of business and the professions have accepted that developing the individual rather than formal training is a more realistic response to the diverse and fast-changing nature of life and work in the twenty-first century. Within education, 'personalized learning' is a policy that incorporates assessment for learning, improving students' higher order thinking skills, and developing strategies for consulting students about their education.[2] These form part of an approach that can be seen as enhancing the 'learning journey' through school: an approach where teaching and learning are seen as integrated processes, with more awareness of the needs of learners, i.e.

> 'The learning journey' refers to a more profound form of educational experience, for whilst successful learning may result in confidence, pleasure and a sense of achievement, persistent failure may lead to low self-esteem, apathy, avoidance or aggressions. Here we are dealing with the cumulative formation of the person as a learner, with each child's sense of themselves and of their capacities – their 'learning identity'.
>
> Andrew Pollard 2008: 171–2

In the business and professional worlds, this broader approach can be recognized in the increasing use of coaching as a strategy for enhancing life and improving work effectiveness.[3] Education is following this trend: in schools coaching is beginning to be recognized as an approach that can enhance the delivery of a 'personalized learning' policy and encourage the development of 'learners for life'.

We are also living through a 'skills renaissance'. It is some years since I heard the prediction that skills would be 'quantum';[4] since then the drive to develop a highly skilled workforce to enable countries to exist and thrive in a competitive global marketplace has become a powerful movement. It has become the driver of government policies and employment practice, which in turn is influencing education and schooling, demanding a significant change of emphasis in what are seen as appropriate outcomes for state education. It has influenced every sector of education, from early years though to lifelong learning.[5]

But the focus on skills is not just to raise the ability of people and countries to compete in a global marketplace, we also have to recognize that we need to prepare young people for a future none of us can even imagine. Change has become the only constant factor we can depend upon. If we cannot conceive of the future ahead of us, the best way we can prepare young people is to encourage them to understand and take responsibility for their own learning. To be able to cope with an unknown future they will need to be adaptable, and have the confidence to learn how to learn in an infinite variety of situations. As Albert Bandura (1995: 17) has put it:

> A major goal of formal education should be to equip students with the intellectual tools, efficacy beliefs, and intrinsic interests to educate themselves throughout their lifetime. These personal resources enable individuals to gain new knowledge and to cultivate skills either for their own sake or to better their lives.

So this book is a response to these trends: the trend to personalized learning, the trend to develop advanced skills for work and life and the need to prepare young people with the flexibility and capacity to live successfully in an unknown future.

The CARE model of coaching has been developed as a response to these needs. In the context of education, coaching has mainly been taken up to improve the performance of teachers and managers. Most books that cover coaching in education deal with this aspect. In this book the focus is on how coaching can be used to develop learning for young people. While this is in response to the trends in the wider world, it is also because of my conviction that a coaching approach provides a realistic response to the varied learning needs which may encompass achievement of academic/vocational qualifications, development of skills or attention to personal, emotional and social development.

> The only person who is educated is the person who has learned how to learn; the person who has learned how to adapt and change; the person who has realized that no knowledge is secure, that only the process of seeking knowledge gives a basis for security.
>
> Carl Rogers and Jerome Freiberg 1994: 152

Focusing on solutions not problems

There must be a vital element missing in the way we educate young people if we take account of the outcomes of our education system. In the UK it's been reported that 120,000 11-year-olds still leave primary school unable to read or write properly, and one in five young people will finish 12 years' education too illiterate and innumerate to function properly in the adult world (Mary Riddell 2007). Closer scrutiny of statistics reveals significant differences in achievements between boys and girls, and between ethnic minorities. Overall, significant increases in spending on education have produced 'almost no acceleration' in the performance of pupils (Anushka Asthana 2007). Sadly, research findings also suggest that the UK has the highest percentage of unhappy young people (Unicef 2006). Unhappiness and unfulfilled potential mean wasted resources – a waste of individual talent and future potential, a loss to communities and countries.

In many ways, these outcomes suggest an education system that has not kept pace with the rapid cultural, social and technological changes of the latter part of the twentieth century: a system that still clings tenaciously to a structure and practices designed for a previous era. Yet while the structure may be slow to change, there is of course widespread recognition that the outcomes of education for young people need to be vastly different to meet the changing social situation:

> Our present 'crisis in schools' partly relates to the collapse of the old factory system and the recognition that successful workers now have to have more than just basic skills and an amenable attitude, which is largely what was required of their parents and grandparents.
>
> John Abbot and Terry Ryan 2000:266

However, keeping a focus on a 'crisis', means focusing on a problem. And the more you talk about problems the bigger and more difficult they seem to become (Jackson and McKergow 2007: 24). Constant analysis of a problem can often lead to paralysis – being problem-focused can serve to make the problem appear so large and intractable that it stifles any positive action. Rather than dwelling on the question 'With all our advantages, why aren't we doing better?' I prefer to ask 'What are we doing now that has the seeds of the solution?' Applying this to individual young people, I believe a coaching approach can nurture the seeds of the solution that are already there. Coaching can provide the additional and vital element – the difference that makes the difference.

Education rather than schooling

Although the term we use for our state system is 'education', what it's really about is 'schooling'. Government policies and the way schooling is organized place emphasis on consistency, conformity and compliance. In one way this is not surprising since schooling as a state 'system' is fundamentally the same as it was 150 years ago. Despite initiative following initiative, and an experience of change being the only constant factor, the basic structure and system of how we organize state schooling remains much the same. Despite general acceptance of the value of personalized learning, there is a tension in trying to establish this as a policy within an education system that can be said to echo the Fordist principles of standardized mass production:

> This means that personalised learning is delivered in a culture of public service which traditionally fits the individual to the system – not the other way round.
>
> Mike Gibbons 2004: 3

Certainly an experience of working in the school system may seem to be one of constant government intervention. Up until the last quarter of the twentieth century, this intervention stopped at the school gate. Since then, and particularly since the introduction of a National Curriculum in the UK, government policy has dictated not just *what* should be taught but – as in the example of the Literacy and Numeracy

Strategies in England – *how* to teach it. So the flexibility to respond to individual needs has been stifled. Inevitably, when state systems become so enormous their operation depends upon systems of control and accountability, the danger is that the systems become rigidly institutionalized.

Of course there are many young people who find the system suits them. Unfortunately, there are also many young people who vote with their feet – who become NEETS (Not in Education, Employment or Training). Not that I'm suggesting coaching should be reserved for those in danger of dropping out. There are dangers also for those who achieve in our formal system – their achievements may be in a narrow 'academic' area that does not necessarily prepare them to cope in a fast-changing modern world. For instance, there has been a long-term claim from business and industry that universities do not prepare students adequately for the world of work – that many students leave university deficient in such basic areas as communication skills.[6] With so many young people not achieving their full potential, we have to conclude that what the state system of schooling is failing to address on a large scale are factors more relevant to the individual learner – what some writers have called issues of 'personal accountability, internal motivation and uniqueness' (John West-Burnham et al. 2007: 12).

Coaching for learning as conceived in the CARE model is a direct way of dealing with these issues, and as such, it falls within the broad category of education, rather than schooling. The definition is vitally important because the principles of coaching place the emphasis on the whole person and their experience – not just the school experience. Taking this broad view is also essential to a solution-focused approach. Rather than focusing on the 'problem' – which might be something about schooling – coaching encourages young people to find solutions by drawing on their own resources and developing their own skill base. Achievement of formal educational outcomes may be a short-term aim of coaching, but there are also over-arching long-term aims relating to learning development and well-being. In this respect it is crucial to recognize that what we understand as learning happens in all contexts, at all times and certainly outside the experience of schooling. The difference between schooling and education has been very neatly described:

> schooling is perceived as an essentially linear process, the school day, week, term and year form a sequence of events. Progression is always age related by cohort and the sequence is automatic. Education, by contrast, is adaptive, contingent on time and place, often unpredictable and the result of complex interactions. Schooling tends to be fragmented by year and subject; education is a holistic experience, integrating all the different facets of developing understanding – moral, social and intellectual. In the same way, schooling has become synonymous with the delivery of a curriculum that is content and information centred. Education relates to the creation of knowledge – personal understanding and meaning. The measurement

of the curriculum experience is invariably quantitative – outcomes, marks, grades and league tables. Education, by contrast, is concerned with more elusive, qualitative processes.

John West-Burnham, Maggie Farrar and George Otero 2007: 24

Who can be coached?

My own experience has been working with young people of secondary school age, and with students in further and higher education. In particular I've worked on the development of the accredited training for Learning Coaches in Wales. Wales has been innovative in introducing this role as part of a unique 14–19 Learning Pathways policy.[7] The aim of the policy is that each learner will experience a *Learning Core* wherever they are learning, and in addition, will have a choice and flexibility of programme to construct an individual *Learning Pathway* to meet their own needs.[8] There has also been, as in other countries, limited alternative provision in further education colleges for young people pre-16 who were disaffected and in danger of dropping out of secondary school. Generally, the 'alternative curriculum' away from a school environment has proved successful in re-engaging young people in education. But a most interesting aspect is that researchers claim that vocational solutions alone may not always be the best way forward. Students who had made a success in further education had done so because of good personal relationships compared with school, and an opportunity to make a fresh start and for motivation to develop (Yvette Solomon and Colin Rogers 2001: 342).[9]

So it's a belief of mine that good personal relationships make a difference, and the quality of the relationship was the first consideration in developing the CARE model. In addition of course, the policies that have been introduced in Wales have recognized that young people have particular needs, and are designed to address them. Indeed, it is because of the particular needs of young people that I initially took this age group as a focus for a model of coaching. I also believe that – in the particular times we live in – the experience of young people is vastly more complex and confusing than it has been for previous generations.

Psychologists have theorized that, as we grow to full mature adulthood, we pass through a series of stages of development.[10] At each stage, we have to address particular tasks and challenges to enable us to successfully reach the next stage towards adulthood. The tasks relate to understanding ourselves, understanding the world we live in and the expectations of society upon us. As Robert Havinghurst (1972: 2) described it:

> A developmental task is a task which arises at or about a certain period in the life of the individual, successful achievement of which leads to his happiness and to success with later tasks, while failure leads to unhappiness in the individual, disapproval by the society, and difficulty with later tasks.

A hundred years ago the expectations upon a young person would have been comparatively simple: there would have been a well-defined social system to guide their behaviour, and their main task would be the transition from schooling to work, probably following the example of their parents in relation to their particular occupation. Nowadays, not only is the period of transition for young people significantly extended, their world is no longer bounded by clear expectations: rather there is complexity, multiple social and peer pressures and an uncertain future. The coaching relationship can provide an anchor in a world of confusion and uncertainty, and the strategies of coaching can help young people, not only to negotiate their immediate transitional task, but also to prepare them for lifelong learning.

Having said that, I introduced this book by saying I had drawn away from devising a model of coaching for learning for use with a particular age group. This stance had been emphasized for me by my observations of learning work with primary school children. On one occasion in particular I was drawn to the conclusion that the learning approach I was observing was more aligned to my emerging concept of coaching, than it was to a traditional concept of teaching. This was a Year 5 class, and the young people had previously been engaged in thinking about how they learned. One aspect they had identified was that they learned from their own, and other people's mistakes. What I was now observing was a confident and lively discussion where Mike their teacher held back from acknowledging a single 'right' answer. Instead, I was conscious that the young people were aware that the range of alternative answers being explored was engaging them in thinking, and was thus expanding their learning. Significantly, Mike admitted that earlier in his career he would have acknowledged a 'right' answer far earlier, because as the 'expert' teacher he would have seen that as his role. It had taken some reflection for him to step out of that role and have the confidence to allow more talk in his classroom. Plainly this had taken a leap of faith, prompted initially by his distress at the children's perceptions when he first engaged them in thinking about how they learned (see Fig. 1).

It seemed to me that this interaction between teacher and students contained more of the features of coaching as I was beginning to define it, than of teaching. The teacher did not hold the stance of the 'expert' with the single right answer, so there was a more egalitarian relationship between teacher and students. A complex interaction of children working in random pairs and larger groups meant they were more likely to derive the clarification they needed from questioning each other than

Figure 1: How children learn (1)

from asking the teacher. The teachers' main input was in the form of challenging questions aimed at getting the young people to work things out for themselves.

It was also very evident that this class had been moved from a position where their perception of 'learning' was something controlled by the teacher, and was undismayed at putting forward ideas that might be construed as 'wrong' answers. 'It's good to be wrong', asserted one young person. Plainly, in this classroom, failure had been reframed as feedback that a problem needed to be approached from a different angle.

I was reminded how the critical school years, not just for socio-economically disadvantaged pupils, were thought to be between the ages of 5 and 10. It had been claimed that children who experience much failure by the age of 10 will have their confidence and motivation destroyed and will be acquiring 'failure identities' (Richard Nelson-Jones 1992: 43, citing William Glasser 1969). This point was more recently highlighted in a major report on behaviour and attendance, where it was considered to be becoming all too obvious that many interventions with pupils who exhibit behaviour and/or attendance problems occur much too late, often after a situation has reached the persistent or crisis stage (NBAR Report Welsh Assembly Government 2008: 6). I later found support for this in practitioner research, where there was consistent reporting by the parents of adolescents that they could trace the start of behavioural problems and 'dropping out' of school back to when the young people were aged between 7 and 9.[11]

Nevertheless, because the experience of myself and those who have contributed to this book has been with the 14–19 age group, I have made this group the focus of the CARE model. You will see later on that the model is conceived as an *intervention* that takes a 'whole person' approach. In so doing it sees no separation between learning to achieve academic or vocational qualifications and learning for social and emotional development. David Reynolds (2008) has written that schools are beginning to be used to achieve some of the social, emotional and civic goals that perhaps society and parents find too hard to achieve nowadays, but these innovations are only just springing up.[12] So while an *intervention* such as the CARE model may be more effective at an earlier age, I don't think we can neglect those young people who have not had the benefit of innovation in their schooling.

But I do need to add a word of warning about the focus I've described. In state education a tremendous amount of policy initiatives have been directed at the 14–19 sector. However, there is a danger that in making this age group the focus of so much attention, it will create an expectation that initiatives for 14–19 will solve all the problems of education.[13] While innovation in education is needed at a younger age, because of the world we now live in we will all need to engage in lifelong learning if we want to keep up with the fast pace of social and technological change. There are many people post-19 who are still uncertain about a future direction for themselves, and even for those who may feel settled in their choice, the likelihood is that they will have to retrain and be adaptable given the fast-changing nature of the modern world of work. And because of what we now know about the brain and how people learn, we know that learning need no longer be the prerogative of youth. As Albert Einstein is reputed to have advocated, intellectual growth should commence at birth and cease only at death!

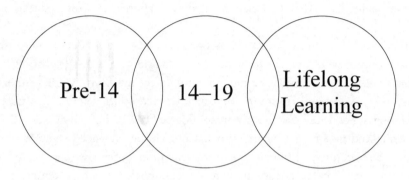

Figure 2: The focus of coaching for learning

So I suppose what I'm saying is that – although the CARE model has developed out of work with young people – the approach can be adopted to help *anyone* raise their self-awareness and develop their capacity for learning. Because anyone at any stage of life may need to improve their ability to live and work successfully – and a coaching approach can help.

How has theory influenced education and schooling?

Compared to other professions such as medicine, the teaching profession has never been firmly based upon the findings of research. Indeed, as David Hargreaves (2005: 22) has pointed out, there is not even an agreed vocabulary about learning, learning to learn and independent learning, either among researchers, or within the teaching profession, or between these two communities. Perhaps the sheer complexity of the average classroom has made it difficult to define a common 'scientific' approach that can account for all the variables. Just in relation to the subject of learning, as you will see in Chapter 2, we can adopt different perspectives: from physical changes in the brain, styles of thinking, to the range of social and emotional factors that influence learning.

Nevertheless we can't ignore the drive to become an 'evidence-based' profession. And even if there are tenuous links between the teaching and research communities, we have to acknowledge that our own 'personal theory' that underpins our practice will have absorbed influences from research at some level. Even though I generally take a pragmatic approach – I am interested in 'what works' and in outcomes – I have to conclude that actions don't come from a void; all actions are influenced by beliefs and values that will have been synthesized from our social, cultural and educational experiences. So before setting out the 'personal theory' that has influenced the CARE model (see Chapter 3), it's also important to be aware of theories and research that have influenced education and schooling in the past. It is always useful to an understanding of where we are now, to be able to understand where we have come from.

Learning as a change in behaviour. As an explanation of how learning occurs, *behaviourism* was the dominant theory at the beginning of the twentieth century. The principles were established from research into teaching animals to carry out simple tasks. The credibility of *behaviourism* was established because many of the findings applied surprisingly well to human learning, although as Geoff Petty (2004: 15) has pointed out, they hardly tell the whole story. Such learning theory that existed in the late nineteenth and early twentieth centuries was generally behaviourist, with features described as: 'people needed rewards to do tasks; our brains were blank sheets awaiting instruction; and intelligence was dimly thought of as being completely innate and inherited (John Abbott and Terry Ryan 2000: 267). There is still plenty of evidence of the principles being applied in schools – at least in part. Effective teachers will use frequent rewards in terms of praise, stickers and positive feedback on completed work. However the best effects depend upon reinforcement in the form of positive feedback occurring as soon as possible after the desired behaviour. If a young person has to wait weeks for work to be marked, it is unlikely to have the same effect as if the work was marked promptly. The use of praise can be selective: when a young person has limited achievements, or is exhibiting challenging behaviour, it may be very difficult to find even the smallest hint of progress to offer praise and encouragement. It's hardly surprising then that some young people become de-motivated and resistant to learning when in their home life or during years of schooling they lack the experience of achievement or any encouragement as a stimulus to learning.

Learning as stages of development. Things have moved on from the dominance of *behaviourism*, however, because we now have the benefit of research that has been carried out in the intervening years: research that deals with thinking – or *cognitive* – processes more than just behavioural responses to stimuli. Perhaps the next biggest influence on the education of children was Piaget, despite the fact that he wrote very little about the educational implications of his theory. His background had been in biology, and his study of the thinking and understanding of children and adolescents formed the basis for a theory of *learning readiness*.[14] The idea that children pass through stages of development, and that they cannot learn or be taught at 'higher' levels before they have passed through the lower ones is evident in both the organization of state education, and in the traditional practice of teaching.

However, as David Fontana (1995: 59) has pointed out, much subsequent research has challenged Piaget's view – not just in relation to the reality of stages of development, but also that he underestimated the abilities of children and the speed at which they can progress. Piaget's research was based on setting children a series of tasks that were explained to them by adults. From a child's inability to complete the tasks he drew the conclusion that they had not reached the stage of mental development to enable them to do so. However, alternative explanations have been offered. For instance, David Wood (1998: 65) describes the claim that the tasks may have been unfamiliar to the children, would have been 'artificial' and outside their own experience, and maintains that this would explain why they made errors. In addition, there seems to have been little consideration of whether the children could understand the instructions of the researchers or of the influence of how the task was set up. In subsequent research when the tasks were adjusted and attention was paid to how verbal and non-verbal language of the researchers could enable the child to 'make sense' of the task, different results were achieved.

In fairness, however, we need to understand the focus of Piaget's work. Since the aim was to *describe* the stage of a child's mental development, his researchers were specifically tasked with avoiding any sort of interaction that would interfere with the child's present thinking. As Michael Shayer (2003: 478) has pointed out, they were to actively avoid saying or doing anything that would change the child's thinking in order to describe the present stage. Subsequently, there have been different interpretations:

> Children's 'failure' to understand the questions and instructions and explanations offered to them by adults is due less to their own shortcomings than to the frequent inability of adults to present these communications to them in a form which is appropriate to the level at which conceptually they are able to function.
>
> David Fontana 1995: 61

This point holds particular interest for us in relation to coaching: it suggests that children's ability to learn can be influenced by interpersonal and social factors and are not necessarily dependent upon their age-related stage of cognitive development.

Learning as the construction of meaning. David Fontana has pointed out that no one has challenged Piaget's basic finding that children's understanding is determined by how well they have formed mental concepts and can build a mental model which is consistent with external reality. There is a general acceptance that for learning to occur in both children and adults, they have to build on their previous understanding and 'construct' their own unique meaning. The other aspect of this *constructivist* view of learning is that, because everyone makes sense of things in their own unique way, there needs to be an emphasis on giving learners responsibility for directing their own learning experiences.

In addition, as you will have seen from the challenges to Piaget's research, others have sought to establish that there are external factors that influence an internal ability to construct cognitive frameworks. The Russian psychologist Lev Vygotsky emphasized the social and cultural influences on children's learning. From Vygotsky comes the term 'zone of proximal development', as described in his words:

> The zone of proximal development of the child is the distance between his actual development, determined with the help of independently solved tasks, and the level of potential development of the child, determined with the help of tasks solved by the child under the guidance of adults and in cooperation with his more intelligent partners.[15]

Thus 'cooperation with partners' suggests opportunities to engage with peers in learning tasks, and 'the guidance of adults' has been interpreted as the 'scaffolding' role of an adult in asking appropriate questions, supporting the learner towards their own understanding. The American psychologist Jerome Bruner has also placed emphasis on the role of a teacher in providing well-structured interactive pupil experiences and guiding the pupil's own discovery through asking focused questions. So in the work of both Vygotsky and Bruner we see highlighted the importance of talk as a learning tool (Steve Bartlett et al. 2001: 137–41).

This *social constructivist* model of learning therefore challenges the emphasis on 'telling' in a traditional didactic approach to teaching. And the need to give young people responsibility for their own learning also presents a challenge to teachers to create effective 'discovery' learning activities within a system of schooling that is geared to standardization and testing. What certainly can't be under-rated is the challenge of shifting from 'telling' to the highly skilled questioning that fits with the *social constructivist* model. In this respect, I was reminded of something I wrote some time ago concerning independent learning:

> the development of independent learning ... is not an approach that reprises the more laissez-faire aspects promulgated by 'progressive' educationalists in the 1970s. Rather, it is an approach that recognizes that an educational project that can give students ownership of their own learning, that is dynamic and exciting, that has relevance because the skills really are transferable to real life, and at the same

time can establish basic skills, requires a much more demanding and inclusive pedagogy than an approach that has the importing of knowledge at its core.

Jacquie Turnbull 2004:80

Learning as emotional growth and development. In some ways, this final approach may have been squeezed out of our system of schooling by the thrust to raise standards – standards defined by the achievement of formal educational outcomes. The *humanistic* model of Abraham Mazlow and Carl Rogers takes a very positive view of human beings. For them, the single most important drive in human beings is a positive drive to maintain, develop and reproduce oneself – to *self-actualize*. In other words, to fulfil individual potential. Unfortunately, the experiences of life may obstruct the drive to become a unique fully functioning individual. One reason is because the need for positive regard from others is a learned need developed in early infancy. So people may develop a view of what they 'should' be like based on what other people value which will work at cross purposes with their own deeper *self-actualizing* drive. Carl Rogers advocated that such blockages to the *self-actualizing* drive were the source of all psychological difficulties, and the cause of people repeating behaviours that did not meet their real needs.[16] Within the school system for example, there has always been a higher value placed on academic rather than vocational achievements. It is understandable that young people can 'internalize' these values, and when their own achievements do not match these values, can acquire the 'failure identities' mentioned earlier.

Carl Rogers' view was that these difficulties could be understood and the motivation towards self-fulfilment released within a relationship that had certain preconditions. When he moved to apply his principles to education, he suggested that the key to classroom learning lies in the teacher-pupil relationship. This should be characterized by a demonstration of empathy, respect and genuineness on the part of the teacher. Thus teachers needed to be more than subject-matter experts; they must offer good human relationships to pupils.[17] It was this aspect that was essential to the process of developing of independent learners:

> Throughout, I have tried to indicate that if we are to have citizens who can live constructively in this kaleidoscopically changing world, we must free our children to become self-starting, self-initiating learners. Finally, it has been my purpose to show that this kind of learner develops best, so far as we now know, in a growth-promoting, facilitative relationship with a person.
>
> Carl Rogers and Jerome Freiberg 1994: 167

Perhaps we can conclude that *humanistic* principles are more evident in primary schools than at secondary level; a primary teacher has more opportunity to build a relationship with a child, and strategies such as circle time are used to develop emotional intelligence. In secondary schools and colleges the situation is more complex: a young person will encounter teachers for different subjects, and a range of other professionals with various responsibilities. If anything this complexity is likely to increase with the evolving 14–19 agenda. With increased flexibility in the delivery of education, there will need to be some core of stability for young people – something perhaps that a coaching relationship can offer.

Reflection

This chapter has set out a wider social and educational context for coaching. It has looked at the drivers for change that are causing the emphasis in educational practice and outcomes to shift. It has also identified how theories of learning have influenced education in the past. This will be followed through in Chapter 3 to show how the theories have influenced the CARE model of coaching.

For the moment, you may find it useful to reflect on how the issues raised impact upon your own working context and practice. Can you recognize the influences that have been identified? What do you think of the separate definition of education and schooling? Can you identify how the theoretical ideas are reflected in your own work? And did you feel comfortable with the broad level of the analysis – do you find that there was a fit with your own style of thinking?

Key points

- Because of the need to be flexible and adaptable in the fast-changing world we live in, the best thing we can do for young people is to enable them to learn how to learn
- Coaching needs to be solution-focused and address the needs of the whole person
- Anybody at any age can benefit from coaching for learning
- *Behaviourism* emphasizes that positive feedback can encourage learning
- *Constructivism* stresses that people make their own meaning, and that they can be supported to do this with appropriate learning experiences and skilled questioning
- The *humanistic* approach says that people can develop and grow within a relationship that demonstrates empathy, respect and genuineness
- Coaching can be the 'difference that makes the difference' to learning.

Notes

1. *The Taming of the Shrew* (1592) Act 1, Sc. 2.
2. www.standards.dfes.gov.uk/personalised learning/bground.
3. According to the CIPD's 2007 learning and development survey, coaching is used by 63 per cent of UK organizations.
4. These phrases are from personal communication with Danny Saunders and Steve Marshall.
5. As in the example of Wales: 2008 saw the roll out of the Foundation stage for 3–7-year-olds with a curriculum that encompasses personal and social development, well-being and cultural diversity, language, literacy and communication skills. This is followed through in a revised skill-based curriculum with a development of 14–19 Learning Pathways where young people can access educational options that suit their abilities and interest. The Welsh Baccalaureate (see note 10) has also integrated key skills, academic and vocational learning.
6. In Wales, the development of a Welsh Baccalaureate has been designed to improve the breadth of education, without diminishing the depth of study of individual subjects. It adds a common core to the study of existing traditional subjects that covers the key skills of IT, numeracy, personal and social education and environmental and political issues concerning Wales and the world.
7. www.learning.wales.gov.uk
8. National Assembly for Wales Circular Number 37/2004.
9. See also the example in Appendix 1.
10. See Erik Erikson's psychosocial stages (1959) and Robert Havighurst's developmental tasks (1972, 1979).
11. Mandy Scanlon 2008, see Appendix 1.
12. See an example in Appendix 2.
13. Baroness Estelle Morris raised this point in her keynote speech at the Dysg Conference in Cardiff 13 March 2008.
14. David Wood 1998:8.
15. As cited by Michael Shayer 2003:470 taken from a (partial) translation of Vygotsky by van der Veer and Valsiner 1991:337.
16. I have drawn on Richard Nelson-Jones 1992, pp. 15–37 for a description of Humanistic Person-centred theory.
17. Richard Nelson-Jones 1992:48.

2 How do we understand learning?

Learning is much more than the flip-side of good teaching and schooling.
John Abbott and Terry Ryan 2000: 262

We are living through a cultural shift that has taken us from an emphasis on teaching, to an emphasis on facilitating learning. You may have asked yourself what has brought this about; how have ideas about learning changed so that we have a different perspective? On a broad level, you have seen in Chapter 1 the idea of differentiating between education and schooling; with education seen as involving a holistic learning experience while schooling being considered content and information centred. At a basic level, we know that young people cannot learn when they are anxious, stressed or have too much 'stuff' going on in their heads. So taking a 'personalized' approach to education, we need to acknowledge that we cannot separate the learning required to achieve academic/vocational qualifications from personal, social or emotional growth. What you will not find featured in this chapter is a section on learning as the acquisition of knowledge or a skill. That is because these are the *outcomes*, and our concern is to understand the *process* of learning. And as we also have the benefit of advances in neuroscience to inform us about what actually happens in the brain when learning occurs, we can now develop a more informed perspective on learning than people were able to have in the past.

As human beings, our background of surviving two billion years of evolution to become the cleverest creatures on the planet has equipped us with a remarkable brain capacity. As Andrew Pollard (2008: 172) reminds us, humans learned for many thousands of years before anyone thought that a 'curriculum' and 'schooling' were necessary – a fact to keep our perspective as professional educators! Evolution has indeed equipped us with a brain capacity and complexity that is quite difficult to comprehend. Even the average brain has a collection of a hundred billion neurons (brain cells) connected by a hundred trillion synapses (the gaps where electrical impulses pass between cells) (Stephen Pinker 2002: 42). To help us grasp the extent of those numbers, there's a metaphor that tries to convey the scale of neural connections possible in the average brain – as many as there are grains of sand on all the beaches in the world.

With all that capacity, there's also little doubt that we don't fully utilize the potential available to us. Estimates about how much brain capacity we use vary from as little as 2 per cent to 25 per cent at most (Alistair Smith 1996: 15). So with that sort of capacity, and with an evolutionary history that has equipped us to be adaptable, there would seem to be plenty of scope for any of us to extend and improve our learning. First though, we need a little exploration into the various ways we can understand learning.

> We will start with two simple assertions: humans are born to learn and learning is what we are better at than any other species
>
> John Abbott and Terry Ryan 2000: 7

Learning and the brain

One way of thinking about learning is to think of a learning experience as creating new connections between brain cells. We know that people learn throughout their lives, and that the products of that learning have to be stored in the brain somehow. We also know that given multisensory stimulation and cognitive challenge connections can be stimulated and learning enhanced. From this perspective, learning *is* a change in the brain.[1]

The interesting thing about the past 20 years or so is how advances in neuroscience are beginning to support things we intuitively knew about learning. By means of brain imaging technology researchers can now map learning as activity within different parts of the brain. The brain can now be 'seen' as 'a flexible self-adjusting, biological system which grows and reshapes itself in response to challenge, or withers through lack of use' (John Abbott and Terry Ryan 2000: 8). Neuroscience is beginning to catch up with psychology by discovering changes in the brain that underlie learning. They can now describe how boundaries between swatches of cortex devoted to different body parts, talents and even physical senses can be adjusted by learning and practice (Stephen Pinker 2002: 45). Thus, significantly for us, as Abbott and Ryan (2000: 27) put it, this new knowledge empowers us to construct models of learning which *'go with the grain of the brain'*.

Perhaps the most interesting aspect from the perspective of this book has been the finding of neuroscientists in relation to the changes in the brain in adolescence. It seems that in adolescence, young people are not just experiencing physical growth spurts, but various features of their brains are also undergoing dramatic changes. Not all parts of the brain have settled into their adult form by puberty as was previously thought. Rather, when adolescents' brains are studied through magnetic resonance imaging (MRI) scientists have found that they actually work differently from adult brains. In particular, they found that teenagers use different parts of the brain to process emotional information, especially if that information comes in the form of verbal threats or comments, or staring. While the response in adult brains comes from the *frontal cortex*, which governs reason and planning, young people mostly use the *amygdala*, a small region deep in the brain that is the source of swift emotional rather than rational responses.[2] (More on this in Chapter 5.)

The interesting thing about these findings in relation to coaching is that the scientist, Deborah Yurgelun-Todd, has suggested that young people should be encouraged to develop the frontal lobe by teaching them to think rationally (Murray 1998). So from this perspective, learning can not only be seen as the creation of new neural connections, but also as the development of the frontal lobe, the brain tissue involved in planning, insight and organization.

Learning and intelligence

The debate about the most potent influence on human intelligence and behaviour – our biological nature or social and environmental influences – has raged for three centuries. Advocates have lined up on both sides: those that thought of intelligence as a single fixed entity that remained stable throughout life, against those who thought intelligence could be influenced by environment and learning opportunities. Some consider that the debate is still alive and kicking, with research data still emerging to support both sides of the argument (Steve Bartlett et al. 2001: 108).

But we do seem to have moved from the dominance of the 'fixed-intelligence' view, to a stage where there is more understanding of how learning can be influenced by both genetic and external factors. Evidence such as the so-called 'Flynn effect' showing how IQ scores have been dramatically rising over 100 years has certainly made it difficult to maintain the idea of intelligence as standard and fixed for life (James Flynn 1987, 2007). We can now see that what IQ tests actually measure is the type of intelligence traditionally most favoured by our education systems: verbal/ linguistic and logical/mathematical.

Our views have also been influenced by conceptions of intelligence as a much more multi-faceted phenomenon. Although the ideas of Harvard's Howard Gardner have attracted criticism, a particularly useful aspect of his work lies in the fact that he uses the term 'intelligence' to describe a range of attributes in his theory of *multiple intelligences* (MI) (Gardner 1993). Gardner's work helps us to regard 'intelligence' as a much more fluid concept: a way of understanding individuality, a way of describing different qualities that can grow and develop. His work has been very influential in education systems, with thousands of so-called 'MI schools' springing up in America, Canada, Australia and elsewhere (John White 1998: 2). Many schools in the UK have also taken up Gardner's idea that pupils 'have quite different minds from each other' (Gardner 1993: 71) and are attempting to raise awareness of the differences.

You will also see later on how beliefs affect young people's readiness to learn. The experience of schooling in particular can have a profound effect on young people's beliefs about their own intelligence. And since beliefs have implications for the experience of emotions, as you'll see in the next section, applying the term 'intelligence' to our ability to handle emotions opens up another aspect of learning.

Learning and emotional intelligence

Strong or negative emotions can be one of the biggest blocks to learning. The reverse is also true; young people need to be in a good emotional state to be able to learn (Susan Norman 2003:32). As we've seen above, research is showing that young people respond more from the 'emotional core' of the brain – the *amygdala* – than adults, who can have a more fully developed rational part of the brain – the *frontal cortex*.

Having said that, Daniel Goleman has highlighted that it's not just adolescents who can be ruled by their emotions. He sets out to help us understand how we all learn emotional habits that can undermine our best intentions, and what we can do to subdue our more destructive or self-defeating emotional impulses. Significantly for us, he believes that what we now know about the brain presents an opportunity to shape our children's emotional habits (Goleman 1996: xii–xiii).

You will no doubt have experience of a young person responding to a situation with a swift emotional reaction. You've probably also known young people who think their emotional reactions are something beyond their control. 'It's just the way I am, I can't help it' is probably a lament you'll be familiar with. But knowing what we now know about the source of emotional reactions we can understand how that can be. The *amygdala* is part of our primitive brain, the part that kicks in with an emotional response much faster than our rational thinking mind. The speed of the reaction would have served our stone age ancestors very well – faced with a sabre-toothed tiger there wouldn't have been much time to consider rationally what action to take. We still need that swiftness of response when we see danger; it's the sort of rapid reaction that helps us to move quickly to grab a child back from an on-coming vehicle.

Then Daniel Goleman tells us of the second kind of emotional reaction, slower than the quick-response, which starts with our thoughts before it leads to feelings. This is the sort of reaction where our thoughts play the key role in deciding what emotions will be triggered:

> More complicated emotions, like embarrassment or apprehension over an upcoming exam, follow this slower route, taking seconds or minutes to unfold – these are emotions that follow from thoughts.
>
> Goleman 1996: 293

A key factor that Daniel Goleman alerts us to is that the emotional mind is 'childlike', and more so the stronger the emotion grows. One indicator is that thinking may be black and white, as when someone says 'I never get things right'. And while our rational mind may be able to accept new evidence and adjust our beliefs, the emotional mind takes its beliefs to be absolutely true, and ignores any evidence that suggests an alternative way of looking at things.

Learning in relation to the emotional mind therefore is concerned with the development of young people's ability to become aware of their emotions, and to understand how the beliefs they hold can influence and stimulate emotional reactions. The good news is that emotional intelligence can be learned (Goleman 1999: 315), and learning to understand and handle emotions can bring improvements in self control, and develop skills in handling personal problems and relationships with other people. In this respect, Goleman poses the question of how can we best educate young people for the world of work:

> For our children, this includes an education in emotional literacy; for those already at work, it means cultivating our emotional competence. All this, of course, demands rethinking the notion of the 'basics' in education: Emotional intelligence is now as crucial to our children's future as the standard academic fare.
>
> Goleman 1999: 313

Learning styles

As far as style of learning is concerned we no longer think that 'one size fits all'. One of the reasons that we think about learning differently is the immense amount of research and theories concerning the different ways people think and learn. Research into cognition (how we perceive, how we learn, how we think) came to prominence in the 1950s when the thinking was that research into styles could form a bridge with the study of personality (Robert Sternberg 1997: 134). More recently, a systematic review of learning styles and pedagogy in post-16 learning – known as the Coffield Review – identified 71 models of learning styles, and categorized 13 of those as major models (Frank Coffield et al. 2004). David Hargreaves (2005: 11) has described the main applications of learning styles models in use in schools and colleges:

> There are very many different schemes for determining learning styles, using different names and based on different questions, though a relatively small number of these schemes accounts for the majority of applications in UK schools/colleges. So a new language of learning styles can commonly be found in schools – or more accurately a range of different languages:
> - Activists, theorist, pragmatists, reflectors
> - Divergers, convergers, assimilators, accommodaters
> - Verbalizers, imagers, analytics, wholists
> - Analysts, changers, realists
> - Visual, auditory, kinaesthetic.

The Coffield Review has been only one source of criticism of concepts and models of learning styles. Concerns have been expressed that there is no overall model that integrates all the theories, and that the concepts appear to be unsupported by evidence from neuroscience to link the theories to activity in the brain. But neuroscience is a fairly young discipline, and those working in the area have themselves admitted that *'functional resonance imaging'* has so far only been concerned with the learning of simple tasks, and therefore the relationship between the elements of learning styles and any brain activation is still hypothetical.[3]

But as my friend Ann commented, 'We didn't have to wait for pictures from space to know that the earth was round, did we?' and indeed, in this respect, perhaps it is that neuroscience has yet to catch up with psychology. But nevertheless, it's also important to have a critical understanding of the claims of learning style theory, so that we can deflect criticisms that, as educators, we too readily pick up and use the latest user-friendly assessment tool that comes our way.

The first aspect to clarify is the crucial distinction between style and ability. As Robert Sternberg (1997: 12) points out, an ability refers to how well someone can do something, whereas a style refers to how someone uses that ability, how they like to do something. People may be practically identical in their abilities and yet have very different styles.

A second aspect is that styles are not good or bad, they're just different. But there is no doubt that some styles fit in our system of schooling more than others. It's a rather large generalization, but since teachers are likely to have been successful learners within the school system, they are more likely to teach in a style that has served them successfully. When a learner's style matches that of a teacher then, unsurprisingly, students are likely to describe the experience as 'effective teaching' (Entwistle and Tait 1990). Conversely, a mismatch between a teaching style and the learning style of a student can be a big turn off for the student. So in any engagement with young people, it's helpful to be able to recognize whether issues of non-achievement relate to learning style rather than lack of ability on behalf of the student. And as you'll see as you read further, successful engagement with young people involves raising your own self-awareness: we all need to be able to recognize and understand our own preferred learning and thinking styles, and develop the flexibility to adjust our approaches to accommodate the various styles of young people.

A third aspect we need to guard against is that psychological theories tend to like to put people into boxes. You will see later on that I have suggested ways to use what is perhaps the most popular of the learning styles categorizations – visual, auditory, kinaesthetic. But in practice it is still a constant battle to stop people referring to them as though they were fixed and permanent categories. They are preferences, I insist. We all use a range of styles, it's just that we may have got into the habit of favouring one over the others. But if we slip into the habit of telling young people that they are '**A** visual learner' or '**A** kinaesthetic learner', then we are doing no more than reverting to the more or less discredited way we used to think about intelligence – as something that is fixed and immutable. Rather, we need to be encouraging young people to develop their capacity for flexibility in thinking – as in behaviour:

> Realistically [...] people cannot be as easily pigeonholed as psychologists would often seem to like them to be. Most people, at least, are more flexible than psychological theories give them credit for.
>
> Robert Sternberg 1997:145

A final point leads on from this tendency to label people. David Hargreaves (2005: 11–12) has pointed out that young people can internalize a label and think of themselves as a certain type of learner who should concentrate on a diagnosed style. In Hargreaves' view, this is poor professional practice that can damage a student's learning and development. A good education does not limit young people to a particular style or type, but gives them opportunities to strengthen other learning styles and so broaden their intellectual development.

Despite the criticisms, the reason that interest in learning styles remains strong is probably that, intuitively, we sense that styles exist, and that they can account for differences in performance that abilities do not account for:

> Styles matter. Moreover, they are often confused with abilities, so that students or others are thought to be incompetent not because they are lacking in abilities, but because their styles of thinking do not match those of the people doing the assessment. Especially in teaching, we need to take into account students' styles of thinking if we hope to reach them.
>
> Robert Sternberg 1997:158

And even though a model we favour might have dubious 'scientific' credentials, if nothing else, there is a value in thinking of descriptions of learning styles as metaphors. The usefulness of a metaphor lies in providing us with a framework and a form of language to help young people understand how they think and learn. It can be immensely empowering for young people to discover that their inability to learn may be because they have become 'stuck' in a particular mode of thinking and learning, that actually it's a preferred style rather than a fixed part of their personality, and that they have the capacity for far more flexibility in order to achieve their potential.

Learning as metacognition

Thinking about thinking about learning styles leads us nicely into thinking about metacognition. The prefix 'meta' means above and beyond, so developing metacognition means going beyond cognition, and being able to think about how we think, how we learn, how we perceive. In other words 'conscious and deliberate thoughts that have other thoughts as their object' (Douglas Hacker 1998: 8). So, as David Hargreaves puts it:

> There is learning, but there is also learning about learning. People think, but they can also think about their thinking. Using the language of psychologists for these phenomena, there is cognition and also cognition about cognition. By metacognition we mean the capacity to monitor, evaluate, control and change how one thinks and learns.
>
> Hargreaves 2005: 7

It is hardly surprising that metacognition is topical and receiving a lot of attention in education. Metacognition is crucial to 'learning to learn' and therefore central to the development of independent learning. As you will have seen in Chapter 1, there has been a shift of emphasis in thinking about the core principles of education. The complexity of our modern world, with change being the only constant factor we can depend upon, means that young people need to develop as independent learners to prepare them for lifelong learning. While there is a role for a learner's experience to be managed, if not dominated by a teacher, as learners mature, their need for independence will increase if they are to be successful learners in further and higher education and in the workplace (David Hargreaves 2005: 19). Indeed, some writers have suggested that enhanced metacognition should be a learning outcome in itself, as well as having a critical impact on the achievement of content-based outcomes (Jennifer Case and Richard Gunstone 2002).

Research into metacognition has become increasingly fine-grained, and the definitions developed can explain why it is crucial to the development of independent learning. *Metacognitive knowledge* is referred to as awareness of one's own personal characteristics, understanding of a particular task and the various strategies available to successfully negotiate a learning situation. In other words, *what* one knows, *how* one thinks and *when* and *why* to apply certain knowledge or strategies (Paris and Winograd 1990: 17). Even with that knowledge, young people may still choose not to engage in a particular learning task, so *metacognitive skills* refers to the ability to self-manage: the sort of thinking about thinking in action that enables creative problem solving.

The point about developing metacognition is that it is a process of raising to conscious awareness patterns of thinking, learning and perception that were previously unconscious drivers of behaviour. If during this process, thoughts and beliefs are revealed that have a irrational basis, there is an opportunity for a coach to challenge the irrationality and foster a more realistic approach. As with all things, awareness has to precede the development of skills.

Learning as belief

As well as thinking about thinking, research has shown the importance of thinking about the beliefs we hold that influence our behaviour. You will see in Chapter 3 that I have taken care to make explicit the beliefs that underpin the CARE model of coaching. In relation to learning, beliefs can have a powerful effect upon achievement, and adopting more productive beliefs can improve motivation and foster empowerment.

Carol Dweck (2000) has used the results of research to devise two frameworks that demonstrate how beliefs about intelligence influence learning and achievement. First, there is what she has called an *'entity theory'* – a belief some people hold that their intelligence is a fixed trait, that it is an 'entity' within us that can't be changed. Second, is the *'incremental theory'* – a very different definition of intelligence whereby people view intelligence as something that can be increased through their own efforts.

Not surprisingly, Dweck's research with young people has revealed very different responses to learning challenges relating to the different beliefs, and identifying two distinct reactions to failure:

The Helpless Pattern: When set a challenging task (even when this followed a series of successes) these young people quickly blamed their intelligence for their failure, saying things like 'I'm no good at things like this'. They became discouraged by the difficulty they encountered and even tended to forget that they had had successes previously. They took the difficulty as an indicator of personal inadequacy, gave up far too quickly and became anxious. Further, more than half the young people in this group resorted to using completely ineffective strategies to try to solve the problem. This reaction to failure seemed to indicate young people's ability to use their minds effectively was impaired by holding this belief.

The Master-Orientated Pattern In complete contrast, the young people in this group did not blame anything for their failures; in fact they didn't even seem to consider themselves to be failing. Significantly, almost all of them engaged in some form of self-instruction or self-motivation in order to improve their performance, such as saying 'I should slow down and try to figure this out'. Far from viewing their lack of success as a failure, these young people welcomed the opportunity to confront and overcome obstacles.[4]

Plainly, a belief that intelligence is something that can be increased in relation to the effort applied is likely to be a motivating factor in encouraging learning. Other writers also have identified aspects of beliefs that can relate to and influence earning competence: [5]

Agency This relates to what young people believe about themselves as learners, for instance whether they are competent or incompetent. In working with young people it is important to foster a belief that they can be self-directed and self-critical learners.

Instrumentality This concerns young people's beliefs about the usefulness of the strategies they use to achieve outcomes. For instance, if they see no use in note-taking, they will be unlikely to adopt it as a strategy to achieve a learning outcome.

Control This relates to young people's understanding that they have the power to direct their own thinking. If this is not encouraged and developed they will look upon themselves as ineffectual as learners.

Purpose This has to do with young people's beliefs about the purpose of their learning. There needs to be positive expectations and success should be valued for young people to be orientated towards learning.

Learning as reflection

One of the valuable aspects of coaching is the role the coach plays in challenging the 'limiting beliefs' a young person may be unaware of. Firstly, a coach can act as a mirror, reflecting back the beliefs they are picking from a young person's language and behaviour. Then a coach can test out the credibility of the beliefs, challenging the lack of evidence to support the belief, suggesting alternative examples that can support more positive beliefs.

As part of developing reflexivity, Barbara Larrivee (2000: 304) has pointed out that discarding long-held assumptions is not an easy process. There can be an initial uncertainty and confusion when familiar thoughts are challenged, and new beliefs are yet to be embedded. Yet this confusion often precedes understanding in any learning process, and an inner struggle is a necessary stage in developing a reflective attitude. Indeed, as Barbara Larrivee indicated:

> this uncertainty is the hallmark for transformation and the emergence of new possibilities. ... Fully experiencing this sense of uncertainty is what opens the door to a personal deeper understanding, leading to a shift in ways of thinking and perceiving.

Reflection as an aspect of learning is of crucial importance to your own development personally and professionally. You will see in Chapter 3 that I stress the importance of experiencing yourself as a learner, in order to maintain your continuous professional development, and also to ensure an egalitarian basis in the coaching relationship. As well as being able to challenge the 'limiting beliefs' of the young person you work with, reflecting on your own practice, and the beliefs and assumptions that underpin it, will guard against being 'stuck' in familiar ways of doing things. It will enable you to approach each new situation as fresh and unique because you will not be limited by a restricted or limited frame of reference. As Larrivee puts it:

> Becoming a reflective practitioner means perpetually growing and expanding, opening up to a greater range of possible choices and responses to classroom situations and individual student behaviours. Teachers have to continually challenge the underlying beliefs that drive their present behaviours.
>
> Barbara Larrivee 2000: 301

Single and double loop learning

It is reflection that establishes the difference between what has been called single and double loop learning. Chris Argyris and Donald Schon (1996: 20-1) originally identified this as an aspect of organizational learning. It works like this: single loop learning is exploring a problem without attempting to consider how we were led to define it as a problem in the first place. Double loop learning, on the other hand, allows us to examine our assumptions and understanding and to question the very definition of the problem, including whether 'it' is a problem at all! (Nigel Bennett 1997: 61)

Single and double loop learning has been explored and written about in relation to how organizations can become 'learning organizations'. Yet plainly, organizations are made up of people, and it is the ability of individuals to 'reframe' problem situations that adds the illumination of the double loop. We all view the world from a personal perspective: we have our own internal 'map' of the world that has been constructed from our past experiences, our personal belief system. Our perception of a young person's attitude or behaviour will be filtered by our own personal 'map': Barbara Larrivee (2000: 300–1) describes this as passing our experience through a series of 'screens' that act as a subjective mediating process. Left alone, what this process also does is filter out the potential of the experience to be interpreted in different ways. So in a busy life of working with young people, we may operate on 'automatic pilot', reacting without giving conscious thought to alternative responses. We may learn at one level from such situations, but that will only be single loop learning; double loop learning occurs when we are able to challenge our screening process, question why we respond in a certain way and consider alternative responses.

However, those who study how organizations can improve their effectiveness have identified that the very structure and practices of organizations can put up barriers to double loop learning. Gareth Morgan (1997: 88) has noted that this is especially true of bureaucratized organizations, whose fundamental ways of working often operate in a way that actually *obstructs* the learning process. As you will have seen in Chapter 1, being a bureaucratized system, education has not really kept pace with the rapid changes in wider society, and still clings tenaciously to a structure and practices of a previous era. So when working with young people, double loop learning can involve recognizing how the structures and norms of an organization may be creating barriers to individual development, and being prepared to challenge them. Gareth Morgan (1997: 88–9) warns how these barriers can be created: employees are usually encouraged to keep to their own place in the organization, and are rewarded for doing so; there will be a need for bureaucratic accountability and systems for rewarding or punishing employees. At a personal level, when people feel threatened or vulnerable, they will often engage in 'defensive routines' to protect themselves:

they find ways of burying issues and problems that may put them in a bad light and deflecting attention elsewhere; they become skilled in impression management to make situations appear better than they really are; they may ignore or fail to report deep-seated problems.

Plainly, at a personal level, single loop learning involves learning from situations within the existing context of individual working practice and the structure of an institution. Double loop learning, on the other hand, means being open to re-framing personal assumptions and defensive responses, and recognizing and challenging the established norms of an organization where they may be prejudicial to the welfare of young people. As Barbara Larrivee (2000: 301) puts it:

> As teachers challenge their screens and consider alternative responses to reoccurring classroom situations, they become open to more possibilities and no possible response is automatically ruled out or in.

Social learning

This last section has led us from considering learning as something that occurs solely within the brain / mind of an individual, to starting to be aware of how learning is influenced by social factors. As far as individual factors are concerned, it is plain that we are much more knowledgeable now than even in the recent past. It is when we include the host of environmental and interpersonal factors that we can gain further insight, both into how the complexity of influences on learning has come to be recognized, and why we now need to view education as more than schooling.

Rhys Griffith (1998: 15–16) has written about his development as a teacher and educational researcher, and reflected on the experience of himself and his colleagues in the 1970s. He concludes that they weren't bad teachers then, not wilfully so. They weren't lazy teachers either – they worked hard to entertain pupils and tried to make lessons as interesting as possible. Yet with hindsight, he considers they were failing themselves and their pupils in their complacency:

> we certainly didn't consider that, as educators, we had any wider responsibilities or that our teaching styles might have implications upon the personal and social development of pupils. Our perspective was blinkered so that we saw only an adults-needs purpose to our work: we trained pupils to pass exams so that they could get jobs. Lip-service may have been paid to the esoteric idea that the sum of a pupil's school experiences should coalesce to form some fuller sense of education, but there would have been a sneer on those lips. It was teachers like us who hid the hidden curriculum.

Moving forward 30 years, we find there is much more recognition of the breadth of environmental and social influences on learning. As Michael Eraut (2000: 131) has illustrated, even taking the context of a formal classroom, the learning of explicit curriculum knowledge is only one aspect of the learning process:

> Pupils are also learning how to present work for assessment; how to participate in shared discussions; algorithms and schemas for reading and problem-solving; a hidden curriculum of orderly, disciplined behaviour, working to deadlines and submission to authority; and a rich array of knowledge, beliefs, attitudes and behaviour from peer group interaction. Can these separately listed forms of learning be separated from each other in practice? It is hard to imagine a formal learning context in which only explicit learning of explicit knowledge takes place. To focus only on the explicit learning of formally presented knowledge is to fail to recognise the complexity of learning even in well-ordered classrooms. The knowledge gained is constructed in a social context whose influence on what is learned, as well as how it is learned, cannot be denied.

Indeed, Michael Eraut (2000: 132) presents an argument that learning is *always* situated in a particular context which comprises not only a location and a set of activities, but is also embedded in a set of social relationships. This raises the question of to what extent learning is really personal. In response, Eraut points to the fact that learning from experience has traditionally been presented as a purely individual activity with other people being part of the experience, rather than part of the learning. However, if we acknowledge the *social* nature of the learning, the learning process becomes more complicated. So the *individual* process of making personal sense of something will be drawing on a wide range of influences, whether they are recognized or not.

There are two aspects of social learning that are significant for our purposes. The first is in relation to what young people learn about themselves from the environment and interpersonal relationships of schooling. The school imposes social roles on students and teachers; schooling is structured and operates in accordance with a value system – a system that defines young people as conformist or non-conformist, successful or not successful. So young people who find themselves negatively defined in respect of the dominant values of the school in terms of behaviour, attitude and academic work, may learn to accept this definition of themselves. The adoption of 'failure identities' mentioned in Chapter 1 may be the result. And in many cases, young people can transform this learned identity to an alternative form of high status achieved by rule-breaking and generally opting-out of the system (Steve Bartlett et al. 2001: 181).

On a more positive note, we have also seen in Chapter 1 that the work of Vygotsky emphasizes the role of interaction with peers and adults in developing learning, i.e.:

learning awakens a variety of internal developmental processes that are able to operate only when the child is interacting with people in his environment and in cooperation with his peers.[6]

So for Vygotsky, the social process is an essential element in order for young people to develop their internal concepts and achieve their learning potential. Similarly, Robert Glaser (1999: 99) has neatly summarized the view that learning is a social rather than an individual process:

> The acquisition of competent performance takes place in an interpersonal system in which participation and guidance from others influences the understanding of new situations and the management of problem solving that leads to learning.

4 Pillars of Learning

Perhaps the most holistic perspective on learning is the definition proposed by the UNESCO report of the International Commission on Education for the twenty-first century.[7] The report considered that formal education systems emphasized the acquisition of knowledge to the detriment of other types of learning, and urged that policy makers should conceive of education in a much more encompassing fashion. Specifically, the report identified that education throughout life was based upon four pillars:

1. Learning to know
2. Learning to do
3. Learning to live together
4. Learning to be.

Learning to know Although this may sound as though it is concerned with the acquisition of knowledge, rather learning to know implies learning how to learn. The report emphasizes that, because of the infinite nature of knowledge, attempting to know everything becomes more and more pointless. To be truly educated, a person now needs a broad general education and the opportunity to study a small number of subjects in depth. Further than that, the process of learning to think is a lifelong one and can be enhanced by every kind of human experience.

Learning to do We have moved on from the industrial model of the twentieth century, and 'learning to do' can no longer mean what it did when people were trained to perform very specific tasks in an economy based on manufacturing. Rather the growth of service industries has meant that the key concept is now 'personal competence', with the qualities of communication, team and problem-solving skills assuming greater importance. From now on, excellent interpersonal skills will be an essential job requirement.

Learning to live together There's a challenge thrown down in relation to this aspect of learning: can we educate young people to avoid conflict or peacefully resolve it? It's a difficult challenge because of a human inclination to entertain prejudices against other people. The recommendations are that formal education should set aside sufficient time and opportunity to engage young people in collaborative and social activities from an early age.

Learning to be Human development throughout life is a process based both on self-knowledge and on relationships with other people. Young people should receive an education that equips them to develop their own independent critical way of thinking to be able to make up their own minds, solve their own problems and shoulder their own responsibilities. More than ever before, the essential task of education seems to be that young people should develop their talents and keep control of as much of their lives as they can.[8]

These categories shift the emphasis from a fairly narrow definition of school learning to a broader concept of the components necessary for education for the twenty-first century. They encourage us to think of learning in terms of what has been described as a broader journey of personal, social, emotional and intellectual growth (Leora Cruddas 2005:6). This is a perspective that highlights a major problem with education systems in separating academic learning from personal growth. It is a perspective that seeks the synthesis of learning for the achievement of formal educational outcomes with preparation for personal growth and citizenship:

> Moral purpose of the highest order is having a system where all students learn, the gap between high and low performance becomes greatly reduced, and what people learn enables them to be successful citizens and workers in a morally based knowledge society.
>
> Michael Fullan 2003: 29

Reflection

This chapter has brought together a range of perspectives on learning. Learning has been considered as processes of individual cognitive and emotional development, and in addition, the importance of learning as a social activity has also been highlighted. Plainly, a narrow conception of learning as the acquisition of academic and vocational knowledge is no longer adequate to prepare young people to meet the challenges of twenty-first century life and work.

You may want to think about how you account for emotional and social factors in your work with young people, particularly in respect of how such factors may be creating barriers to learning. And what do you think of the arguments for and against theories of learning styles? Can you see how ideas about learning styles may be helpful for young people, but that there is a danger of encouraging labelling? Overall, this chapter has sought to demonstrate the complexity of human learning, as a way of illustrating that an overly narrow focus on school learning is no longer sufficient to prepare young people for their future.

Key points

- The immense capacity of the average human brain has the potential to improve and extend learning
- Research in neuroscience has discovered changes in the brain that occur in adolescence
- There is now less acceptance that intelligence is a fixed and stable entity; alternative views look upon intelligences as different qualities that can grow and develop
- The development of emotional intelligence is as important as academic learning
- Learning styles can provide a framework for young people to understand how they think and learn
- Developing metacognition is crucial to learning to learn
- Learning always takes place in a particular context, and is embedded in a set of social relationships
- The 4 Pillars of Learning offers a broad perspective on learning that is not confined to academic and vocational learning.

Notes

[1] Stephen Pinker 2002:45.
[2] The work of Martin Teicher and Deborah Yurgelun-Todd as reported by Misia Landau in *The Harvard University Gazette*. www.waldorflibrary.org/Articles/Adolescence2.pdf
[3] Thies 2003:52 cited in the Coffield Review 2004:26.
[4] Ibid., pp. 9–10. A version of my summary of Dweck's patterns also appears in *The*

Learning Coach: Coaching for Learning, a module on the learning coach accredited training course, Welsh Assembly Government.

5   Paris and Winograd 1990: 28–9 also cited by Val Klenowski 2002:34.

6   Lev Vygotsky 1978: 90 cited by Michael Shayer 2003: 465.

7   *Learning: The Treasure Within*. UNESCO 1996.

8   Summarized from the description of the 4 Pillars of Learning at www.unesco.org/delors/fourpil.htm.

3

How do we define coaching?

Too much instruction makes young people too dependent on the teacher.
John Abbott and Terry Ryan 2000:270

Chapter 1 tried to answer the question 'Why' in relation to coaching, and Chapter 2 considered the 'What' in relation to learning. This chapter follows on to consider 'How': not the fine detail of the CARE model yet – that will come later. But with terms such as coaching, mentoring and helping used interchangeably, it's important to set out a particular definition of coaching. We also need to explore how coaching fits with a traditional definition of teaching. You may look for this sort of clarification if you're the type of thinker who needs to understand the reasoning behind something before you move into action. For you, it may be important to know how the model has been influenced by theory, and the beliefs and values that underpin it. Perhaps you're also wondering whether the CARE model will be relevant for your own particular work context. So this chapter will also be answering the 'Who' question – who is it aimed at, and is it an overall approach that you can use in your own work with young people?

The drivers of change in our fast-changing world have resulted in changing practices of working with young people. The trend towards personalized learning, and the skills agenda have been just two that were identified in Chapter 1. Workforce re-modelling has also meant that there are now many more people working in class-rooms to support the work of teachers. We have a range of 'paraprofessionals' assisting young people in their learning – whether called teaching assistants, learning support assistants (LSAs) or learning mentors. In Wales, a new role of *learning coach* has been introduced and since 2007, within the 14–19 *Learning Pathways* policy, all young people in Wales have an entitlement to support from a learning coach. (See Appendix 3 for case studies from learning coaches.)

There has also been a widespread movement of support for young people from other sources. There is an international student mentoring movement; to varying degrees universities in different countries have trained their students as mentors to provide practical help for young people in schools. The National Mentoring Pilot Project in the UK was an example; starting in 1999, it emerged from a conviction that universities should be improving learning and raising aspirations in schools in their catchment areas (Alan Evans 2003: 6–7).

Whatever their job title, a large number of people working in educational environments – teachers, LSAs, mentors, counsellors – would probably say that they also 'coach' as part of their role. But it's the wide range of job titles that makes it even more important to have a clear sense of what 'coaching' is. So in this chapter I'll be trying to tease out and clarify my definition, as well as how I see the role for coaching in relation to young people and learning.

One thing I want to do is draw back from further compartmentalizing work with children and young people. My approach to coaching is not to see it as a specific job description that fits a particular job role. Rather my approach is to see coaching as an overarching philosophy, a set of principles that can be applied within a range of different job roles, a skill set that can enhance work with young people in general. It is an approach to developing learning that is influenced by what we now know about how people learn, and how skill in the use of language can influence the development of thinking.

Michael Shayer (2003: 465–85) has pointed out that, before one can dream of an ideal solution to school learning, one first must tackle the problem of the Western environment that has produced a 'cultural deprivation' whereby so many young people cannot benefit from schooling once it goes beyond the primary level. He cites the results of a survey of 14,000 children aged 10 to 16 that indicate that the range of mental development in any one year group is far, far wider than anyone dreamed. Significantly, the survey indicates that in any one year group or class of 12-year-olds of mixed ability, maybe no more than 20 per cent will be functioning at their true mental potential.

Shayer suggests the notion of *intervention* as an intermediate tactic to increase the proportion of children who can attach a mental level at which they can process their learning during the course of ordinary instructional teaching. I interpret that as achieving the capacity to realize potential and facilitate independent learning. He claims there is ample evidence to show that this tactic can be successful, and further suggests that, perhaps in 30 years' time when intervention methodology has been practised with all age groups and most children realize their potential, 'good teaching practice' will have evolved to a seamless integration of instruction and intervention. That, indeed, would be an exciting prospect.

While I can relate the CARE model to the notion of an *intervention*, a framework and an approach that can be applied in support of instructional teaching in order to achieve unrealized potential, there are two very important issues that need clarification. The first is twofold: defining the difference between coaching and mentoring, and how coaching fits with teaching. The second stems from the traditional nature of coaching as being 'non-directive' and whether this feature can, or should, be applied to work with young people.

The difference between coaching and mentoring

This first difficulty lies in the fact that the terms mentoring and coaching are used interchangeably. Some people think that the words mean the same anyway, but for me there are essential differences that need to be teased out. Mentoring is a very old established practice – the term itself derives from the name of an experienced and trusted adviser charged with tutoring the young son of a king of Ancient Greece. But the trend towards the practice of coaching is so persistent that it must mean that there are subtle but important differences.

So as a starting point, Figure 3 is an attempt to express the differences between coaching and mentoring, taking the 'traditional' idea of mentoring, and a 'non-directive' model of coaching. It may be that not everyone will agree with the analysis, others may say that what they do in practice is a bit of both. It's certainly not a case

Coaching	Mentoring
Generic helping skills that can be applied to different contexts	Expert knowledge/experience in a particular area
Depends upon creating a sharing trustful relationship	Relationship depends on different status between mentor and mentee
Avoids giving advice	Gives advice
Maintains a belief that people can find their own answers	Offers answers from their own experience
High level of skills in precision questioning and reflecting	High level of skill in their area of expertise
Coachee has ownership of change and development	Mentor provides a role-model for potential change
Provides a blend of support with high challenge	Provides a blend of support with advice
Takes the perspective of the whole person in order to focus on solutions	Takes a focus on specific issues/tasks

Figure 3: Coaching and mentoring table

of either/or as practices may merge. And even though in this book the case is being made for coaching, neither is it a case that coaching is superior to mentoring. Both have a role to play, but they do have different relationships and different skill sets, so it's important to tease these out.

This definition evolved from much debate and discussion with colleagues, and there were two aspects in particular that caused concern. First, some thought that because of the different status in a mentoring relationship, a mentee could develop a dependence upon the mentor that was not helpful to their development as an independent learner. It is a point made by Will Thomas and Alistair Smith (2004: 28):

> Arguably one of the dangers of mentoring advice is that there can be a difference in status between the mentor and the person they are mentoring. This can lead the mentee to feel that they must take the advice even if they feel unsure about it.

Of course, this might be a danger with coaching also, if the coach does not adhere to an ultimate aim of the independence of the learner. A power differential in working with young people has to be acknowledged, and can very easily result in the creation of dependency. But at the simplest level:

> coaching is a process and relationship within which the person being coached decides what the course of action will be and devises their own solution.
>
> Will Thomas and Alistair Smith 2004: 28

This second issue – whether coaching for learning for young people can be 'non-directive' – requires much more discussion, and warrants a section of its own. But first I want to explore how I see a model of coaching fitting with teaching.

How does coaching fit with teaching?

I've already indicated that I see coaching as an intervention sitting alongside instruction in enhancing the portfolio of professional practice of a teacher. All decisions a teacher makes requires professional judgement, and when and where to employ a coaching strategy will form part of that judgement. So it may help to lay out the features of teaching against coaching, as I did with mentoring.

Of course this is a fairly simplistic approach and you can get hung up on arguing that teaching is much more than the activities that appear in that column. You can argue that many teachers already engage in the activities that come under the

Teaching	Coaching
Subject-specific expertise	Generic helping skills that can be applied to different contexts
Relationship of different status between teacher and student	Depends upon creating a sharing trustful relationship
Gives advice	Avoids giving advice
Offers answers from their own 'expert' position	Maintains a belief that people can find their own answers
High level of knowledge in their area of expertise	High level of skills in precision questioning and reflecting
Gives guidance on the acquisition of subject knowledge and skills	Coachee has ownership of change and development
Provides a blend of support with advice	Provides a blend of support with high challenge
Takes a focus on specific subject knowledge a skills	Takes the perspective of the whole person in order to focus on solutions

Figure 4: Teaching and coaching table

coaching heading. But as with mentoring, there is a core of essential difference between a coaching approach and a traditional teaching approach – and the core essential difference lies in the relationship.

In my experience it involves a significant shift of mindset for some teachers comfortable in a traditional didactic style to step back from the role of 'expert' to adopt a coaching role. As Mike Hughes (2006: 61) surmises, although a great many teachers have considerable experience of mentoring, few have extensive experience of coaching. And further:

> Coaching requires a very different range of skills and techniques, and therefore, for many teachers, represents a significant shift in mindset ... after many years of making judgements, having opinions and giving advice, the first instinct of many people is to tell. Moving into coaching involves, for many teachers, breaking the habit of a lifetime.

Yet I've also seen that when teachers have adopted coaching strategies that encourage students to talk, learn from each other and explore their own learning styles, there has been surprise and delight at the enthusiasm for learning they've been able to stimulate.

Clearly, teaching is a highly complex activity where a teacher may have to make a thousand decisions a day. A teacher who has developed professional flexibility will choose from a range of behaviours to suit each situation. Some of those decisions may involve switching from one role to another as needs dictate, i.e. teacher, mentor or coach. The important factor is that these choices are underpinned by a clear understanding of the difference in the roles. I've sought to demonstrate that coaching is not mentoring, and it is also different from teaching. Nevertheless I've also found that the application of coaching within the portfolio of teachers' skills can improve teacher/student relationships and achieve outcomes in respect of the development of student independent learning.

Can coaching for learning for young people be 'non-directive'?

Trying to tease out the difference between coaching and mentoring, and coaching and teaching, raises a particular dilemma. A mentor – traditionally – is an older, more experienced person who can offer support and guidance to a younger person. A teacher – traditionally – is also a more experienced person who can offer instruction from a basis of expert knowledge. Plainly these definitions fit comfortably with a practice of adults working with young people. A coach, on the other hand, does not necessarily have knowledge in a specific area, but has an understanding of the influences on learning and development, and a high level of expertise in generic helping skills. A highly skilled coach would be able to work in any context. The focus of coaching will be supporting people to move in the direction of personal growth, without imposing 'advice' on what that direction should be.

And therein lies the tension. Can coaching really be 'non-directive' in work with young people? Because of their youth and inexperience, don't young people *need* advice and guidance?

*(I'm reminded here of a comment from a headteacher friend. The occasion was some years ago when we were attempting to define the role of learning coaches in Wales. 'What our young people **don't** need', said the head, 'is another expert'.)*

I've spent a long time debating this issue. So I'll try to play devil's advocate in addressing some of differing *Points of View* that have arisen in my discussions with colleagues. In devising the CARE model of coaching, I've had to think this through very carefully, and these are responses to some of the arguments that have been raised.

POINT OF VIEW: Young people don't know everything so they need to be **given the information** they need.

Is giving information the same as getting people to think?

Take the example of health information that is available to young people. All the evidence is that campaigns that rely on giving facts – such as about the dangers of smoking, drug taking, drinking, sexually transmitted diseases – have very little effect. People only make healthy choices when they become engaged in thinking about the issues in a personal way. In the face of facts about risks to health, people can always come up with reasons why they should continue a less-than-healthy habit. Young people continue to be drawn into smoking for instance, despite lurid warnings printed on packets and legal bans on smoking in public places. Do you recognize any of these reasons that people use to justify a habit?

- My grandfather smoked 60 a day all his life and lived until he was 90.
- It's the only pleasure I have.
- I'd be a lot more stressed if I didn't smoke.
- All my friends smoke – it's the only time we get together for a chat.

Evidently there is far more to smoking than a habit where knowledge of the dangers has the potential to change the behaviour. Particularly for adolescents, smoking can represent a (sometimes rebellious) rite of passage into the adult world and an assertion of autonomy (Ian McDermott 2007: 36). So behaviours such as smoking can be associated with issues of identity, issues that need to be addressed at a deeper level than merely at the level of factual information.

Coaching can encourage a *different level of thinking* than mere consideration of facts.

POINT OF VIEW: Young people don't know what they don't know so **need instruction**.

Do all young people do what they are told to do?
Does everyone learn when instructed?
Of course young people – because of their youth and comparative inexperience – may need advice and information. They can also be surrounded by people whose main purpose and practice is to give them advice and information. Unfortunately, it's when advice is framed as instruction that many young people rebel and reject the advice and information out of hand. Because of their emerging drive for self-management young people may opt for a non-conformist stance, or alternatives outside the control of the school system (see Chapter 2).

Rather than just being another person to give instruction, a coach is concerned with the *process* of engaging the young person to think for themselves.

POINT OF VIEW: Young people **cannot be left to learn by themselves** without the guidance from some one older.

Learning is something we all do naturally. Learning is part of life. It's not that young people cannot learn by themselves; as they grow older, they may be choosing to learn only what has relevance for them. Most of us learned to walk on our own: we may have had some support but generally it was by trial and error and reaching out for the support we needed. Unless there is some physical, mental or social impediment, all children will learn to talk: they will grasp the intricate grammatical structure of their language without any formal instruction.

Unfortunately, as we grow older this natural ability to learn can become stifled: there may be external barriers or we may unconsciously impose our own internal barriers. Early failure at school learning may be one reason for a young person to reject further formal learning experiences.

Coaching can address *barriers to learning*, in order to release the natural ability in young people to learn for themselves.

Finally you may also be wondering about how the non-directive aspect of coaching fits for a teacher needing to have a learning objective for a lesson? And as I've previously said that coaching is *solution-focused*, doesn't that mean that some direction has to be set?

In answer to these points, this is the way I have defined a non-directive approach. Firstly, of course a teacher would have a learning objective for a lesson because they will have an overview of the learning that needs to be attained. Plainly also the learning objective needs to be shared with the class in a way that they see themselves engaging as partners in the learning activity. But using a coaching approach, the pathway to that learning objective will evolve out of the learning *process;* the pathway may go in different directions as teacher and student interact, with the teacher using skilled questioning to encourage the student's own exploration of different alternatives. So while the teacher has a learning objective, the pathway to the objective emerges from the interaction between the student and the teacher, and this is the aspect I would deem to be non-directive.

Older teachers may say this is how they used to teach anyway. But it may be that the imposition of a prescriptive National Curriculum, and the pressure to raise standards, has indeed squeezed out this approach from a teacher's professional portfolio. There are also essential, more up-to-date differences. As you will have seen in Chapter 2, nowadays we know more about how people learn, and we also know more about how the craft of skilled and precision questioning can influence learning and understanding.

If we think about the non-directive aspect in relation to coaching as a separate activity, in a traditional model of coaching a solution will not be imposed by the coach. But if you work in education you will be familiar with the pressure to improve outcomes by raising attainment and achievement. So you may be thinking that the sole outcome for coaching for learning needs to be achievement of formal academic and vocational qualifications.

However, you will have seen that young people are involved in emotional, social and intellectual development as they search for identity and meaning and make the transition to adulthood. You will also know that emotional state and issues of self-esteem can significantly impact upon a young person's ability to concentrate on formal educational attainment.

So solutions that evolve in coaching may not merely relate to the attainment of educational outcomes. Rather the solutions may need to consider the complex interaction of achievement in three areas:

- Academic achievement
- Personal development
- Social and life skills.[1]

Having a broad approach doesn't mean that coaching is lacking in purpose. On the contrary, having a focus on solutions is very purpose*ful*. But again, it's not the coach who sets a particular direction from their own perspective; the direction *evolves* out of the interaction between the coach and the young person. Young people need to have ownership of a solution to be motivated to achieve an outcome. So the role of the coach is to encourage that ownership by allowing a solution to emerge from the coaching process.

This is why coaching is such a highly skilled enterprise. Coaching takes a view of learning encompassing all three dimensions. Rather than viewing academic or vocational learning as a single goal, a solutions focus may develop an understanding of how personal and social skills development impact upon academic achievement. In taking a holistic view, a coach can encourage young people to view learning as part of life, and to gain confidence by recognizing their learning successes, wherever they occur.

Coaches take a young person through the *process* of working on solutions – they don't provide the answers.

Thinking Space 1

As the agenda in schools switches from teaching to learning, it is wholly appropriate that there should be a parallel transitions from training to coaching as coaching is much more than short-term improvements in performance; coaching, fundamentally, is about learning.

Mike Hughes 2004: 31

An 'adult learning' approach

I studied many theories of learning while researching this book, including concepts of adult learning. The notion of 'andragogy' was popularized by Malcolm Knowles in line with his conviction that adults learned differently from children. For Knowles, there were some basic assumptions about adult learners that were different from the assumptions about child learners on which traditional pedagogy is based:

1. **Self-concept:** Adults mature from being a dependent personality towards being a self-directed human being

2. **Experience:** Adults accumulate a growing reservoir of experience that becomes a resource for learning

3. **Readiness to learn:** As adults mature, they become increasingly orientated to the tasks of their social development

4. **Orientation to learning:** As adults mature their orientation shifts from one of subject-centredness to one of problem-centredness

5. **Motivation to learn:** As a person matures the motivation to learn becomes internal.[2]

It seemed to me that these assumptions fitted with my approach to coaching for learning for young people. I could recognize these emerging features in young people negotiating the transition to adulthood. I could also see the difficulties that could be encountered when these features were not accommodated in approaches to learning; such as when the urge for self management becomes so strong that it leads to open rebellion against forms of adult control in schooling. Time and time again I was to find examples of practitioners who were able to motivate previously disengaged young people by creating a mutually trustful relationship; of young people who responded, not just to a different learning environment, but to being treated 'like adults'.[3]

It was when I looked at how writers have described the environmental factors that favoured adult learning that I felt there was an overlap with the assumptions of the CARE model of coaching. For adults, the learning environment must be physically and psychologically comfortable; adults need to know the reason they need to learn something or how it will benefit them; previous bad experiences in schooling may affect self esteem; adults bring a great deal of life experience to formal classroom learning.[4] All these fitted with my own understanding of conditions for learning. Even though young people may lack the wider experience of older adults, they still have experiences outside schooling that can be drawn upon for the benefit of formal learning. And crucially, there was a recognition that, since adults are moving into a self-directed learning mode, there must be some way of helping them with this transition, which was exactly how I saw the role for coaching for learning for young people.

Values of the CARE model of coaching

So far I've been trying to articulate how the features of the CARE model have been influenced by theoretical concepts and social influences. No human behaviour emerges from a vacuum; all behaviour and activities will be influenced by external factors that influence a basis of underlying beliefs and values. We may not often talk about our own specific beliefs and values – we may not even be aware of them consciously – yet they will be evident in our behaviour and the way we conduct our lives.

But when it comes to justifying specific behaviours – such as in the CARE model – it's important to be *explicit* about beliefs and values. Part of being a reflective practitioner will be examining beliefs and values to check they are consistent with our behaviour. As Anne Brockbank and Ian McGill (2006: 9) put it:

> The method of mentoring or coaching is likely to be influenced by the philosophy that underpins it, and in general the theoretical base is implicit and undeclared. [...] Because the philosophy that underlies any approach will impact on its outcome, we recommend that practitioners take time to examine their philosophy, however embedded it may be, and make this known to prospective clients.

Being explicit about the philosophy of coaching is important not just in considering outcomes, but because, if there's a mismatch between our deeply held beliefs and values and our behaviour, then in our relationships with other people we will not come across as credible trustworthy people. I'm sure you will have had the experience of hearing someone say something, but knowing in your heart of hearts that they didn't really mean it. This is because at an unconscious level we pick up 'leakage' of the real meaning from a person's body language. As you read further you will learn more about how we all read body language clues to give us assurance that people mean what they say. So it's not enough to acquire a new set of behaviours, we have to ensure that the behaviours match our beliefs and values, so that there is consistency between what we say and what we do. To start with we need to identify the influences on our beliefs and values; whether they have grown out of our practical experience of life, or whether they have been informed by the findings of research or theoretical concepts.

Like everyone, I suppose I can say I have an eclectic mix of influences on my own beliefs and values. I've already identified a reference point in the review of psychological theories in Chapter 1, and the different theories of learning in Chapter 2. Then I've had practical influences from my own training experiences, particularly in relation to the models of Neuro-linguistic Programming and Brain-friendly Learning. And of course we all have our own 'practice-based evidence' – our discoveries of what works in practice will have fed back into our beliefs and values. A final influence has been an appreciation and recognition that perhaps the features of adult learning can be more applicable for young people negotiating the transition from childhood than the features of traditional pedagogy.

Thus the statements below are a 'beliefs benchmark' for the rest of this book. I believe they are principles that give the CARE model of coaching an aligned purpose: to help young people achieve their potential as fully functioning human beings, and at the same time develop ourselves personally and professionally.

Human beings are unique and individual in ways of learning

As you will have seen in Chapter 2, we have a proliferation of research and ideas on learning 'styles' and 'preferences' to choose from; they reflect a consensus that has moved away from thinking that everyone learns in the same way. The era of 'personalized learning' outlined in Chapter 1 indicates that policy makers also recognize the individuality of young people, and of their ways of learning. Even so, there is still quite a way to go before the unique individuality of every person is accommodated within the vastness of state systems of education. It is still too convenient to put young people into sets, classes, categories, routes of progression – fitting the person to the system rather than having enough flexibility in the system to accommodate the individual.

This is not the same as saying that everyone should expect to be able to promote their own individuality at the expense of others and the system they have to work in. Human beings evolved as social animals, we will have to live and work with various groups of people throughout our lives. The balancing act of getting along with people and working within social systems, while at the same time developing their individuality, will be an important learning for young people.

Applied to coaching, having a belief about human uniqueness helps us avoid stereotyping young people – and that doesn't just apply to the danger of too readily allocating them into categories of low achievement. The categorization of 'gifted and talented' is just as harmful if it creates an intellectual elite and blinds us to the uniqueness of the individual.[5]

So this belief reminds us to approach every young person with a fresh pair of eyes and ears, and an enthusiasm and interest in discovering and encouraging their unique patterns of thinking and learning.

People have to construct their own personal meaning for learning to occur

This belief stems from the dominance of *constructivism* as a theory of learning (see Chapter 1). It also fits with my understanding of the phrase 'the map is not the territory'[6] which philosophers have used to describe how we all have our own internal mental 'map' of external reality. So 'new' learning needs to be related to and use the learner's existing experience and knowledge, their own 'map' of understanding. Learning is not something that can be 'done' to someone else without their participation, it needs the learner's active engagement in the process.

From the *social constructionist* model we see how interaction with another person can help someone develop their learning. So in coaching, the craft of using precision language is directed at helping young people become aware of their own 'map' and making meaning for themselves.

People can develop their potential in a relationship of empathy and respect

At the core of coaching is the quality of the relationship with the young person. From the *humanistic* model is drawn an understanding that people can develop and grow when they encounter conditions of *unconditional positive regard* (see Chapter 1). A coach needs to demonstrate empathy and respect for a young person, and be a real person within the relationship. You will see as you read further that one of the skills of building rapport is 'matching' – a coach can demonstrate empathy with a person by matching their language patterns, or body language (see Stage 1). Again it's a careful balancing act: demonstrating empathy by matching while avoiding being drawn into artificial 'mateyness'. Matching doesn't mean being 'like' the other person – in fact a young person would soon 'suss out' a false friendliness. Being a 'real' person is essential to establishing trust. Being able to demonstrate understanding and empathy for another person while maintaining your own individuality needs a mature, principled and well-developed attitude.

People have all the resources they need

Of course this doesn't refer to access to material resources, rather to the personal resources that we all have, which for many people can remain largely untapped.

Unless there is a physical disability that hinders their progress, all children will learn to walk, and to talk. They will be born with an urge to explore and learn about their environment. Unfortunately, as they grow, and social factors impact upon their development, this innate capacity for learning may become inhibited or directed towards activities that are not in tune with their inner drive towards self-actualization.

From what we now know about the brain, we also know that we only utilize a percentage of the creative capacity at our disposal (see Chapter 2). We can also acknowledge that young people have many 'learning' experiences that they can draw upon – although they may not yet have made the connection that enables them to recognize the learning skills they already have. Having this belief means we can encourage young people to recognize the resources they have, and to overcome the barriers to learning they may have developed through their life experiences.

The coaching relationship is a partnership of learners

Coaching is different from mentoring in that a coach does not have to be an 'expert' in a particular subject area. The expertise of a coach lies in highly developed coaching skills. Linked to the first belief that everyone is a unique and individual learner, it's evidently an area of expertise that needs constant attention to ensure the practice of coaching is relevant to each individual young person. If we also recognize that we live in a world where change is the only thing we can depend upon, then plainly continuous professional development must be a permanent feature of our working life. Experiencing ourselves as learners is a means of maintaining the egalitarian basis of the coaching relationship, and being open and receptive to new interpretations and challenges. As an attitude that is part of your 'professional identity' it will include:

> the overarching beliefs and values you hold about yourself, other people and the whole social environment in which you live and work. It's from this personal value-base that you invest meaning into the roles you enact.
>
> Jacquie Turnbull 2007: 21

Fundamental differences between coaching and other ways of working with young people

You may already be trained to work with young people, and you may have considerable skills in that area, so at this stage you may be wondering how coaching in general is different from what you do already. I've tried to build a picture of how coaching is different from giving instruction and information, and to summarize I'll give what I believe are core features of the CARE model that may differ from other ways of working with young people. The CARE model of coaching for learning:

- *Deals with a different level of thinking*

  The CARE model encourages metacognition – or thinking about thinking. Helping young people to recognize and gain their own understanding of how they think and learn features strongly in coaching for learning.

- *Is concerned with process*

  The relationship between coach and coachee is the core of the CARE model. An egalitarian relationship where the coach comes across as a genuine person is essential to establish trust and openness. The process involves the practice of a high level of skill in precision questioning.

- *Addresses barriers to learning*

  Barriers may be a complex mix of past experiences, low self esteem, fear of failure, issues of identity, discriminatory practices. Helping young people to understand that their personal barriers don't have to be permanent fixtures, and gaining the confidence to challenge external barriers, is an essential element.

- *Combines high support with high challenge*

  Support alone will not stimulate motivation, and challenge without personal support can be demotivating for many young people. The combination of the two means that coaching can create conditions of support within which challenging goals to realize potential can be established.

Overview of coaching approaches

Of course there is no 'one way' of coaching and in this chapter I've tried to outline the particular philosophy of the CARE model. It's also useful to consider different approaches in order to further clarify the differences between coaching and the way you may be working already.

Functionalist	An objective goal to be achieved with little or no exploration of the coachee's personal world
	Suppresses challenge and questioning in order to maintain the status quo and social equilibrium
	Process is didactic and directive
	Learning outcome is single loop and limited to improvement
	Reinforces existing power relations and can reproduce social inequalities
	Coach serves the 'needs' of the organization by unwittingly ensuring power structures remain intact
Engagement	Recognizes the subjective world of the learner
	Broadly humanist approach in order to achieve functionalist objectives and minimize opposition
	Power relations in the social context are largely ignored and kept invisible
	Hidden agenda is maintenance of status quo
	Learning outcome is single loop with potential for some reflection
	Non-directive in helping people to learn rather than teaching them
Evolutionary	Acknowledges and respects the subjective world of individuals
	The coachee is seen as resourceful
	Generates ownership of goals by the coachee
	Taking individual responsibility for learning and development may involve challenging discriminatory behaviour and the prevailing power structures that may inhibit learning
	Reflective dialogue has the potential for double loop learning and transformation
	The coach and the coachee are equals in the coaching relationship

Figure 5: Coaching approaches

Source: Anne Brockbank and Ian McGill 2006: 12–14/95–104

The descriptions derived from the analysis of Anne Brockbank and Ian McGill can be thought about in different ways. We can think of the different approaches as representing the development of society generally in our modern world; from being structured and ordered through to more recognition of the individual. We can also consider the approaches from the perspective of education systems: moving from systems that emphasize control and compliance to a more egalitarian ethos. Then we might consider that at first glance the stages map across the focus illustrated in Fig. 2 The Focus of Coaching for Learning: with perhaps the Functionalist approach being relevant for pre-14 students, the Engagement approach suitable for 14–19 students, and the Evolutionary a fitting approach for lifelong learning.

However, if a policy of personalized learning is not merely to be tokenism, we have to accept the challenge of developing strategies for consulting students about their education (see Chapter 1). If we are serious in an intention to prepare young people for an unknown future, we have to encourage their confidence and adaptability, stimulate their awareness and their ability to be self-directing. The Evolutionary approach to coaching may seem a significant shift from older established ways of working with young people, but it is representative of the shift in cultural values and social relations in wider society: shifts away from overt authority and expertise, shifts in power away from producers of goods and services towards the consumers and clients, shifts away from formality towards informality (Norman Fairclough 1992: 148–9). Of course in working with young people, there remains a tension in that these wider cultural shifts may be in conflict with the pressures on schools to improve efficiency and reach targets. In addition, while it may be easy to embrace a person-centred approach intellectually, a great deal of practice may be needed to eradicate ingrained patterns of behaviour (Brockbank and McGill 2006: 204).

Nevertheless I see the CARE model as being aligned to the Evolutionary approach in respect of the overarching philosophy. An important factor for me is that, as a person-centred approach, it provides the opportunity to realize potential, and in addition to help young people in the difficult developmental task of negotiating the transition from childhood to adolescence. As an intervention that sits alongside instruction, it can address this latter aspect that perhaps has been somewhat neglected during the overly prescriptive demands on teaching and schooling since the 1990s.

Reflection

This chapter has defined the features of coaching in general. In particular, it has teased out the differences between coaching and mentoring, and identified how coaching fits alongside traditional didactic teaching. It is important to be aware of the differences because coaching, as well as encompassing a very different skill set from other behaviours, is based upon a very different set of assumptions. These assumptions have been presented as a series of beliefs and values. All human behaviour is an expression of underlying beliefs and values, and this chapter has sought to identify how the particular beliefs and values of the CARE model have been influenced by research and practice.

You may want to consider whether you recognize the beliefs and values as being similar to those that influence your own practice. Do they feel quite 'natural' to you; can you recognize that they influence the way you currently operate? Or is there anything you would find problematic if you were to attempt to put them into practice? Can you see how the changing cultural patterns in wider society are reflected in approaches to coaching?

Do you find the case for a 'non-directive' approach challenging? Or do the arguments seem persuasive? And what do you think of the adoption of a 'solutions' and 'adult learning' focus? All these issues coalesce into a particular approach that warrants consideration before moving to examine the detail of the CARE model.

Key points

- There are many people working to support the learning of young people, many of whom would say that they 'coach' as part of their role
- It's important to recognize the differences between coaching and mentoring
- Teachers can enhance their practice by incorporating the assumptions and practices of coaching into their portfolio of skills
- Coaching does not involve giving advice or instruction – rather it is an intervention that can work alongside instruction
- Coaching encourages metacognition – thinking about thinking
- A coach is concerned with the process of learning, and with addressing barriers to learning
- The solutions-focus of coaching may have to consider the interaction between academic achievement, personal development and social and life skills
- The assumptions of adult learning can be more appropriate for young people negotiating the transition to adulthood than the assumptions of traditional pedagogy
- The beliefs and values that underpin coaching need to be made explicit
- The philosophy of the Evolutionary approach to coaching fits with the CARE model for coaching for learning.

Notes

1. Julie Anne Ryan 2007: 559.
2. Adapted from Mark Smith 2002: 6.
3. See Appendix 1.
4. See Ron and Susan Zemke 1984.
5. See John White 2006 for an argument that deplores the UK government's 'Gifted and Talented' initiative.
6. Alfred Korzybski 1933.

4

The stages of the CARE model for realizing potential

We need a new framework to show how personal needs can be taken into account within universal equity and excellence in education.

Charles Leadbetter 2004: 6

> This chapter sets out the framework of the CARE model for coaching for learning. You will have already seen in Chapter 3 that there are a particular set of beliefs and values that underpin the model. In professional practice it is important to have both these elements: a set of beliefs and values that are influenced by theory, knowledge and practical experience; and a framework that provides a guidebook to all the important aspects to be covered. Without these guiding principles, there is a danger that professional practice can be reduced to a series of routine-ized actions. You will also have seen from Chapter 3 that I have suggested the CARE model could be used in two ways. Firstly, I see its potential as an *intervention* that sits alongside instruction in the portfolio of a teacher's professional practice. Secondly, there is its use as a stand-alone model for those working with young people in a dedicated coaching role.

Thus the framework of the CARE model is designed with a two-fold purpose: to provide a guidebook of techniques and behaviours to encourage learning, and to ensure the beliefs and values that underpin the model are put into practice. Further, you will see that the framework is broken down into stages, and in addition cross-cutting themes run through all stages. A further element, of course, is that in any initiative we need an ultimate aim to keep in mind: a very high-level outcome that encompasses all work with young people; whether at individual, group or institutional levels.

I see this high level ultimate aim as the development of *independent learning*. It is about learning all we can about learning for ourselves, and sharing that knowledge with young people through a coaching process so that they can develop their own understanding. The CARE model is only one starting point in this more general movement towards independent learning, a movement that is really in its early days of development. As David Hargreaves (2005: 19–20) has put it:

> Our knowledge and understanding, in both science and professional practice, of how independence in learning is best developed from one educational stage to another are currently limited. More needs to be done in science and in educational practice to discover what independence in learning involves and how it is best supported. Our present state of knowledge indicates that any specification probably includes:
>
> - The positive regards for, and personal valuing of, enhanced mastery
> - The will to learn
> - The ability to form clear goals and objectives for learning
> - The capacity to persist in adversity
> - Knowledge of learning processes and their management
> - Basic skills of information processing (literacy, numeracy, ICT skills, search skills)
> - The capacity to collaborate with other learners
> - The capacity to manage evaluations of performances and of progress and the capacity to use feedback constructively
> - The capacity to identify new horizons and to be creative and flexible in journeying towards them.

What I take from this comprehensive assessment is that the individual outcomes can be clustered under the three headings already mentioned in Chapter 3: so that solutions in coaching need to take account of the complex interaction between:

- Academic achievement
- Personal development
- Social and life skills.

A staged framework

Achievement and development under these three headings are therefore the middle-range outcomes of the CARE model. In relation to the stages, the usefulness of a staged model is being able to judge both the stage of development of the coaching intervention, and the strategies to adopt at any one time. In this respect, the framework can be applied both as a guide to structure a single session, and as an overarching framework of a long-term coaching relationship. However, it's also important to recognize that coaching is not something that runs in a specific linear manner, starting at Stage 1 and running in an orderly fashion through to Stage 4. For one thing, learners will not develop in a steady consistent manner, and there may also be social or emotional factors that impede the progress of learning. Everyone is different and each young person will have different needs. As Carol Magnus has commented:

> Coaching needs some managing/framework/best practice but is too personal to be controlled. What's needed is a framework that's open and flexible enough to allow organic growth.[1]

So while it can be helpful to have a sense of an overarching framework, in practice a coach will need to be flexible enough to switch backward and forward between the stages to accommodate the needs of the learner. For instance, rapport needs to be maintained throughout the coaching process, so if as a coach you pick up a sense that this aspect needs attention, you will need to slip back to Stage 1 to give extra attention to re-establishing rapport. In respect of the young person, the process of learning will involve the creation of new understandings. When this happens, they may need return to issues to examine them in light of their raised awareness, to repeat a learning process to build a deeper understanding.

You may therefore find it a useful metaphor to visualize yourself as a juggler managing a series of plates spinning atop bamboo poles. A juggler will set up the plates in order, setting them spinning one after another. But in order to achieve the outcome of keeping all the plates spinning at the same time, the juggler will need to

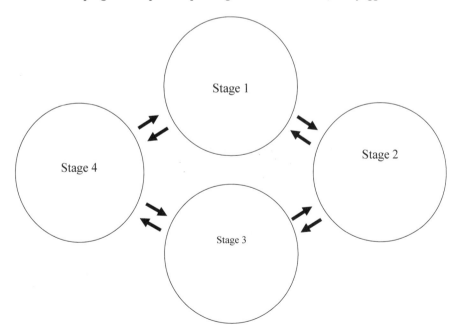

Figure 6: Stages of the CARE model

dodge back and forth, giving a touch here and a tweak there. Similarly, to keep the coaching process successfully on track, you may need to move back and forth between the stages, listening and looking out for where you may need to apply a different strategy.

An integrated approach

For me there is a further aspect to the stages: that is the potential to integrate your professional development with the necessary personal development that will ensure confident and assured practice. In relation to professional development, as you saw in Chapter 3, the idea that coaching can be considered an 'intervention' that integrates with instruction may appear a radical initiative for many teachers. In respect of their own model to promote higher-level thinking, Philip Adey and Michael Shayer (1997: 180) have acknowledged the impact on professional development:

> We have emphasized throughout that intervention methods demand a radical departure from normal teaching practice, requiring the development of skills designed to stimulate and stretch the student mentally which need a separate description as skills of intervention. Widespread adoption of such an art will require a substantial professional development programme for teachers.

Even acknowledging that point, we also have to recognize that in our modern fast-changing world, it is not enough to depend upon formal programmes of training to keep our practice relevant and up to date. The importance of developing reflective practice has already been stressed: the theme of reflection is carried throughout this book, and it also needs to be an approach that is integrated into coaching to ensure professional development is continuous.

But developing professionally is not just about acquiring new skills and practices – that would be merely reducing professionalism to routine-ized behaviours. Rather, developments in judgement, attitudes and abilities to cope with a wide range of situations and people, involve our development at a personal level. We all need an open and receptive attitude to our own learning, and to have the flexibility to adapt and change, if we are to survive successfully in a fast-changing modern world. Apart from the benefit to ourselves, the subtlest way we can influence young people to develop as learners is to demonstrate these attributes ourselves.

So as 'lead learners' those of us working in education need to take full advantage of learning and communication practices, and in addition to the intellectual and cognitive domains, we need to be strong in emotional intelligence (Turnbull 2007: 7).

As Barbara Larrivee (2000: 293) has emphatically put it, nothing else will serve, particularly for teachers dealing with the dynamic and complex state of today's classroom:

> More students are coming to school neglected, abused, hungry, and ill-prepared to learn and work productively. To combat increasing student alienation, and meet the scope and intensity of the academic, social and emotional needs of today's students, those entering the teaching profession will need to find a way to create authentic learning communities by adjusting the power dynamics to turn power *over* to power *with* learners. These changing demands call for teaching styles that better align with emerging metaphors of teacher as social mediator, learning facilitator, and reflective practitioner. Being able to function in these roles begins with teacher self-awareness, self-inquiry, and self-reflection, not with the students.

So from this perspective, the stages represent a progression of learning, both for young people and the coach. Each stage features skills and strategies that build on the previous and prepare for the next. And as already mentioned, the stages can also be experienced as a balancing act:

- A balance between the learning to achieve academic/vocational outcomes and that for personal development
- A balance between self-awareness and awareness of the influence of social factors
- A balance between learning for young people and professional development for the coach.

Stage 1 – Creating Comfort

Stage 1 is about creating the basis for a mutually beneficial coaching relationship. It involves awareness and attention to the physical and interpersonal features that encourage an optimum environment for learning. A major focus for attention in Stage 1 is on establishing *rapport*: the ability to relate to others in a way that creates a climate of trust and understanding (Sue Knight 1995: 122). It is something we normally accomplish intuitively and don't often think about until we become aware that it doesn't exist between ourselves and another person.

If we think about rapport as being able to 'connect' with other people, we can all recognize how that feels. There are some people with whom conversation flows freely, there are no misunderstandings, and with whom we feel at ease. Sometimes this appears to happen without any effort on our part, so we assume that some people are just more likeable, more easy to get along with, more trustworthy, and others are just 'difficult'.

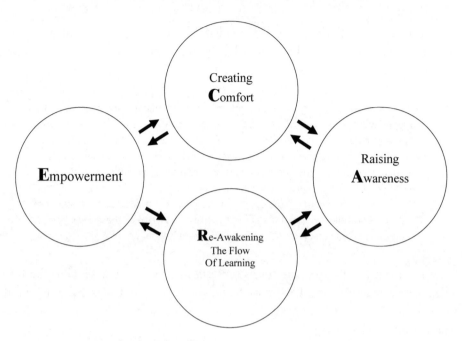

Figure 7: The CARE model for realizing potential

When our relationships with other people are good, we tend to take rapport for granted; we are not consciously aware of what is happening between us that is creating rapport. But because rapport is a 'process' between people, something must be happening to establish it. It therefore follows that if rapport is absent, the features that create it must be missing. When we understand those features that happen *unconsciously* in the good relationships, we are able to *consciously* replicate them when we want to 'create' a good relationship – as in coaching.[2]

Rapport warrants special attention, not just because it is crucial to good relationships, but because rapport – of itself – can influence outcomes. You only have to think about how much easier it is to go along with a suggestion from another person if you feel an affinity towards them: even when perhaps you don't wholeheartedly agree with the suggestion! Sue Knight (1995: 122) even suggests that most business decisions are made on the basis of rapport rather than on technical merit; not only instant rapport but rapport that has been built up in a relationship over time.

Plainly not every young person we meet up with will be likeable, responsive and easy to talk with. But liking another person is not a prerequisite for rapport (Genie Laborde 1998: 29). Rather Stage 1 is about the subtle strategies that you can use to create rapport and establish a climate of trust – even in the most challenging and difficult situations.

Trust is the other feature of good relationships that has similar qualities to rapport. As Robert Solomon and Fernando Flores (2001) have described it, although trust often seems invisible, it is the result of continuous attention and activity. It often only becomes noticeable when it has been challenged or violated. As with rapport, trust can be initiated and cultivated; as something which we can create and maintain as well as destroy, it is something for which we bear a responsibility.

As well as giving attention to establishing the features of good relationships, Creating comfort also refers to creating a physical and emotional environment conducive to learning. As you saw in Chapter 2, at a basic level of understanding of how people learn, we can appreciate that young people cannot learn when they are anxious, stressed or have too much 'stuff' going on in their heads. Neither will young people learn if they are bored, switched off or unmotivated. So Stage 1 is about creating the physical and interpersonal environment to encourage an optimum 'state' for learning.

By 'state' we mean the mental, physical and emotional conditions that combine to create our overall sense of ourselves at any one time, and which has a profound effect on our ability to learn. Kimberley Hare and Larry Reynolds (2004: 30) have stressed that when people are in an unresourceful state, learning is simply not possible, and the alternative is essential:

> A resourceful state is an absolute prerequisite for effective learning. The most important thing a facilitator can do is enable learners to get into a resourceful learning state.

For many young people, there will be a lot of groundwork to be achieved before 're-awakening the flow' that is a feature of Stage 3. We can be active in *state management*. We can take a fresh look at the physical environment we share with young people. What sort of message is it sending out? Is it saying that they are valued? Is it welcoming? Is it a relaxing yet stimulating place to be? We can be alert to how physiology is as important as psychology. We may not have a direct influence over whether young people have had enough food, water or sleep, but we can help them to be aware of how their physical condition affects their mental functioning. And we can also be sensitive to how their emotions may be affecting their aptitude for learning, help them to recognize the effects and acquire strategies of *state management*.

Key Words for Stage 1: Rapport – Trust – State management

Stage 2 – Raising Awareness

One thing 'Raising Awareness' is *not*, is raising awareness of problems. As you read in Chapter 1, constant analysis of problems can make them appear so large and intractable that it leads to paralysis and stifles positive action. Some young people may appear apathetic for just this reason: the difficulties they face seem so overwhelming that they give up on the will and energy to overcome them. (*I even notice this with professional colleagues: how often to you hear people start sentences with 'The problem I have is ...' or 'The difficulty is ...'? One result of a constant focus on problems or difficulties is that it drains energy and initiative.*)

Rather, the first focus for 'Raising Awareness' is on solutions rather than problems. Having a *solutions focus* can be quite a shift even for mature people, and when young people lack a wider experience of life to draw on, raising their awareness that there are different options, different choices, different paths to take can be the first step in generating motivation.

Yet even for mature people, this mental *reframing* can be quite a challenge. One reason may be that over the years we develop patterns of thinking and behaving: patterns that become so habitual that they feel 'part of us' and not something within our power to change. This may be due to a function of the brain called the 'habit system' that underlies our tendency to produce certain responses habitually (Steven Pinker 2002: 40).

Habits of thinking and behaviour we may indeed have, but the point of *meta-cognition* is getting us to think about our patterns of thinking, learning and perception, so that we can judge whether they are the most productive means of achieving solutions. Awareness has to precede the development of the skills of self-management, so helping young people become consciously aware of what were previously unconscious patterns of thinking has to come first. Metacognitive knowledge – the awareness – has to precede the development of metacognitive skills – the ability to self-manage (see Chapter 2).

Certainly reframing how we think to discover there are different options and different ways of thinking about current reality can create a certain amount of mental conflict. So it may seem strange that I'm suggesting for Stage 2 something that may disturb the mental or emotional 'comfort' I'm advocating for Stage 1. But as I've often quoted – 'confusion precedes understanding' – and it does seem that we have to 'disrupt' established patterns of thinking before new approaches can be accommodated. Similarly, in describing a classroom 'intervention' Michael Shayer (2003: 483) suggests it is a teacher's role to induce 'cognitive conflict' where energy flags or where young people have become complacent at too low a level of mental processing.

Peter Senge (1990: 142) makes a similar point at a broader level. He writes that when we get a vision of what we want, and we have that alongside a clear sense of our current reality (where we are in relation to what we want to be), then it generates what he calls 'creative tension'; a force to bring them together caused by the natural tendency of tension to seek resolution. He also sees learning how to generate and sustain this creative tension as the essence of personal management and control – in his terms 'personal mastery'.

Key Words for Stage 2: Solutions Focus – Metacognition – Reframing

Stage 3 – Re-Awakening the Flow of Learning

Another way of thinking about 'personal mastery' is to think about it in terms of 'self-efficacy'. This is a concept that lies at the heart of Albert Bandura's work in psychology, where he describes it as:

> the belief in one's capabilities to organize and execute the courses of action required to manage prospective situations.
>
> Bandura 1995: 2

The core of the theory is that people's level of motivation, emotional state and actions are based more on what they *believe* than on reality. The beliefs about ourselves that we develop throughout our lives exert a powerful effect upon our ability to manage our lives and achieve outcomes. Self-efficacy theory is comprehensive in that it addresses the origins of beliefs, the processes through which they operate, and provides explicit guidelines on how to enhance and develop efficacy.

One of the strongest effects that beliefs about ourselves can exert is the extent to which they can be 'limiting'. As you saw from the work of Carol Dweck in Chapter 2, beliefs about intelligence can have a significant effect on young people's motivation. The source of the 'failure identities' that many young people acquire (see also Chapter 1) will be the self-beliefs they derive from their life experience. Beliefs are also often irrational: they are based on assumptions of what we think we 'should' be like and 'should' be able to achieve. Such core beliefs can drive behaviour in unproductive directions, and because they are inferred from our interpretation of our experience, they often remain largely untested (Barbara Larrivee 2000: 302–3).

So just as 'confusion precedes understanding' challenging untested and assumed beliefs will need to precede the development of the skills of self-management. Bandura believes that self-efficacy can be learned, and that there is a role for social persuasion: verbal encouragement from others can help young people overcome self doubt and gain confidence in gathering 'mastery experiences'.

Therefore there is a role for *affirmation* in Stage 3 and it will be twofold: firstly to challenge limiting beliefs and expose their irrational basis. Inability to achieve at a task or a piece of work does not mean a person is totally unworthy, but this may often be the interpretation young people place upon failure. The second role for affirmation will be to boost confidence by identifying the positive elements of a young person's work and behaviour. Realistic feedback can raise awareness of elements that young people may have become blinded to as a result of the overwhelming self-defeating power of self-beliefs. Affirmation is also significant in defining the difference between the person and the behaviour; confirming the worth of the individual while giving realistic feedback on the behaviour. Adopting the interpretation 'there's no failure only feedback' will enable young people to face difficulties as challenges to be overcome rather than to give up on.

As well as seeking to encourage self-efficacy and give positive affirmation, in a Stage entitled 'Re-awakening the Flow of Learning', we also need to have an awareness of developmental aspects of young people in relation to their *learning readiness*. You will remember the use of the term in Chapter 1 in relation to Piaget's theory of stages of mental development. Piaget used the term 'operations' to describe the mental activities and strategies used by children, which progress in a series of stages. While younger children are pre-operational, between the ages of 6 and 12 years a child will develop concrete operations, and will be able to cope with mental strategies such as addition and subtraction. At age 12+, in the stage of formal operations, young people develop the capability to deal with abstract ideas and things outside their immediate experience (Steve Bartlett et al. 2001: 124–5).

For our purposes, I am taking a wider sense of the term learning readiness. As you also saw in Chapter 1, although no-one has challenged Piaget's basic assumptions, subsequent research has suggested the stages may be too confined, and that he may have underestimated the abilities of children and the speed at which they could progress. Early studies of readiness influenced educational practice to the degree that a practice of holding back children's school progression until they were ready to learn became common practice. However, Rita Watson (1998: 156) cites subsequent research that claims there is no evidence whatsoever that educational postponement in the early years can in any way enhance children's chances of success. Indeed, it's suggested that the negative social and emotional consequences can have adverse effects on a child's overall functioning.

A second reason for a broader approach is because Piaget did not consider any further development from his adolescent stage, and thus there is an implication that 'development' has come to an end. No such end point is imaginable in learning,[3] particularly as we are taking learning as a lifelong activity.

The findings of research also draw attention to other factors. You will remember from Chapter 2 the fact that in adolescence young people are experiencing brain growth spurts, and that not all parts of their brains will have settled into their adult form by puberty as was previously thought. An additional factor is that the major brain-growth spurt around 11 years of age is three times greater in girls. Then there's a reversal in a later brain growth spurt at 15, which is more substantial in boys (Philip Adey and Michael Shayer 1994: 141). So there's a gender factor that also needs to be taken account of in relation to learning readiness.

Thirdly, Adey and Shayer also note that the brain growth that occurs is not an increase in the actual number of cells in the cerebral cortex, but an increase in the 'connections' – the dendrites that allow transfer of the electrical impulses between neurons (see Chapter 2). Since this type of growth depends upon stimulation from the environment, presumably, if a young person has lacked an appropriate stimulating experience to encourage new growth, this will limit new connections being made. Thus, we can factor in the effects of limited social and emotional experience to a broad concept of learning readiness.

Overall, an awareness of all these factors informs our ability to engage in a crucial aspect of coaching intervention – to stimulate a re-awakening of the flow of learning and help young people move to the 'next level'. Mike Hughes (2006: 139) expresses it in simple terms:

> if a student is at 'level 3' she has to be working at 'level 4' in order to progress; 'level 2' is too easy, 'level 3' is stagnation (this is different from consolidation) while 'level 8' is over-optimistic. Few would argue that getting the level of challenge right for each student is a key challenge for the teacher. When work is too easy, students become bored; when work is perceived as impossibly hard, they switch off.

Key Words for Stage 3: Self-Efficacy – Affirmation – Learning Readiness

Stage 4 – Empowerment

Affirmation can play a part in encouraging motivation, but as our overall aim in coaching is to encourage independent learning, plainly the degree to which young people are able to *self*-motivate will be crucial. There was a particular reason for naming Stage 3 *Re-awakening* the Flow of Learning: it relates to the fact that, however they may appear to us, young people are not born de-motivated or disinterested. Rather, we were all born with a natural curiosity and a drive to explore our environment. David Fontana (1995: 149–50) explains how we can come to lose that innate interest in learning as we mature. Firstly, the response of others to our natural curiosity helps determine how it develops. If attempts at exploration are met with adult disapproval then such attempts are likely to become less frequent, to be replaced by apathy or random purposeless activity. Secondly, there is a close link between curiosity as a motivator and the degree of interest that can be derived from the learning experience. To the self-motivated, nothing is 'boring'. (Boring is just a place I've been to – it's in Oregon.) Probably the reason some things capture our interest and others do not is because of the degree of relevance to our daily lives. For many young people though, their school experience may not inspire this level of interest:

> the problem with much school learning is that it appears to lack this relevance. It takes place in an environment distinct from the outside world, and much of what it teaches is a preparation for tasks way ahead in the future, rather than in the present (or tasks which the child meets only in school and nowhere else).
> David Fontana 1995:150

So the first two features of Stage 4 are closely linked. To fulfil our overall aim of generating independent learning, *self-motivation* is essential. To become self-motivated, young people need to be able to relate to the learning aims; to see them as having purpose and relevance to their own interests. When imaginative teachers do this, they are able to hand over *ownership* of the learning to their students.

Plainly ownership of learning is much more than a simple handing over of tasks for students to complete single-handed. You will have seen that the coaching stages have been working towards Empowerment by addressing the complex interplay of cognitive, emotional and social factors. Bandura (1995: 18) refers to this aspect in pointing out that the implications for self-regulated learning have been one of the major advances of the study of lifelong cognitive development. Until recently there had been a heavy focus solely on how the mind worked in processing, organizing and retrieving information. But social cognitive theory has widened the viewpoint by advocating that people must develop skills in regulating the motivational, emotional and social influences on their intellectual functioning as well as the cognitive elements.

The stages of the CARE model take this wider perspective. It is not the case that a person-centred approach is unrealistic, rather it is essential to an effective education for the twenty-first century. Adey and Shayer (1994: 180) make a similar point in arguing that keeping the development of cognition in mind will not interfere with the instructional goals of the curriculum. Rather, their view is that good instruction and the promotion of higher-level thinking can be promoted throughout the curriculum. Similarly, fostering self-awareness and self-belief has to be integrated into educational practice if young people are to acquire the capabilities to educate themselves throughout their lifetime. If knowledge is power, then self-knowledge is empowerment. Or as one dictionary definition puts it: 'Something that is empowering makes you more confident and makes you feel you are in control of your life'. Achievement of such an aim, for both young person and coach, will indeed be a cause for *celebration*.

Key Words for Stage 4: Self-Motivation – Ownership – Celebration

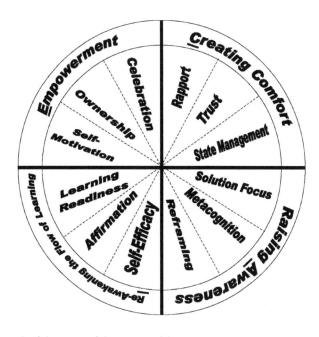

Figure 8: Key words of the stages of the CARE model

Themes of the CARE model

Language

Language is perhaps the most important theme, because the expert use of language is such an essential part of coaching. The theme of language encompasses all the channels through which we communicate. At a basic level, we will not come across as trustworthy credible people if there is a mismatch between the verbal and non-verbal messages we give out. You only have to think of an occasion when someone promised you something, but that you intuitively felt they didn't mean it, to appreciate that.

Until we start to analyse it, we tend to take both verbal and non-verbal language for granted. We will have formed habits of speaking and acting that have become so much a part of us that we are completely unaware of them. We may think that our body language is just the way we are; we may think of verbal language as merely a tool to manage relationships and get things done. And yet the forms of language we use carry clues to our mental frame of reference – in many ways, if we change our language, it opens up new possibilities so that we change the way we think. If we change our posture, we will feel different, and we will give out a different message to other people. Even subtle changes we can make to our words and phraseology can influence meanings for ourselves and for other people. That's why the essential part of coaching will be to provide a new language for the young person; if language can open up new horizons, the biggest new possibility that a coach can provide is in language (James Flaherty 2005: 30).

It is because our forms of language seem so much a part of us that, before we can develop a high level of skill in coaching language, we need first to raise awareness of how we currently use words and phrases and the emphasis we put upon them. In particular, we need to be conscious of the power differential that exists between adults and young people within the formality of schooling that is conveyed through the language we use, the way we speak and the subtle, or even blatant, ways that we can influence other people. For instance, Leora Cruddas (2005: 81) has pointed out the difficulties if we just try to define effective communication:

> An adult who shouts at children, admonishing them for their behaviour, is undoubtedly communicating with them, but the communication is unhelpful, demeaning and disrespectful. However, this communication may be perceived as effective if it results in the children's compliance. But in person-centred practice, this would clearly not count as effective communication.

In advocating a critical study of language, the aim of Norman Fairclough (1989: 233) has been to help increase consciousness of how language contributes to the domination of some people by others, because consciousness is the first step towards emancipation. Given that my stated aim for coaching for learning has been the development of *independent* learning aligned to an evolutionary approach (see Chapter 3), our use of language needs the constant critical appraisal that Norman Fairclough is suggesting. Critical appraisal can help us recognize the contradiction in such familiar teaching styles as teachers engaging in structured question–answer routines with students to elicit predetermined information, and that this style may be purporting to be asking students when they are in fact telling them (Norman Fairclough 1992: 70).

A theme of language is therefore multi-faceted, with many elements warranting attention and reflection, i.e.:

- Raising awareness of how you currently communicate in verbal and non-verbal language, and the effects of your language on other people
- Noticing how young people communicate: their styles of verbal language and their body language
- Adjusting your own language to match the language styles of young people in order to create rapport
- Reflecting on whether your language is aligned to the beliefs and values of a coaching model, or whether there are subtle ways that you maintain young people in 'subject' positions
- Developing skilled coaching techniques, particularly in the use of questioning.

Well-being

However we look at it, we are living through a paradigm shift that is encouraging us to take a person-centred approach in education. At a broad level, government policy in the UK (e.g. *Every Child Matters* in England, and the *10 Entitlements of Young People* in Wales) includes being healthy, staying safe and achieving economic independence as broad outcomes for the well-being of every child and young person. Within education, the 'personalized learning' policy is looked upon as a way of making services more responsive to the individual. It's a move away from the culture of the 1980s and 1990s, with the emphasis on seeing schools as machines to be worked harder and 'improved' (Charles Leadbetter 2004: 8).

John West-Burnham et al. (2007: 5) have worked in Australia, the US and England and report that this shift appears to be global in acknowledging that merely 'improving what is' will not meet the challenge of securing excellence and equity for every child. They also acknowledge that such a significant global move to focusing attention on the broader social environment of the learner is likely to elicit different responses:

> For some this is liberation from the current somewhat exclusive emphasis on the technology of teaching and learning within the classroom context; for others it is a challenge.

As far as schools are concerned, this means recognizing that they cannot work in isolation; rather they must forge new relationships with their communities, and rethink how they engage with other professional groups.

So while 'Well-being' as a core theme for the CARE model of coaching is an acknowledgement of this wider cultural shift, what does it mean in practice for the individual teacher/coach? It's a recognition that we need an awareness of a two-way relationship. Firstly, that raising standards of achievement and approaches to learning will impact on well-being, economic prosperity and social justice (John West-

Burnham et al. 2007: 109). And the reverse is also true: we cannot isolate a concentration on raising standards of achievement from issues of well-being and social justice.

Plainly a teacher/coach cannot be all things to all people, any more than a school can meet all health and social needs. But as I've stressed throughout this book, young people will not be able to learn if there are social and emotional factors that are impeding their learning. A 'person-centred' approach will enable us to recognize this, and also to identify the difference between those factors that fall within our ability to assist, and those that require us to draw on other resources – whether other professionals or any part of the community and agency network that forms a network of support around a young person.

'Well-being' is also a theme running through the CARE model because it encompasses the general well-being of a young person, the well-being of ourselves as professionals and our ability to self-manage and also the health and vibrancy of the institution of which we are a part. That health and vibrancy will be determined by the degree to which the walls of the school are permeable: opening up its practices to both the local community and other professional communities, and welcoming the resources that can support a common purpose of ensuring the well-being of young people.

Goal setting

Goal setting is a theme rather than a feature of a particular stage because of the way setting goals influences all aspects of the development of independent learning. Bandura (1995: 7) has noted that there is now a large body of evidence to show that explicit challenging goals will enhance and sustain motivation. Having goals is useful to prompt self-monitoring and self-assessment of performance; and because goals specify the requirements for personal success, they can increase young people's cognitive and emotional reactions to performance outcomes (Barry Zimmerman et al. 1992: 664).

Goal setting is also integrated throughout the stages because of the range of goals that are possible: there can be academic performance goals, skill development goals, emotional intelligence goals, short-term goals, aspirational goals. But of course, there are certain *qualities* that goals need to have to ensure they will be effective in moving young people towards self-motivation and independent learning.

Firstly, there needs to be clear agreement on a goal, with young people having *ownership* of the goal. Goals need to emerge out of the coaching discussions so that they are stated in terms that young people can appreciate. If young people cannot see the relevance of the goals they are unlikely to take action towards them.

Secondly, goals need to be stated in *positive* terms, rather than in terms of what someone is NOT going to do. If I say to you, 'DON'T think about a blue elephant with pink spots' what comes into your mind? Plainly you will have to think about what I am asking you NOT to think about before you can NOT do it! Similarly, a goal that 'I am not going to fail the exam' sets up a line of thinking about failure rather than realistic success. All negative goals can be re-phrased in positive terms, e.g. 'I am going to pass the exam.'

Thirdly, even the smallest goals need to be worded in such a way as to be SMART, i.e.:

- Specific
- Measurable
- Agreed
- Realistic
- Time-related.

Thus, 'I'm going to pass the exam' would need discussion until an agreed form of words emerged that was specific, measurable and time-related, e.g. 'I am going to achieve Grade C in my Biology exam by the end of this school year'.

Successful goal setting is therefore an element of the balancing act of coaching. As John Whitmore (2002: 61–2) puts it:

> If a goal is not REALISTIC, there is no hope, but if it is not CHALLENGING, there is no motivation. So there is an envelope here into which all goals should fit.

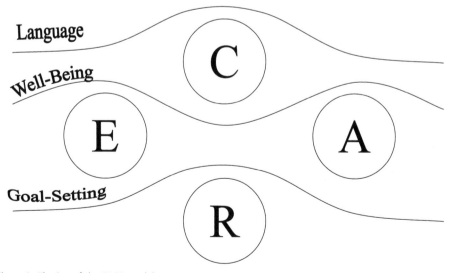

Figure 9: Themes of the CARE model

Reflection

This chapter has provided a framework for coaching for learning with young people. The ultimate aim of the model is to encourage independent learning and as such, it has relevance for our own professional development as 'lead learners'. Since personal development is integral to developing professional capability, as reflective practitioners, we can use the framework to recognize and enhance features of our own development. If we are in rapport with ourselves and have trust in ourselves, it will generate the basic self-confidence to adjust the power differential between ourselves and young people. We need to be able to understand how our mental, physical and emotional conditions combine to create our 'state', and be able to manage it to ensure optimum performance. With a solutions focus we will avoid getting bogged down by constant analysis of problems; we will be able to practise reframing problems to create solutions. We need to be able to challenge 'limiting beliefs' we may hold unconsciously that may be hindering our personal development, and which will also impact upon our effectiveness in our professional role. Our self-motivation to be committed to both our professional role and to our own development as a learner will be a source of energy to inspire the same in others.

Overall, the stages provide a *framework* rather than a definitive set of practices for working with young people. In the *Appendices* you will find descriptions of a range of people who are working in different environments and whose work can be described under different titles: mentors, learning coaches, tutors, peer counsellors. The individual practices may differ, but there is a clear theme of common beliefs and values, and a purposeful aim to support empowerment for young people. The stages of the CARE model are just one way of articulating these common beliefs and aims to provide a guidebook both for your own practice and your personal and professional development.

Key points

- The stages provide a framework for coaching for learning for young people
- The stages can also be applied in reflection on personal and professional development
- *Stage 1* is about establishing the optimum environment and 'state' for learning
- *Stage 2* encourages 'thinking about thinking' and a solutions focus
- *Stage 3* tackles limiting beliefs as a way of developing self-efficacy
- *Stage 4* seeks to celebrate the self-motivated independent learner
- *Language* is the most important theme because of the high level of skill needed
- *Well-being* ensures continued awareness of a person-centred approach
- A range of *goals* can be agreed throughout the coaching process to sustain motivation.

Notes

[1] Carol Magnus, Head of Learning and Development, Alzheimer's Society cited by Ann Knights and Alex Poppleton 2007: 3.

[2] I've written elsewhere about creating rapport – see Jacquie Turnbull 2007.

[3] Philip Adey and Michael Shayer 1994: 3.

PART II – THE PRACTICE

5 Stage 1 – Creating Comfort

The environment is everything that isn't me.
Albert Einstein

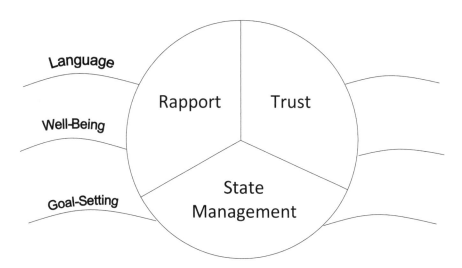

Figure 10: Key words for Stage 1

While *Creating* Comfort is about establishing a basis for coaching, what it is NOT about is sticking in a familiar 'comfort zone'. The CARE model advocates nurturing the 'well-being' of a young person throughout the coaching process, but this has to be balanced by an appropriate level of challenge. The aim for coaching after all is to find the leverage to enable young people to accelerate their learning and maximize their potential, and that won't happen by sticking to familiar and comfortable ways of doing things.

We can use the illustration of a sports coach to think about high challenge for a moment. The idea of coaching really began in a sports context, and some people still consider that coaching for learning should be the same as coaching for sporting achievement. For myself, although I think there are similarities, there are also crucial differences, because – as educators – we know a lot more about learning in general than we can apply.

For instance, an ex-Rugby player now in journalism has written 'There has to be fear and respect for your coaches and your management. That's what sport is all about'.[1] Obviously I wouldn't be advocating that you instil fear in young people, but how about generating 'respect'? The experience of the Wales Rugby Union team gives a dramatic illustration of the difference coaching can make in sport when respect is involved. In 2007 the team won only 5 out of 15 matches, and crashed out of the World Cup at the group stage, beaten by Fiji. As is often the case, this poor form was accompanied by a lot of back-biting and Chinese whispers. Then along comes a new coaching team, Warren Gatland and Shaun Edwards, with more importantly, a new attitude. The coaches were fearless in team selection, dropping players and rotating the team so that no player was secure in their place. Alongside this toughness was honesty; if a player was dropped they were told why, then it was their choice whether to strive to do better or sulk. The honesty was a thread that ran through all the coaching interventions: mistakes were highlighted but there was also an explanation of what the player needed to do to get back into the team. The result was that the Wales team were shifted out of their comfort zone, a new sense of self-belief was created, and they improved their performance to the degree that they beat all opponents to win the Grand Slam in the Six Nations tournament the following season.

What can we take from this example to inform our own practice of coaching for learning? The main thing for me is the honesty. Perhaps not as brutally honest as in the tough male world of Rugby Union; rather, for our purposes, an honesty tempered with sensitivity to the needs of particular young people. A difficult balancing act; and getting the balance right will be different with each individual. But in my experience, an open and honest attitude, not avoiding key issues but rather giving helpful yet challenging feedback, engenders respect in a coaching relationship. Remember it's the quality of the relationship that is the core of coaching (see Chapter 3) and the respect has to be mutual for relationships to be productive. And being honest with yourself about yourself will be the starting point for gaining respect from other people.

Rapport

There was a very good reason for making the previous point about being honest with yourself and establishing yourself as a 'real' person before leading on to the 'how to' of creating rapport. As rapport is created by being able to *match* another person to the degree that you can understand their world – their map of reality – it's vitally important to be able to recognize the difference between 'being yourself' and being drawn into 'being like' another person.

As Anne puts it she 'holds her own space' which is her way of expressing that she has a clear sense of her own identity. From this 'grounded' position she can exhibit a range of behaviours to meet the needs of the young person she is coaching. When people say to you 'I can't be any different, it's just the way I am', it's a good indicator that they haven't understood the basic difference between the *person* and the *behaviour*. My response is usually to say 'It's not you, it's just a behaviour, and behaviour is something that can be changed'. Creating rapport is about behaviours; it's not about trying to be *like* another person – that would be mimicry rather than matching. Matching is something that happens unconsciously and instinctively when we have an affinity with another person. It's when that 'connection' doesn't exist that we need to think about how we can *consciously* create it.

Matching to create rapport 1 – body language

Genie Laborde (1998: 27) has written that the greatest part of establishing rapport is often accomplished non-verbally. Our body language is an important part of the *process* of communication. Because most of the time our attention will be on the *content* of our communication, it can be quite challenging to start to think about the *process* at the same time. Indeed, in coaching there's a reversal of what we would do in ordinary communication or in instruction: there's more emphasis on process than on content.

I once had a piece of video I used in training to illustrate aspects of body language. It was from a time I was teaching in high school, and my students were involved in a peer support project. We'd gone to a local primary school so the students could introduce themselves and tell the schoolchildren a bit about what they could expect when they went up to high school. After their set piece to the whole class, the students mingled with the children and chatted informally. I filmed one student as she talked to several children seated around a table. She had knelt down beside the table so she was on the same level as the children. This was in marked contrast to other students who had chosen to remain standing, seeming a little uncertain about how to behave. But for this particular student, it was an intuitive choice to 'get to their level' physically which plainly helped to ease the conversation. When I showed the video later, I asked her what had prompted her to kneel down. She said she hadn't even thought about it, she just did it.

'Getting on the same level', 'getting along with someone' and 'seeing eye to eye' are all metaphors we use that show we recognize body matching is a key part of having an affinity with another person. The Native American saying 'To understand a man, you have to walk a mile in his moccasins' is saying the same: to get a feel for someone, we have to put ourselves in their position.

In my experience, matching some aspect of body language is the quickest way to set up rapport when it's needed. It's a routine with me now in any interview to notice how another person is seated and settle myself in a matching position. Sometimes matching may feel a little strange because it feels like stepping outside your own way of doing things, your own comfort zone. But the way we do things – whether it's the way we sit, stand, move or talk – is not a fixed part of us, it's just a habit of behaviour, a habit we have practised so much that it now seems part of us.

Matching of course is not blatant copying – that would be disrespectful and anyway matching is a much more subtle strategy. Plainly it needs to be so when there may be particular physical differences between people, such as an adult working with a much younger person. The starting point is to notice the way a young person is sitting or standing, how their weight is distributed, any particular inclination of the head, how their shoulders are held. The subtlety can be relevant when we begin to notice how they hold their arms and hands, and whether they use any gestures, particularly if they regularly use certain gestures to emphasize specific things they are saying. Trying to match such movements exactly may appear too obvious. But we can make smaller matching movements with hands, or even fingers, to match the speed and frequency of their own movements. And it conveys a particularly strong impression that you are with them, if when repeating their words to test your understanding, you can match their own gestures along with the words.

While matching someone's breathing may seem the most subtle strategy of all, it can also be the most powerful – as you'll see below in the section on Pacing and Leading. Nothing new here – the fact that our word 'conspirator' is derived from a Latin word meaning 'to breathe with' indicates a long-held notion that people who breathe together reach agreement. On a lighter note, while people who join a choir may initially do so to participate in music-making, they also appear to experience a comradeship and bonding over and above the shared love of music. Breathing together has significant side-effects.

When you first try it out, noticing a young person's breathing rate may seem a little difficult. Good indicators will be the rise and fall of their shoulders, and the pace of their speech. And since a person's state will affect how they breathe, being able to match their rate of breathing is a powerful strategy for understanding their experience.

Matching to create rapport 2 – voice

Voice matching can feel the most natural of the body language channels: when someone has a pronounced accent I've noticed I feel drawn to match it – not deliberately, it just seems to be something that happens that's outside my conscious control. And it seems I'm not alone in this: there was an interesting example I spotted during a television programme. It was a documentary about John Barrowman, actor and singer, and his search to understand the source of his sexuality.[2] John had been born in Scotland, and had moved to the States with his family at the age of eight. Since most of his formative years had been spent in the States, he spoke with a distinctive American accent. Part of the programme showed him talking to his parents: both had retained particularly strong Scottish accents despite living many years in America. The interesting thing was that when John talked with his parents, the American accent slipped and he adopted a Scottish brogue. Whether this was conscious on his part it was impossible to say. But it certainly seemed to be an expression of his strong affinity with his parents.

There's so much about the voice that can be matched quite apart from regional accents. You'll probably notice a lot of matching of volume amongst young people, and speed is another aspect where you may have found yourself falling into matching mode. If someone is talking quite fast, it's difficult to resist speeding up along with them. It's an interesting exercise to start consciously tuning your ear to how young people use their voices, noticing the variations and trying out how you can make use of voice matching to create rapport.

Matching to create rapport 3 – language

Just as we have acquired habits in the way we sit and stand, how we use gestures and how we speak, we also make habitual use of particular words and phrases. An associate of mine once set about gathering a list of phrases used regularly by each of the people she worked with. It was the subject of much laughter at a social gathering, mainly because nearly everyone identified the particular individuals correctly when she read out the phrases.

I'll be reminding you about matching language in Stage 2 when we consider thinking styles. Part of Raising Awareness will be becoming consciously aware of patterns of thinking, and noticing how patterns of thinking can be detected in the language we use. For the moment, though, I ask you to start giving special attention to the language that young people use. Noticing their choice of particular words means you can use them back to them – which is one way of demonstrating that you're listening and you understand what they are saying. NOT using their own words but choosing to use your own can have a reverse effect of *mis*matching. Such as if a young person says to you 'The Maths teacher does my head in' and you respond 'So the Maths teacher is irritating you?' Using your own words is an indicator that you're replying from your own map of reality rather than trying to understand theirs. 'Doing my head in' may not be a phrase you would normally use, but you can try to understand what it means for the young person:

'The Maths teacher is doing your head in – how exactly does that make you feel?'

Thinking Space 3

In any field, very experienced professionals can acquire an intuitive knowledge to inform their behaviour. Teachers with a class of 30 children can have a sense of what is happening in every corner of the classroom – sometimes even to the extent of being able to 'see' what's going on behind them. Trainers I have worked with will adapt their training plans in a moment when they get a sense that the 'climate' in the group needs a switch of emphasis to maintain interest and attention. Nurses have told me that they have had the experience of 'knowing' something was not right with a patient – even when all readings such as temperature and blood pressure gave an indication of stability. And it also usually turned out that their 'instincts' proved to be correct.

Guy Claxton (2000: 37–8) suggests intuition stems from a *heightened sensitivity to clues*. Saying that someone is 'very intuitive' can imply that they have the capacity to

---

notice more, and extract the maximum amount of information from the environment. The information may not even be registered consciously, but the ability to be attentive to fine detail, whether consciously or subliminally, may underpin what we view as the clinical judgement of an experienced professional.

One estimate has put it that we have two million pieces of information available to us via our senses at any one time. So it is hardly surprising that we don't register all the details at a conscious level. Yet the complexity of our brain and nervous system is so immense that we have the capacity to be registering this information unconsciously.

Is this heightened sensitivity – what I would call *sensory acuity* – something that is innate in some people only, or can it be learned? Genie Laborde (1998: 78) thinks that sensory acuity is the most important and far-reaching skill you can learn. For most of us, it does need practice to shift ourselves out of our personal preoccupations and turn our attention outwards. Matching elegantly and subtly will mean first noticing minute details about the people around you. You could start practising by noticing a certain feature of everyone you come into contact with in a day. Do they regularly sit or stand a certain way? Do they have particular habits in movements of arms or legs, do they foot tap or fiddle with pens? How do they hold their head – on one side or bent down? What is their facial expression – do they make eyebrow movements, smiles, frowns, grimaces? What sort of eye contact do they make; in which direction do their eyes move when they are talking to you? And what can you notice about voices – tone/pace/inflection/accent? Once you start noticing what you notice, you'll begin to recognize more and more how people change from minute to minute.

Creating rapport 4 – pacing and leading

If you've ever been in conversation with another person while walking, it's likely you would both be walking at a similar pace. Should one person start to speed up or slow down or even stop, if you're *getting along*, it's likely the other person would do the same to maintain the conversation. All of the matching strategies mentioned so far are about pacing another person in their experience. It's also about being able to acknowledge another person's beliefs and values without trying to convince them they are wrong. Pacing is not the same as agreeing; you don't need to take on the beliefs of others as your own, only acknowledge that they are important for the other person (Ian McDermott and Joseph O'Connor 1996: 24).

Pacing is important for Stage 1 because you are providing a bridge to take a young person from where they are to a better learning position. Going straight to a motivated and enthusiastic learning state is likely to be too big a jump, a step too far. But once you have paced a young person and have rapport with them, you will be more able to influence their 'state'.

Matching and pacing are also powerful tools when a young person is in a state of high emotion. You may well feel instinctively that the way to deal with strong emotions is to remain calm and talk in a soothing voice in order to placate the other person. But think about it for a moment. Have you ever been dealt with in that manner when you've been very upset or angry? And have you ever felt *more* angry the more a person remains calm? Or *more* frustrated because they don't seem to be acknowledging your feelings, just trying to shift you out of them?

Alternatively, matching and pacing a young person in a highly emotional state means you could try matching their posture, voice tone, facial expression and breathing. What you are *not* matching is the actual emotion; but you are showing that you recognize their feelings and empathize with them. Then, once you've established a connection, you can lower your voice, relax your body and breathing and are more likely to lead them to a calmer state because you've *first* demonstrated an understanding of how they are feeling.

> **Thinking Space 4**
> * Resistance in another person is a sign of lack of rapport
> * Increase the flexibility of your communication and the resistance disappears[3]

Trust

Resistance in another person is also a sign of lack of trust. Generating trust is crucial because, as Mike Hughes (2004: 42) puts it:

> Trust is coaching cement; it holds the entire process together.

Trust is also a vital part of human relationships for Robert Solomon and Fernando Flores (2001). For them, trust doesn't just happen as a result of good luck or mutual understanding; rather it is something that can be cultivated by skill and commitment. Although trust may often seem invisible – or transparent – it is the result of continuous attentiveness, activity and change. Indeed, very similar to creating rapport. Put simply, telling the truth establishes trust and lying destroys it. To establish trust, nothing else will do but *keeping your word* – if you say you are going to do something being sure to do it. Even more significantly, Solomon and Flores describe trust as emotion: trusting people – like loving them – not only appreciates and depends upon the other people, it *changes* them, and usually for the better. And further, trusting changes both the person trusted and the person who trusts.

I remember an example that illustrates just this point. A teaching colleague of mine told me that two of my sixth form students had gone to her for advice on a day I was absent from school. I'd given them a contact of a district nurse, and together we'd fixed a date and time they could interview her as research for their project work. It was only later they realized there was a clash with something else they needed to be doing with another teacher. They came to tell me, or rather what they really wanted was for me to intercede with the other teacher and explain the importance of their interview appointment. As I was absent, they sought help from my colleague. She didn't really want to interfere, so she suggested they needed to go away and think about what they should do. Sometime later they came back. They'd thought about it and decided they should keep the appointment, and they would go and tell the other teacher they were sorry, but they thought that was the right thing to do.

For me it was interesting the way my colleague related this to me the next time I was in school. Plainly we were both pleased that the students – with a little prompting from my colleague – had taken responsibility for their own actions, and dealt with it themselves without the aid of a teacher. But I also gained a sense that, had they been her own students, she may well have interceded and dealt with the problem for them. Because they were another teacher's students, and she didn't want to interfere, she had been prompted to trust them to make their own decision. And I detected a sense of pleasurable surprise that, having been trusted to do so, they had done the right thing. I gained the distinct impression that trusting her own students would be something she would be much more open to in the future. As Solomon and Flores say, trusting changes both the trusted and the person who trusts.

Congruence

There are lots of elements that combine to enable us to encourage a sense of trust between ourselves and other people. Being secure in our identity as a person will enable us to come across as genuine and authentic. A sincere desire to create rapport and understand another person's map of the world is another. And overall, we need to convey an impression of *congruence* – something we achieve when our channels of communication are consistent and aligned to the same message.

Congruence is a bit like rapport in that we usually only become aware of it when it's absent. Like when someone says something to us and we get an intuitive 'gut' feeling that they don't really mean it. The words they're saying may sound perfectly reasonable and factually correct, and yet – there's something about the way they say it that doesn't ring true. You may have asked someone how they were feeling, and had the reply 'I'm fine thanks', but you've had a sense from their slumped shoulders, their downcast eyes, the hesitant tone of their voice that they're anything but fine.

It shouldn't really be much of a surprise to us that we're able to have this 'sixth sense' about people. Body language was the first language we learned; as small children, before we understood the words people were saying to us, we could grasp meanings from their tone of voice and their facial expression. Then we learnt to use words ourselves, and words became such a dominant feature – particularly in our schooling – that we came to think that verbal language and content were the most important factors in communication. Yet we hadn't lost that early ability to interpret meanings from body language, and in fact, when we are in any doubt, we tend to take the body language message as the true message.

People who are vulnerable also appear to be more tuned into body language messages. Patients receiving diagnostic information from a medical professional will check whether there is any 'leakage' through the other channels that will conflict with the verbal message. Young people in an emotional state may similarly be more sensitive to body language. I've certainly experienced many young people who have become quite agitated at a mere 'look' from another person. It could well be that, due to their youth, young people are more tuned in to these channels than older people anyway. That would certainly explain how they appear to have instant recognition of those teachers they can play up and those with whom they won't get away with unruly behaviour.

The crucial importance of body language factors has also been supported when psychologists have studied what makes people effective communicators. In a much-quoted piece of research, Mehrabian (1971) identified the elements of effective communication as:

- 53 per cent posture, gestures and eye contact
- 38 per cent voice tone and inflection
- 7 per cent content.

This research is saying is that 93 per cent of what makes us effective in communication comes down to body language factors rather than the content of what we are saying. As other writers have put it, 'Probably more feelings and intentions are communicated non-verbally than through all the verbal methods combined' (Thomas R. Tortoriello et al. 1978: 23). Of course, in saying that only 7 per cent of effective communication depends upon *content*, it's not saying that what you say doesn't matter. Plainly in jobs such as teaching accurate information is an important factor. Rather it's saying that *how effective* you are in conveying that information depends more upon your posture, gestures, eye contact and how you use your voice than on the words you use.

Being genuine and authentic is also about being open and honest, even acknowledging your feelings. As you saw in the example above, trying to mask feelings with words doesn't work because people 'see through' them. Being able to say things like 'I'm feeling a bit unsure about this' carries more credibility with young people than trying to act as if you have all the answers. As Daniel Goleman (1996:

90) tells us, credibility stems from integrity: and integrity – acting openly, honestly and consistently – sets apart outstanding performers in jobs of every kind.

So our own integrity – our ability to be open and honest with ourselves and with others – will carry credibility in our dealings with others. Our integrity will be conveyed predominantly through body language – and the fact that our non-verbal messages are congruent with our verbal language. And when we are congruent in communications, people will be more able to find us worthy of trust.

Active listening

The reason active listening appears in Stage 1 is because it is one of the building blocks of effective coaching – as it is for communication in general. And it appears in a section on Trust because *ineffective* listening is the biggest barrier in communication, and therefore to our ability to engender trust. Active listening is not something that we learn to do well naturally. In fact, the reverse is more likely to be true, as Colin Riches (1997: 174–5) has described:

> Listening is a most difficult skill to learn. Perhaps this is because, throughout our lives, we develop improper listening habits and become expert in the art of not listening when appearing to listen, having an interested expression when all the time we may be thinking about something entirely different!

In my experience, for many teachers it involves quite a stretch to move away from the dominance of teacher talk and start listening actively rather than talking. For some, I suspect, the habits of a working lifetime will be so entrenched that active listening will be a task they never really accomplish successfully. Developing the skill of listening effectively demands constant vigilance. It's as different from hearing as the Atlantic Ocean is from a puddle on the pavement. Rather than being a passive process involving only our ears, it's an active whole body and mind process.

In setting out to listen actively in coaching, your first attention needs to be to your own body:

- Do you have a relaxed open posture that is sending out signals that you're receptive and paying attention?
- Have you uncrossed your arms and legs so there is no barrier between you?
- Have you stopped any potentially irritating gestures such as playing with a pen?
- Are you maintaining relaxed eye contact and are you able to resist glancing at your watch or a clock?

- Is your facial expression conveying interest?
- Are you nodding your head in encouragement?
- Can you limit your own talk to murmurs of encouragement and resist jumping in with your own opinion?

At the same time as maintaining your own body language messages, you keep your attention on the other person:

- What are you seeing?
- What is their overall posture?
- Are they making any gestures as they talk?
- Have you identified a body language feature you can match to create rapport?
- Are they fidgeting?
- How about eye contact – are they avoiding making this connection with you?
- Is there a mismatch between what they are saying and the message you're getting from their body language?

Your attention will also be on what they are saying:

- Are you noticing any patterns in the way they use words?
- Are you hearing a lot of detail, or are you picking up that there are things that are *not* being said?
- If you notice this, can you use a question as a prompt to encourage the other person to say a bit more?

And what are you feeling?

- Are you gaining a sense of what it must be like to be the other person?
- Can you resist interpreting your own meaning of what is being said and listen for the other person's meaning?
- Do you feel you can associate with their own experience?

You will probably gauge from this outline the extent to which being an effective listener needs constant attention and practice.[4] But it is practice well worth the time and effort if it convinces young people they can talk to us, and establishes our trustworthiness in a coaching role.

State management

All the aspects of Stage 1 already mentioned have the potential to influence how young people will be feeling. Paying attention to building rapport and listening attentively will be part of creating a 'climate' conducive to learning. In addition, our environment plays a significant part in influencing the emotional and social climate we share with young people. We may not have direct control over how people feel, but we can take control of aspects of our physical environment to create a positive influence.

Just a thought about influence before we go further. Genie Laborde's (1998: 201) approach is that we can influence with integrity, but she recalls someone questioning whether that was possible; isn't influencing with integrity a contradiction in terms? Laborde disagrees. She thinks we all influence. Indeed, to influence well and in an appropriate way has been the concern of thinkers through the ages. Our increased knowledge has made us recognize we have superior tools for influencing. The use of these tools and the integrity of that use is in your hands. So while in coaching we are aiming to be non-directive, we cannot *not* influence; we just have to ensure that our influence is positive rather than negative, an encouragement for learning rather than a barrier.

Physical environment

To be able to recognize the influences, take a fresh look at where you work with young people. First impressions are important; your place of work may have become very familiar to you, but you can try entering as though you were visiting for the first time. The sensory acuity you've developed from watching and listening to other people will be just as useful to gain a sense of whether it appears a stimulating learning environment, or whether there are aspects that could have a negative effect on young people.

It's quite some time since I taught in high school and physical conditions for teaching have much improved since then. But I well remember how my heart sank on my first morning when I saw the room I'd been allocated. There was no outlook; the only windows were high on the walls. The room must have faced north, because I don't remember a glimmer of sunshine ever lightening the gloom. It looked as though it had managed to escape the attention of decorators for some considerable time, as the paint was peeling from the walls. No interactive whiteboard; just a blackboard worn grey from years of use. And apart from the tables and chairs the only other furniture was a metal grey cupboard.

A bad enough impression on my first day, but midwinter brought a fuller realization of the negative effects of the environment. The room was the last in the corridor, immediately adjacent to two doors leading directly outside. Two things I learnt that first winter: some young people never learn to shut doors, and there's no way you can keep a room warm when people are continually leaving doors to the outside open. In addition, the room was at the end of a long corridor, which appeared to be a step too far for the ageing central heating system, so the radiators never really warmed up.

As I'm writing this it sounds really Dickensian. But believe me, it wasn't all that long ago! The amazing thing was the expectation that young people would be able to learn in that environment. Rather my class used to shuffle in, huddling into their coats, little spark of enthusiasm for what I had to offer.

In my lowly status I had little power to change the room, but I did what I could to temper the negative influence. I had plenty of potted plants at home so they were brought in first; at least they softened the lines of the grey cabinet. Some posters next to cover the peeling paint and add splashes of colour. Finally music; upbeat lively 'coming in' music, then something calming when they were working on tasks. Oh, and I made a point of standing at the door and greeting them individually with a smile when they entered, and similarly when they left.

> **Thinking Space 6**
> 'The essential understanding here is that teachers are a huge part of the environment. The 30 or so other brains in the room filter what the teacher says and how he or she acts. It may not be fair to put all of this on a teacher, but it's true. Teachers are the mobile, shifting environment for learning ... Teachers are not merely influenced by the overall school climate; they create their own microclimates in the classroom. Learners in a positive, joyful environment are likely to experience enhanced learning, memory, and self-esteem.'
>
> Eric Jensen 2008: 97

There are probably not many rooms nowadays that are as bad as my experience, but the way we set up environments that accommodate young people still warrants close attention. We still herd young people into large halls, silent and empty except for spaced out tables and chairs, remove anything they may find it comforting to fiddle with and tell them seriously and sternly they must stay still and observe the rules. These procedures serve the needs of systems for the examination of individual knowledge, but they completely ignore individual needs in relation to maximizing potential performance. People learn from negative experiences as well as from positive ones, and for many young people the learning from this experience will be that examinations are stressful and anxiety-provoking, or even that they are experiences to be avoided. (More below in Thinking Space 7 on how to alleviate these effects.)

Anchors for the emotional brain

The Reptilian Brain
The oldest part of the brain. Centred on the brain stem and controls the body's basic survival systems, such as heart rate, breathing, temperature. Also the source of the 'flight or fight' response.
* The Key Motivator for the reptilian brain is *survival/avoiding harm*.
* Under negative stress the reptilian brain dominates which means the learner will resort to 'fight or flight' responses, and resist new information

The Limbic System
The 'mid-brain' that sits on top of the reptilian brain and routes information to where it is needed. The site of the amygdala, responsible for the emotions and immune system and plays an important part in long-term memory.
* The Key Motivator for the limbic system is *hunt for pleasure*
* Information with a powerful attachment to emotions or feelings will 'stick' in the long-term memory. Therefore an experience with a strong emotional association will be easier to remember

The Neo-cortex
The 'thinking cap' that sits on top of the mid-brain, and is separated into two hemispheres. The 'new' part of the brain that evolved most recently, concerned with problem-solving and abstract thought.
* The Key Motivator for the neo-cortex is *quest for novelty*
* The neo-cortex searches for meaning. Learners will not cognitively understand or learn something until they can create a personal mental model[5]

Figure 11: The triune brain

As you saw in Chapter 2, the discoveries of neuroscience are enabling us to understand more about the functioning of the brain that we can apply in encouraging learning. Fig. 12 is a simplified outline of something that is so immensely complex it is difficult to grasp outside the boundaries of neuroscience. Susan Norman (2003: 16) writes that apparently neuroscientists no longer find the concept of the 'triune brain' useful, but since it ties in with emotional intelligence it can be of interest to educators. More importantly, involving young people in their learning means giving them a language to understand their own physical and mental functioning, and the concept of the triune brain is a way of presenting complexity in understandable terms.

You will also have seen in Chapter 2 that neuroscientists have identified that teenagers are more likely to process emotional information using the amygdala in the mid-brain, than the frontal cortex, situated in the newer 'thinking' part of the brain. This is a crucial finding for us as Joseph LeDoux (1998: 168–70) describes the amygdala as the *'hub in the wheel of fear'* because it receives information from a range of sources. There will be low-level stimuli from our senses (things we see, hear, touch, smell or taste), inputs from the parts of the brain dealing with memories and the emotional brain is also highly tuned to symbolic meanings. Through its connections to other parts of the brain the amygdala is involved in appraising the emotional meaning of present or remembered experience: 'It is where trigger stimuli do their triggering' (LeDoux 1998:169).

The suggestion from neuroscientists mentioned in Chapter 2 was that young people could be encouraged to develop the frontal lobe by teaching them to think rationally. But before we can move to the more rational activities involved in planning, insight and organization, for Stage 1 an important focus is to recognize the immense power of the emotional brain to influence the functioning of the rest of the brain. Andrew Pollard (2008: 198) urges us to remember that learning can be emotionally challenging, and is certainly not simply cognitive and rational. The key factors for us to be alert to at Stage 1 are that the brain is designed for survival not for formal learning, and under conditions of negative stress the amygdala will dominate (Alistair Smith 1996:13–16). This means that new information will be resisted, or as Daniel Goleman (1996:83) succinctly puts it:

Anxiety undermines the intellect.

Therefore in Creating Comfort, the focus is on 'keeping the reptilian brain happy'. We can't of course predict the 'state' of young people when they arrive; the potential sources of negative stress are unlimited: arguments with parents, bullying, limiting beliefs, illness, lack of sleep/food, inability to understand the relevance of school work, etc. But we can seek to ameliorate the negative effects and stimulate more resourceful states by setting up 'anchors' for a positive learning environment (see Mandy's strategy in this respect in Appendix 1).

I have a picture of my baby granddaughter as the screensaver on my computer. So when I switch on each morning, and I see her sleeping peacefully, I just have to smile. When my children were at home, they always played loud and lively music in their bedrooms as they were getting ready to go on a night out. When my daughter was even smaller, she wore the silky label on her teddy bear completely away because she caressed it with her fingers every night as she went to sleep. When I unpack the shopping and I get a whiff of freshly baked bread I just have to have a slice straight away. I can never resist old-fashioned puddings like spotted dick – especially with custard – because the taste reminds me of my childhood.

Anchors are part of our lives. They are things that we see, hear, touch, smell or taste that trigger different states, and different behaviours. Some will be individual to us, like those of mine above. Others will be purposely used by advertisers and stores to induce us to spend our money: bakeries carefully sited at the rear of supermarkets so that the smell of freshly baked bread drifts throughout the store for instance. Yet others we may not even recognize consciously as anchors until we make changes and realize that certain habitual behaviours had been triggered by something in our environment.

Thinking Space 7
Are you always in a good state for coaching?

Or are there times when you feel tired, listless, mentally distracted: when the last thing you want to do is try to relate to stroppy teenagers?

Anchors work using the principle of 'association'. We can make the principle work for us by setting up anchors to shift ourselves into a more resourceful state.

Is there a picture or photo that always gives you a warm glow when you look at it, or which has a calming effect?

Which piece of music always makes you feel energetic, even though you felt tired the moment before you heard it?

Is there something small you can carry – like a smooth pebble, a crystal, a special coin – something you can touch to evoke a memory of a time when you were at your most resourceful and competent?

Which perfume makes you feel confident when you wear it?

How does even thinking about the taste of a particularly well-loved food make you feel?

Just as these can work for you, young people can create their own anchors to access resourceful states when they need them. Examinations for instance: encourage young people to associate successful learning with something they can take into the examination with them. It could be a small talisman they hold while they are revising. As they bring sections of information to mind, suggest they pause, look at their talisman and feel it, while they are thinking about the information. Then do the same in the examination when they need to bring the information back to mind. Or it could be a perfume that they wear or small phial of scented oil that they keep with them, that will become associated with their successful learning of material.

Anchors, of course, can have negative as well as positive effects. Appalling as it may seem to us now, one of the early experiments in *behaviourism* (see Chapter 1) applied the principles established with animals to humans by stimulating fear in a small child by association.[6] As far as the physical environment in which we work is concerned we can aim to eliminate potentially negative anchors. Things about ourselves may not be so easy to deal with. I remember a teacher colleague who had a particularly shrill and high-pitched voice. One occasion when my students were working on a task we could hear her in the next room. I spotted one of my students shiver, and whisper to the fellow student sitting next to her, 'I *hate* that woman's voice'. I suppose the only answer to whether something about ourselves may be setting up negative anchors is to be constantly vigilant to the effects we notice in young people. Being flexible and responsive in our own behaviour will help to avoid any negative effects.

So on the positive side, you can check how you are anchoring a multi-sensory learning environment:

- Are there posters, pictures, banners, learning materials displayed? Are they fresh and attractive, changed regularly?
- Are there flowers, plants?
- Have you carefully selected the music? Lively for 'coming in', calming for working on task, lively for a lift of energy.
- Are there any objects that can be touched, held, felt?
- Is the air fresh? Or could you use a burner with essential oils, or pot pourri, or a spray?
- Is the environment saying 'Come on in, this is a good place to be learning!'?

Then you can use your own habitual behaviour to set up expectations:

- Move to the same position every time you deliver information
- Sit in your 'active listening' posture when you want to encourage talk
- Adjust the volume and tone of your voice to distinguish between conveying facts, ready to discuss and open to listening.

Remember the rituals! The reptilian brain is responsible for ritual behaviours, and used properly they can enrich and support a learning experience (Alistair Smith 1996: 69):

- Greet young people at the door with a smile when they enter
- Remember their names and use them
- Keep to the same music for different moods

- Find a short fun activity and regularly use it as a goal: 'If we complete this learning, we should have five minutes for ...'
- Encourage attentive curiosity: 'And in a moment ... not yet ... we'll be ...'

We can also set up positive peripheral influences. Presenting key learning points on posters provides visual reinforcement as well as being pleasing to the eye. And this can also be an effective way of presenting positive and motivating messages. Making them colourful and laminated so they stay fresh, placing them at eye level or above, left alone they present powerful subliminal messages. In addition, they can be picked up on and integrated into coaching as a trigger for discussion. Fig. 12 lists some I've used; you'll have favourites of your own I'm sure, and an internet search will bring up plenty more.

---

* No Failure only Feedback
* When you stop doubting ... what is left is confidence
* 'Remember, no one can make you feel inferior without your consent': *Eleanor Roosevelt*
* Believe in yourself and expect good things to happen
* 'Aerodynamically the bumble bee shouldn't be able to fly, but the bumble bee doesn't know it so it goes on flying anyway': *Mary Kay Ash*
* Stress depresses memory
* 'It's not the mountain we conquer, but ourselves': *Sir Edmund Hillary*
* 'It is not a crime to make a mistake; what is a crime is failure to learn from a mistake': *Walter Wriston*
* It's never too late to become who you want to be
* 'If you think you can or think you can't, you're right': *Henry Ford*.
* Brain functioning depends very much on what you've eaten for breakfast: *Richard M. Restak The Brain: The Last Frontier*
* Many of life's failures are people who did not realize how close they were to success when they gave up: *Thomas Edison*
* Even if you're on the right track, if you just sit there you might get run over: *Will Rogers*
* *Albert Einstein*:

  'It's not that I'm so smart, it's just that I stay with problems longer.'
  'We can't solve problems by using the same kind of thinking we used when we created them.'
  'Anyone who has never made a mistake has never tried anything new.'

Figure 12: Inspirational sayings for peripheral learning

Social and emotional environment

When he delivered the Wales Education Lecture in 2005, Professor Tim Brighouse set out to define what made an especially successful teacher. He argued that in addition to the usual competences, beliefs, attitudes, purpose and behaviour that can be expected from all good teachers, successful teachers brought something more. He reminisced about Mrs Lewis, a primary teacher who in the 1960s effortlessly practised what the government now calls 'personalization' – she got the very best out of *all* the children and was at pains to utilize all the behaviours that made her practice 'personal' rather than 'impersonal'.

Professor Brighouse conceded that it was easier for Mrs Lewis than for her secondary colleagues, who could teach between 200 and 300 difficult young people every week. Yet he described how many secondary teachers spend a lot of preparation time – often before the autumn term starts – putting names to faces so that they can use names in greeting young people in corridors during breaks as well as in lessons. They determine seating arrangements to maximize shared learning rather than leaving student's free choice. They share questions fairly in a manner that affirms individual confidence. They have a range of classroom management tasks for students to carry out. They deploy marking practice that makes students feel special, and give full and explanatory feedback so that all students know exactly what they have to do to progress.

Successful teachers as Professor Brighouse described them were not immune to the unpredictability of teaching: they had the experience of something working 9 out of 10 times and then unaccountably not working. But that was the first definable feature of their specialness. They didn't give up:

> When these teachers encounter a pupil with whom they cannot connect – whose mind and heart they do not meet – they go our of their way at the weekend to find an artefact or an article that is related to the youngster's private interest and on the Monday, they stop them in the corridor and say 'Sean, I saw this and thought of you'.

The practices of successful teachers described are well outside teaching to meet the requirements of the subject curriculum. Yet the significant thing is that, according to Mrs Lewis's headteacher, all the children in her class learned to read, she got the best out of the children – *all* the children. Similarly, with a secondary teacher Professor Brighouse described, Saima Rana: she expected all her young people to get a higher grade GCSE – even those with statements.

For many, these are practices and approaches that would be additional to instruction, yet they are crucial to maximizing the potential of all young people. They are practices that fit with a model of coaching for learning rather than teaching as instruction. As Professor Brighouse described it, they are in addition to the intellectual and cognitive domains, and what makes these teachers outstandingly successful is that they are strong in emotional intelligence. Their emotional intelligence means they recognize the importance of the social and emotional elements of learning and structure their student's learning to be positive social and emotional experiences. In other words, for them, 'creating comfort' is the foundation for realizing individual potential.

Themes of the CARE model – STAGE 1

Language

Coaching involves using language in a different way. Before we do that, we first need to be aware of the powerful effect of some simple everyday words that we are accustomed to using.

Let's take 'BUT' first. Have you ever had a discussion with someone who continually says 'Yes, I hear what you're saying, but ...'? And has it felt as though the 'but' seems rather dismissive of what you are trying to say? A usual response can be that we try to reinforce the point we are trying to make. So you may come back with another 'yes ... but' and round and round you both go 'yes ... butting' each other.

Using 'but' can engender resistance, and it can also be de-motivating. Think about the following as feedback to a student:

> 'That's a very good essay, **but** it would be even better with a stronger first paragraph.'

For the student, the 'but' can cancel out the first (positive) part, and they will often only interpret the feedback as criticism.

Simply substituting 'and' for 'but' can avoid the sense of criticism and make it sound more like feedback:

> 'That's a very good essay, **and** it would be even better with a stronger first paragraph.'

Then there's 'IF'. Since the brain is always open to suggestion and readily fills in gaps, using 'if' plants the possibility of failure in a learner's mind:

'**If** you learn how to do this well, you will succeed in the test.'

Substituting 'When' prompts the learner to visualize a positive outcome of their efforts. The brain is always open to suggestion ...

'**When** you learn how to do this well, you will succeed in the test.'

CAN'T is a word that needs to be banned from coaching for learning discussions. Every time a young person expresses an 'I can't ...' it can be questioned to seek the source of the limiting belief, and help the learner reframe it more positively, e.g.:

What would it be like if you were able to ...?
What is it that's stopping you from ...?
What do you need to be able to do to ...?

TRY is another word that sets up a mental possibility of failure, e.g.:

'I'll **try** to get it finished by Monday.'

I used to joke with students that I didn't want them to 'try', I wanted them to 'do it'. **Try** is really giving themselves a let-out clause. They can always allow themselves *not* to succeed by saying 'Well, at least I tried ...' Like **Can't, Try** can be challenged, e.g.:

What needs to happen for you to get it finished by Monday?
What do you need to do to be sure of finishing it by Monday?

Well-being

The emotional brain is highly attuned to symbolic meanings (see above). That's why metaphors are so powerful: they work by conveying meanings that transcend the particular content. They work particularly well in our context of coaching, because young people will not always have the words to express how they are feeling.

If you ask a young person how they are feeling you could perhaps get a shrug of the shoulders, and a muttered 'OK'. Numbers are metaphors, and scaling is a useful device that allows a person to express their experience without the need for words:

'On a scale of 1 to 10, 1 being the worse you've ever felt, and 10 being the best, how energetic/ happy/ready for learning/focused do you feel at this moment?'

Say you get 5 as a response, you can next ask:

'OK, so tell me about a time when you were at 7?'

Just telling you about being at 7, the young person will have to 'associate into' being at 7. And you can help them bring to mind how that feels with the next question:

'So what needs to happen now to move you towards 7?'

Alternatively, you can get different sorts of information by using different metaphors, as with this question:

'If you were to think of yourself as an animal, which animal would that be and why?'

Over the years, I've had a range of responses to this particular question, e.g.:

I'd be a mouse, because I feel a bit timid and shy today.
I'd be a spotty dog, bouncing all over the place.
I'm a cat, I feel lazy and want to curl up in a warm place.
I'm a monkey, a naughty one I think!

As you will notice, it's not the particular choice of animal that's important; it's the additional information you get about the emotional state of the person, information that you may not get just asking a straight question.

Goal setting

In addition to giving young people a new language to understand themselves and how they learn, a powerful feature of coaching is enabling them to reframe their limiting beliefs and visualize new opportunities and potential futures. A good way of doing this is by use of the 'Miracle Question'.[7] Adapted for our purposes, it could go like this:

'Imagine that when you go home this evening, you go to sleep, and while you are asleep a miracle happens. The miracle is that everything you don't feel good about concerning your learning is changed for the better. When you wake up in the morning, you don't know the miracle has happened because it happened while you were asleep. What would you notice that would tell you the miracle had occurred? What would be different? And what else ...?'

I once used the Miracle Question when I was doing some research about what young people thought about school. They absolutely loved it. Just the question and a few repeats of 'And what else ...?' was enough to trigger an animated and interesting discussion with a small group of Year 10s. And they also took it really seriously: no airy-fairy ideas, but realistic and sensible thoughts on what could make school better for them. It triggered thinking that went beyond our initial discussion: some time later I was walking along a corridor when a teacher called out to me from her classroom doorway, 'Mrs Turnbull, could you come back some time, Janine has just said she's thought of something else.' This is a key feature of coaching: recognizing that the thinking and learning goes on after the direct coaching activity has ended.

The point of the Miracle Question is that it triggers thinking about future possibilities, then the role of the coach is to track backwards to present reality to find a small thing that is achievable for the learner, to make a start on the journey towards the future potential. Setting large long-term goals needs to be resisted at this stage. Rather you need to seek out something that might be really, really small, but something which can give a quick sense of success as a first step towards the visualized future potential. Something which allows you to say,

'I'll be interested to hear how you got on with that next time.'

Remember also that the features of the Stages are not set in stone in a linear fashion. The Miracle Question is valuable at any stage where thinking may have become blocked and progress is stagnating. Adapted to meet individual circumstances the principle serves to open up new possibilities for a learner.

Reflection

Reflection on our own capabilities needs a twofold direction. As we become more aware of ourselves, we also need to be able to turn our attention outside ourselves to notice more about other people and our environment. A heightened sensitivity to minute clues will help us be more responsive to other people. It can be challenging to acknowledge that if young people are not responding to us, it may be because we are not doing enough to create rapport. Yet people are different, and we need to increase our flexibility by trying different strategies with different people.

Our approach to emotional intelligence also needs to be twofold. More and more I hear leaders in education commenting that developing emotional intelligence is a key factor both for learning and for teaching. Sharing our knowledge with young people is a first step towards engaging them in the development of their own emotional intelligence. We also need to be strong in emotional intelligence ourselves, not just to help young people realize their potential, but to enable us cope with the complexity of working in teaching and coaching for learning.

> The Stage 1 strategies can be used to ensure we are in a good emotional 'state' for coaching. The creation of a pleasant and positive learning environment will encourage our own learning as well as that of young people. We can use the principle of association to anchor productive states and keep our energy and enthusiasm flowing. We need to 'create comfort' for ourselves as a foundation for realizing our own potential as coaches and educators.

Stage 1 – Practice pointers

- Sensory acuity is an extremely important skill to develop
- Sensory acuity will enable subtle matching to create rapport
- Rapport, of itself, is influential
- We cannot *not* influence, but need to aim to influence with integrity
- Integrity will be established if we are trustworthy
- Trusting changes the person trusted and the person who trusts
- Congruence conveys trustworthiness
- Congruence in communications means matching what we say with what we do
- 93 per cent of effective communication is conveyed through body language
- Active listening is a whole body and mind process
- In conditions of stress, the reptilian brain will dominate
- The physical environment will affect emotional state
- Emotional state can be influenced by anchoring positive associations
- *Creating Comfort* is a foundation for realizing potential.

Notes

1. Jonathan Davies 2008.
2. 'The Making of Me' shown on BBC1 24 July 2008.
3. Two of the presuppositions of neuro-linguistic programming.
4. For a fuller account of active listening see Jacquie Turnbull 2007: 117–32.
5. See Alistair Smith 1996:13–23 for a full account of the brain in learning.
6. *The Case of Little Albert*. See Watson and Rayner 1920.
7. The 'Miracle Question' was created by Steve de Shazer, originator of Solution-Focused Brief Therapy, adapted from a strategy used by Milton Erickson.

6

Stage 2 – Raising Awareness

When awareness increases, new sustainable futures are created.
Will Thomas and Alistair Smith 2004: 13

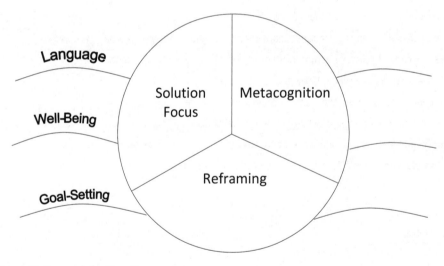

Figure 13: Key words for Stage 2

Throughout the CARE model the primary focus is on the *process* of learning. That in itself will be a considerable shift given the outcome and target focused environment in which we work. There will be goals of course; goals stimulate action and are a practical way of realizing potential. Without action any enterprise would be just an empty theoretical exercise. But a constant focus on educational *outcomes* can have negative implications for young people, as Michael Brearley (2001: 2) reminds us:

> Seeing learning as outcomes camouflages and distracts our attention from the process of learning and sends many students away from school surrounded by negative beliefs about themselves. It is not the destination any school wants, but it is where many end up ... Students are not able to consider their relationship with learning because it is clouded by what they are being driven to achieve.

A focus on the 'relationship with learning' also shifts our attention from concentrating on problems. Seeing learning issues as problems is really adopting a deficit model, i.e. lack of progress in learning is because of something 'wrong' with the young person. Rather, we need to be alert to the seeds of solutions that are already present: helping the learner build on 'what works' for them, and from there, helping them gain the confidence to expand and enhance their learning strategies.

You'll remember from Chapter 3 that solutions in coaching may need to evolve out of the complex interaction of three domains: academic achievement, personal development and social and life skills. This gives a framework to shift for the seeds of change – those things that a young person does well, things that you can help them recognize they're already doing well, skills and attributes that can be transferred across to other areas to develop solutions. *Raising Awareness* for the coach means that you will be searching for the areas that will make the most difference; the area where small steps can result in leverage for more extensive change. What is their approach to subjects they enjoy that they can transfer to enhance subjects where they may be struggling? How can they use the skills they have developed in their part-time work to maximize their study strategies? How can you help them identify the success they've achieved in one domain – however small – and transfer it to another? Overall keeping an approach that fits with 'education' rather than 'schooling' (see Chapter 1), as Andrew Pollard (2008: 170) reminds us:

> A reflective professional has two major concerns – there is a short-term focus on pupil performance in relation to curriculum tasks, but there is also a longer-term responsibility to foster each child's personal confidence as a learner.

Stage 2 is not by any means an easy or comfortable option. It is a stage of challenging thinking, deliberately inducing 'cognitive conflict' (Michael Shayer 2003: 478). 'Confusion precedes understanding' I have often reassured students when they feel overwhelmed by new information, new ways of thinking, when new options are opening up. Albert Einstein focused on solutions: he is reputed to have said that you can't solve a problem with the same sort of thinking that created it, you have to use a different sort of thinking. So changing ways of thinking has to come before the realization of potential. Stage 2 is the time when the twin aims of coaching – high challenge and high support – both peak together. So hold fast – it's the pain before the gain!

Solution focus

Having said the above, we still don't want too swift a move from the comfort of Stage 1 to the more challenging Stage 2. I have not seen the stages running in a strict linear fashion in any case (see Chapter 3). It's tempting to want to encourage a learner towards a potential solution, but there's a danger in doing this before exploring all possible actions. Heightened sensory acuity and active listening will be crucial to allow you to pick up the clues you need to help the young person identify the seeds of solutions.

Paul Jackson and Mark McKergow (2007: 128–30) provide a useful set of tools for working in a solution-focused way. They have termed the start of the process as *Establishing a Platform*. Converting a problem to a platform involves a shift of perspective; from something that is problematic, to an opportunity, a point of departure.

From the platform they shift attention to the *Future Perfect*. In the Future Perfect, if the problem doesn't exist, what would be happening instead? (Up to now, this is similar to our Stage 1 process: setting up a positive relationship can be seen as a platform and the Miracle Question will elicit the Future Perfect.)

The next stage is to seek elements of the desired future that are happening already or have happened before. These will be *Counters*: resources and skills that will count towards the solution. These may be small aspects that may appear insignificant to a young person, so it's important for a coach to *Affirm what is Helping* so they are not underestimated.

Finally, and only after considering all possible options, there is selection of the *Small Actions* to bring about the desired results. Like the CARE model, these tools do not just work in a linear fashion. When small a step is achieved, it provides a further counter towards a solution, so there can be a circling back for further affirmation and choice of a new small step.

The question is the answer[1]

Stage 2 is where we start to appreciate the value of questions in the coaching process: questioning is the most important skill in a coach's portfolio. They will not be the sort of questions where there is one right answer being sought, rather they are forms of questions that open up new channels of thinking for the young person.

Shifting from a problem to a solution focus involves *reframing*. More on that below, but first let's address one of the challenges of working with young people, the fact that we may at times have to face negativity, lack of motivation and a reluctance to share information.

Open questions are generally better than closed questions in this respect because they require a fuller answer. For instance, the response to 'Did you have a good weekend?' can only be 'Yes' or 'No' unless the person chooses to tell you more. Whereas 'What did you do at the weekend?' invites more information. There are also subtle ways of enhancing open questions so that they gently probe a bit further, as in the following alternatives:

Young person: 'I'm not bad at English, but I've never been any good at Maths.'

Coach: 'What's behind that?'
                  'Where might that have begun?'
                  'How long have you thought like that?'
                  'When did you start thinking like that?'

                  Or:

                  'What *specifically* is that about?'
                  'How *exactly* did that start?'

There are several things to keep in mind that influence the effectiveness of questions. Firstly, the formula needs to be a mix of curiosity and empathy. The curiosity is not a nosiness to know for yourself; rather it is a curiosity to find the keys that will open up new channels of thought for the young person. The empathy should not tip over to the 'Oh dear' of sympathy; rather it is a genuine concern for the well-being of the young person.

Secondly, it's the way you say it! It's about remembering Stage 1 and the importance of body language in effective communication, keeping the rapport going, being sensitive to clues that give you an indication that the form of question is useful for the young person, trying another tack if you suspect otherwise.

Thirdly, you'll notice that the questions do not refer specifically to 'not being any good at Maths'. That would be reinforcing the limiting belief; it's the seeds of the solution you're looking for rather than focusing on the problem. In that respect, whenever you get a 'never been any good at ...' comment, a really good question can be:

'Never, never ever?'

With the patience you've learned from practising active listening you'll be more prepared to wait for answers. Some coaching questions take more time to process than questions requiring straightforward factual answers. It's fine to repeat this if you get a quick response that suggests the young person hasn't thought about it long enough, though don't jump in too soon. And you could do so in a light-hearted challenging way as long as you have the rapport to do so:

'You've never, *ever* been good at Maths?'

As Paul Jackson and Mark Mckergow (2007) remind us, no 'problem' happens all the time. The likelihood is that there'll be some occasion, sometime, somewhere, however small, when the young person has had an experience of 'being good at Maths', and when they recall it, there you will find the counter towards the solution. So once you've found the 'one time' you can turn the negative to a positive, and shift for the first small step:

'What exactly were you doing when you were being good at Maths?'

Thinking Space 8

Ann G. recognizes awareness overlaps the formal boundaries of a coaching session. During the initial welcoming chit-chat, walking into the room, fixing a drink, she will be looking for ways to match for rapport, listening for any patterns of speech, feeling her way into the relationship. She's also conscious that thinking goes on after a coaching session has ended. Processing new ideas and ways of thinking takes time. Awareness isn't instant: it more likely comes after a long period of unconscious processing to accommodate new concepts into a person's mental map. Ann also knows she needs to reflect on a session, checking on her own reactions, thinking through the language to check for the seeds of a solution. So when she meets the young person the next time, she can be alert to any pick up any signs of changed thinking, and will have thought about any adjustments she needs to make to her own approach.

Jackson and McKergow (2007: 81) also suggest questions are useful for their stage of *Affirming what is Helping*. A compliment can be wrapped up in a question in order to avoid sounding patronising. So this could be a way of helping a young person recognize what they do well in one subject to transfer it to progress in another:

'How are you learning in English so well?'

Or to transfer skills from one domain to another:

'How are you organizing your time so well that you do all that training?'
'When did you learn to relate to other people so well?'
'How do you concentrate so well when the shop is busy?'

As well as seeing questions as keys to open up new channels of thought for a young person, they are also the signposts to the first small steps. Small steps come about from noticing what works, and need to be something that can be achieved straight away. As you'll see in the next section, for a young person, noticing what works means first raising awareness of the unique and individual way they do their learning.

Metacognition

As you saw in Chapter 2, there is learning, and there is also learning about learning. One aspect of our human evolution that makes us unique in the animal kingdom is that we have self-awareness, we can think about how we think.

You will also have seen in Chapter 2 the extensive range of ideas about how people learn: 71 models of learning styles identified by the Coffield Review, with 13 of those being major models. Indeed, there can hardly be a school in the land that has not been exposed to these ideas in some shape or form; there is a proliferation of training courses, questionnaires and internet resources available.

So many resources, in fact, that you may have found it confusing to try and identify their usefulness and relevance for your particular context. So many models of learning styles also, that this is not the place to explore each and every one. Rather, it is better to seek to deepen our understanding of the practical use of certain theories of learning, while at the same time not being constrained by a notion that one size fits all, or one model has all the answers. The other important aspect is that we are seeking to give young people a language to understand how they learn; an understanding that will help them realize their potential. If a model can do this, it will be a practical test of its usefulness as an explanatory framework. It can also be part of our role to cut through the confusion and aim for clarity, as David Hargreaves (2005: 4) reminds us:

> In many schools there is also no agreed vocabulary in which teachers might talk with their students about their learning, even though this is at the very heart of professional practice.

Left brain/right brain

The fact that the brain has two hemispheres and that each appears to deal with a different form of mental functioning is a good starting point for understanding how people think and learn differently. In 1981 Dr Roger Sperry won a Nobel Prize for 'discoveries concerning the functional specialization of the cerebral hemispheres' (Susan Norman 2003: 18). Since then much has been written about 'left' and 'right' brain thinking and learning, and how individuals may favour the type of thinking and learning that originate in each hemisphere:

> Within the neocortex, parts of the left hemisphere have been found to be particularly significant for analytical capacities such as language, logic, pattern recognition and reflective thought; whilst much of the right hemisphere is associated with more intuitive and representational capabilities such as visualization, imagination, rhyme, rhythm and expression.
>
> Andrew Pollard 2008: 186

We can also think in very simplistic terms of the right brain taking a global view, and the left brain preferring details, but we need to be cautious about over-simplification in aligning functions to one or other of the hemispheres. To begin with, advances in brain imaging tell us that the brain is a much more complex integrated system. Secondly, the hemispheres are not separated; they are linked by a thick band of nerve fibres called the corpus callosum that passes messages between the two sections and means the brain can work in an integrated way.

Having said that, the concept of left brain–right brain provides a useful metaphor for understanding how different young people may think and learn in different ways. It is also one way of understanding how some young people may not fit comfortably in a system of schooling:

> In reality, schools and most formal teaching situations are geared towards the traditional concept of the logical 'left-brained learner' and it is the so-called right-brained learners (those who don't follow the step-by-step logic easily and need a big picture and seem to make intuitive leaps of understanding) who are often failed by the system. Teachers, almost by definition, are those who have flourished in the system, and it is not always easy for us to understand that there are people who need to learn in different ways. Therefore, if the concept of the R/L brain gives us a justification for taking a significantly different approach to teaching for at least 50% of the time, then it is a useful concept.
>
> Susan Norman 2003:18

Plainly developing approaches that assist young people with a right-brain preference will enhance their learning, but since the brain has the facility to integrate all forms of learning, using integrative strategies will also stretch people with a left-brain preference, even though they may already be comfortable in formal teaching situations. Providing a stimulus for 'whole-brain' learning is all the more important for work with young people as the corpus callosum develops at a fairly slow rate and often does not mature until the late teens (Eric Jensen 2008: 20).

Gordon Dryden and Jeannette Vos (2001: 125) record an interview with Colin

Rose where he gave an example of how the different aspects of the brain can work together in an integrated way:

> If you're listening to a song, the left brain would be processing the words and the right brain would be processing the music. So it's no accident that we learn the words of popular songs very easily. You don't have to make any effort to do that. You learn very quickly because the left brain and the right brain are both involved – and so is the emotional centre of the brain in the limbic system.

The example of Albert Einstein provides dramatic illustration of the potential of left-brain–right-brain integration. Carla Hannaford (1997: 145) believes that Einstein was originally a right-brain learner because he didn't talk competently until the age of seven, and he graduated from Federal Polytechnic University in Switzerland without any particular acclaim. But he sought out holistic learning situations that fed his curiosity and lust for understanding, and in later life he frequently referred to the fact that his ground-breaking scientific insights had started with images and visualization.

In Stage 1 you will have already begun to establish an environment to assist right-brain learners and nourish the integration of left-brain/right-brain capacities:

- A multi-sensory learning environment
- Peripheral posters – using words, colour, images
- 'Mood' music
- Things to fiddle with.

There is all the more reason to maintain all the features of 'creating comfort' since recent research in neuroscience has shown that connecting area of the corpus callosum is adversely affected in children exposed to stress (Julie Anne Ryan 2007: 561).

At Stage 2 we can add in strategies to 'exercise' the brain, and encourage left-brain/right-brain integration. Terry Horne and Simon Wootton (2007: 89) tell us that activities that involve remembering and repeated recall involve an extensive network of neuron connections. The density of neuron connections in the brain is not only increased by learning new things, the connections increase by tackling tasks that use different parts of the brain in combination. You will already have your own favourites, of course, below are just some examples. The important thing is sharing the knowledge you have acquired about the brain will mean that young people will be able to understand how these strategies work, and in particular what works for them. Then you can be creative together in coming up with new ideas that suit individuals:

- Creating a rhyme (Thirty days hath September ...)
- Setting information to a song or rap
- Using mnemonics (as in 'Richard Of York Gained Battle In Vain being used to remember the colours of the rainbow – red, orange, yellow, green, blue, indigo, violet)
- Making memory maps, spider diagrams
- Moving about while reciting information
- Physically pacing out a diagram/geometric angle while reciting its name
- Creating games – card sorts, adapting snakes and ladders
- Creating crossword puzzles, wordsearches
- Cutting up cartoon strips for groups to work out the order
- Integrating stories (How many stories have you noticed inserted into the text of this book?)
- Using metaphors (e.g. scaling, thinking of yourself as an animal in Chapter 5)
- Making models
- Visualization (the more funny, outrageous or bizarre the images connected to pieces of information, the more likely they are to be remembered)
- Creating computer presentations that combine text, images and sound

---

Thinking Space 9

I used to teach 16-year-olds taking a vocational course in health and social care. Some had excellent interpersonal skills, and all had a desire to work in a caring profession. Not all, however, had an ability to complete written work to match their level of skill.

They particularly needed some practice to improve their basic spelling – but I didn't want to make it a tedious exercise. So one day when I'd finished a lesson a little early I latched on to an idea. 'We've got 10 minutes left,' I announced, 'so we're going to play a game.' Attention that was already drifting towards where they had to go for the next lesson turned back, intrigued to hear the rules of the game. 'I will read out a word', I said, 'and if you know how to spell it you need to come out to the front, pick up a pen and write it on the board. The rest of the group will then decide if you've spelt it correctly. If you have, they will give you a round of applause. If you haven't, it will be for them to tell you the correct spelling. Everyone has to have a turn, so if you know a word, it's best to jump up quickly and get your turn over with.'

On the whole I applied the rules scrupulously, leaving it for the group to decide if the spelling was correct, or to suggest corrections. I did, however, make one exception.

For our purposes I'll call her Zara. She was a tiny Muslim girl, permanently hunched into her black coat and scarf, doing her best not to be noticed in the group. When I first met her, I'd attempted to get her to join a group discussion. But the response from the rest of the group had been swift, 'Miss, Zara doesn't speak'. I'll leave aside how she had managed to get through 11 years of schooling without speaking, suffice to say that at that stage she didn't – not without a hesitant stuttering, a reddened face and seeming to shrink even further into her coat and scarf.[2] Nevertheless, I didn't think that was a reason for Zara to be excluded from the spelling game, so I was prepared to manipulate it.

Nearly all the group had taken their turn and, not surprisingly, there had been no move from Zara to take part. So I picked on a five-letter word that I thought was an easy option. Rather than calling it out to the whole group, I deliberately aimed it in her direction and said quietly 'Come on Zara, have a go'. Fortunately the rest of the group quickly caught on to my strategy – like I've said they had good interpersonal sensitivity. In light of the calls of 'Yeah, come on Zara', she had no other option than to step up to the board.

Silence fell as she picked up a pen. She stood so close to the board and wrote in such tiny writing that we couldn't see what she was writing. Then she stepped away, anxious to get back to her seat, and we could see that she'd spelt the word correctly.

They were a great group; if I had stage-managed the response I couldn't have asked for better. The room erupted with cheers and clapping and shouts of 'Yo Zara!' And I can still see her face. She had blushed to the roots of her hair and her eyes had filled, but the smile was the first I'd seen since I'd known her.

My 'game' was a simple enough strategy, but it proved popular. There were often requests from the young people 'Can we play the spelling game Miss?' followed by groans of disappointment if I said we didn't have time that particular day. Each time we *did* play it, Zara took part without any special urging. A simple enough strategy, but when I think about it now I can identify the elements beyond the mere reinforcing of correct spelling:

* The use of words associated with their subject matter would have helped their fluency in writing assignments

* Current thought is that spelling is best taught by writing, and is best remembered in the fingertips. It is the memory of the moving pencil writing the word that makes for accurate spelling (Gordon Dryden and Jeannette Vos 2001: 377)

* In addition to individual writing, there was display of all words on the board, and oral recitation of correct spelling, which according to Terry Horne and Simon Wooton (2007: 65) would not only give the brain a memory upgrade, but would expand general cognitive capacity

* There was an emotional element in the 'public performance' (having to stand up and walk to the front of the class)

* The element of feedback and affirmation from fellow students would have boosted individual self-esteem

Visual – Auditory – Kinaesthetic

As a model VAK provides a useful explanatory framework for helping young people think about how they think and learn. As well as being popular and in widespread use, it has additional benefits for a coach. It suggests how we can use our sensory acuity to pick up external clues to young people's mental processing.

The VAK model suggests that our thinking works like this: we receive information from the outside world via our senses – what we see, hear, feel, taste and smell. Then we reproduce these processes internally to *re-present* reality mentally for ourselves. So we construct our conscious thought using the three main representational systems – by generating pictures (Visual), by hearing sounds (Auditory) or by means of physical sensations and feelings (Kinaesthetic) – or a combination of these that will be unique to us.

For example, if I were to ask you to think of something – say something everyday like COFFEE – some of you would see a picture of a cup of coffee or a jar or a percolator, others would hear the word, or someone asking if they wanted a cup, yet others would 'feel' like a cup of coffee or have a feeling of distaste if they didn't like coffee, some could even get a whiff of coffee brewing, or experience the taste. The point is that although 'coffee' is a word we would all understand, we would all *represent* it in our own unique way of thinking.

We all use these different ways of mental processing – by means of pictures, sounds or feelings. As well as these non-verbal forms of thought, of course, we mentally talk to ourselves, and this way of thinking stems from the physical activity of speaking, which becomes internalized to create verbal thinking. Thus, all forms of thought are *activities* (David Wood 1998: 29).

While we potentially all use each of the representative forms of thought, for some people what may start out as a *tendency* to favour one or other of the forms of thought will, through habit and practice, become established as a *preference*. Using a questionnaire is one way of helping young people explore whether they have a preference in the way they think and learn. Discussion about questionnaire results would be one way of developing their metacognition and there are lots of resources available.[3]

From there, young people would be able to appreciate the type of methods and resources they believe help them learn. For a predominantly visual thinker:

- Diagrams that explain text
- Memory maps and spider diagrams
- Visual displays
- Coloured pens and highlighters
- Film and video
- PowerPoint, flip chart and whiteboard using colours and visuals
- Making montages/collages
- Note-taking using visual formats

For a predominantly auditory thinker:

- Group and paired discussions
- Listening to a teacher
- Taped lectures
- Music
- Rhymes and raps

For a predominantly kinaesthetic thinker:

- Frequent breaks to move around
- Making lots of notes
- Hands-on activities
- Plenty of time to process
- Making models.

Health warning!

A major benefit of the VAK model is that it provides young people with a language to understand how they think and learn. Even so there are two aspects for a coach to be cautious about.

The first is the danger of putting young people into boxes and letting them think about themselves as **A** visual learn or **A** kinaesthetic learner. As you saw in Chapter 2, stereotyping like this would be as bad as the more or less discredited way we used to think about intelligence – as something it is not possible to change or develop. Since we *all* use *all* the systems of thought the only value of knowing whether someone has developed a strong preference for one or the other is to use that information to help them enhance their learning.

Secondly, where a young person *has* developed a strong preference, it can be reassuring for them to understand that that's a pretty efficient way for them to learn, and they could probably increase their efficiency by playing to that as a strength. However – and it's a very big 'however' – to *really* maximize potential, we need to encourage young people to enhance their learning potential by developing other attributes that may be underused. That is one reason why the creation of a multi-sensory learning environment is vital – in appealing to all the senses it opens up opportunities for multi-representational thinking. So, just as we can encourage activities to develop left-brain/right-brain integration, we can encourage young people to reach out from the comfort zone of their thinking preference and try out different strategies that will develop their learning capacity. As with left-brain/right-brain inclinations, it is the *combination* of processes that has the potential to enhance learning.

Using sensory acuity to detect mental processing – listening to language

I started this section by saying that VAK was a model that enabled us to pick up external clues to young people's mental processing; indeed how people use language can give very illuminating insights into the way they are thinking.

As well as using language to communicate with other people, it's also our means of expressing the thoughts in our heads. It works the other way as well; sometimes the thoughts will be vague and unspecified, and they only become meaningful to us when we attempt to put them into words. Hence the neat line on the last page of *Howard's End* by E. M. Forster 'How do I know what I think until I hear what I say?'

So it would seem to follow that, if we are using a particular representational mode of thinking, i.e. pictures, sounds or feelings, it is likely that the words we use will indicate that particular mode. The way we use language can therefore give an indication of the *process* of our thinking as well as the content.

As you are practising your active listening, you may notice that people use particular words and phrases, and you may also pick up that they use the same 'type' of words so consistently that they sound like patterns of speech, e.g.:

- 'I get the *picture*', 'I *see* what you mean', 'That *looks* good', 'I need to *see it in black and white*', 'can you *show me* what you mean ...', I'll *focus* on this part of it', 'The future's *looking bright.*'
- 'I *hear* what you're saying', 'I like the *sound* of that', '*loud and clear* ...', *Music* to my ears ...' '*Rings bells* with me ...', 'I'm into the *rhythm* of it now ...', '*Listen* ...'

- 'That makes *sense* to me', 'Things are really *moving* now', I like *concrete* ideas I can get to grips with', 'I'm *feeling the pressure*', 'I'm trying to *shape up* these ideas', 'I've got a *feeling* ...'

(I smiled to myself as I wrote the first paragraph for this sub-section. I have a strong preference for visual thinking, and when I'm struggling to articulate an idea I tend to revert to my comfort zone. So when I wrote 'illuminating insights' it made me smile to think how this was an example of what I was trying to write about. I could have said something about 'how people use language means you can hear how they are thinking', or 'sense how they are thinking' to appeal to people with other preferences, but I left it to provide an illustration – oops, there I go again!)

Apart from enabling us to get a sense of which thinking process a young person may be accessing, there's a further use we can make of language clues. Chapter 5 dealt with how you could match language to create rapport, and when you begin to notice language patterns that indicate thinking processes, you can use this as a further opportunity to match to demonstrate your understanding, e.g.:

| Young person: | I can't see the point of this. |
| Coach: | You can't see the point of this; what do you need to be able to get a glimmer of understanding? |

| Young person: | This doesn't strike a chord with me. |
| Coach: | It doesn't strike a chord with you; let's discuss it and see if we can phrase it another way. |

| Young person: | I can't seem to grasp this. |
| Coach: | You can't grasp it; what would need to happen for you to get a handle on this? |

The alternative, of course, is that we stick with our own processing and therefore our own language patterns. This would mean that, at the very least we would lose the opportunity of engaging with the young person, at worst we could turn them off altogether due to a mismatch of language. You can think about how that might feel by reflecting on the example above of my own choice of visual words and phrases; whether the words worked well to hook you in to an understanding, or whether the alternatives I could have used would have worked better for you.

Using sensory acuity to detect mental processing – watching body language

It's become more recognized now, but perhaps the thinking process that has traditionally been overlooked in education has been kinaesthetic – the need for touch, movement and emotional impact. Perhaps one of the major impacts of the VAK model has been the recognition that learners who process predominantly kinaesthetically may not just be 'messing about' if they fidget – they actually *need* to move to think and learn (Mark Fletcher 2000: 58).

The other interesting thing when you start watching body language is how you begin to see more and more the differences in people when they are engaged in serious thinking.

I remember Lisa: when she was thinking about something her eyes always went upwards, usually to her left. In discussions, she talked very fast, and she used a lot of gestures – it was almost as though she was drawing out a picture she had in her mind. I could always tell when she'd lost interest because she would either start to doodle or stare out the window.

Then there was Tracey: she seemed to work best being able to talk things through in group discussions. Tracey would always be the one listening intently to what I had to say, usually with her head on one side. She had plenty of questions also; I soon understood that Tracey needed me to *tell* her how she was doing.

David was different again. He was a tall lad, with a deep voice and he spoke quite slowly and deliberately. He would usually be slouched back in his seat, legs stretched out, looking down at the floor. On other occasions he would take lots of notes; too many notes it seemed to me at the time.

So, just as we can get clues to how young people are mentally processing from the words they use, we can learn a great deal from 'the way they say it'. The different ways that people speak, the way they sit and stand, how they use gestures will all give clues to their mental processing. In the examples above, their styles could give an indication that Lisa was processing visually, Tracey had an auditory preference and David had a kinaesthetic preference. Of these non-verbal factors, one of the most dramatic indicators can be the way people move their eyes while they are thinking. In very general terms, 90 per cent of people will look *up* to the left or right if they are visually processing, look *to the side* when auditory processing, and look *down* if they are processing kinaesthetically.

It can be quite amusing to think about how these young people may have been dealt with in schooling in the past. For Lisa, looking up could have brought a response from a teacher 'You won't find the answer on the ceiling, you know!' whereas, for Lisa, as she needed to look up to think about the answer, the ceiling is just where she would find it. Tracey may have been the class chatterbox and may have been told to be quiet, whereas talking and listening would have helped her to learn. And I wonder how many times David had been told 'Look at me when I'm talking to you!' when in fact he needed to look downwards to be able think.

I hope you are beginning to comprehend how heightened sensory acuity can give you so much more information about people. When we can see, tune into and sense young people's learning preferences we can use this information to raise their own awareness of how they think and learn.

Dominance Profiles

Helen had never really found the VAK model particularly useful. She tried different learning style questionnaires, but for her, they never seemed to give the complete picture; she was always on the lookout for something more. Then she read *The Dominance Factor* (Carla Hannaford 1997) and things clicked into place for her.

A Dominance Profile is a method of assessing learning styles that is based on the individual's pattern of dominances; that is, which hand, eye, ear, foot and brain hemisphere is dominant. There are 32 possible profiles. I asked Helen what exactly it was about the profiles that attracted her. Firstly, she liked the fact that Carla Hannaford was a neuroscientist who also worked with children in education, and whose work was therefore both rigorous and practical. Secondly, the profiles are richly complex and throw light on some of the structural reasons for particular learning styles. Significantly for coaching for learning, Dominance Profiles help explain why an individual's learning preferences will change in different situations, for example when under stress.

Helen explained to me how it might work: each brain hemisphere communicates with and controls the opposite side of the body; for example the right hemisphere communicates with the left hand, eye, ear and foot. And we favour those senses and physical movements whose dominance is opposite the dominant brain hemisphere. These are more likely to be fully accessible to us even when we are under stress. For example, if a learner has a *dominant right eye* opposite their *dominant left brain* hemisphere, but the dominant left ear, hand and foot on the same side as the dominant hemisphere, they are likely to *favour vision* as means of learning, especially under stress, because the flow of information from eye to brain and back has the most direct route. (Communications between a dominant left brain and a dominant left eye would always have to go via the right brain first – a longer route.)

Interestingly, Hannaford believes that Einstein's profile was one in which the dominant brain hemisphere was on the same side as all the other dominances (all on the right) – a profile with excellent potential for creative and intuitive thinking but which may involve difficulty in communicating when under stress. Note that Einstein was not able to talk capably until he was seven.

OK so far, but I needed to try it out for myself. So I roped my family in and we all had a go at working out our Dominance Profiles following Carla Hannaford's instructions. Hand first, then eye, ear, foot and, finally, brain hemisphere. Helen was right, working out our profiles was physical and fun! I could see how young people would enjoy the process and testing out to what extent the predictions are true for them. One school that Helen was involved with had their entire Year 10 students working out their profiles.

For each of the profiles, Hannaford offers detailed advice on the optimum learning conditions for students which includes which area of a classroom would be most beneficial for them to sit, whether background noise is likely to be a hindrance or a help to them and what sort of activities would encourage learning. In particular, there is an emphasis on physical activities that encourage whole-brain integration, such as Brain Gym (Paul Dennison and Gail Dennison 1994; Carla Hannaford 1995).

So I could see how Helen had found Dominance Profiles illuminating in working with learners. And I liked the fact that Carla Hannaford gives a similar warning to my own above: '... please do not label learners. Dominance Profiles do not present the full complexity of any person nor do they indicate the infinite adaptive strategies that people develop to expand their capacities as they grow and learn' (1997: 37). Nevertheless, for young people to work out their Dominance Profiles is another option for raising awareness of how they currently think and learn. And the process would generate a lot of physical activity and discussion – and enjoyment even!

Reframing

If we think of 'reframing' as a shift in perception, we have already seen one example in this chapter – shifting from a problem to a solution focus. Reframing is not merely looking at the world through rose-coloured glasses; issues still have to be worked through to find solutions. However, the more ways of looking at issues young people have, the more options they open up for themselves.

Another example of reframing has been the way we no longer think of learning as a single thing that is the same for everyone. As you saw in Chapter 2, there are many different ways we can think about learning. The examples above are useful in providing young people with different ways of thinking about styles and preferences in learning.

Also in Chapter 2, you will have seen that the notion of intelligence has become reframed from something that was thought of as a fixed entity which was stable for life, to something that can be influenced by external factors. Howard Gardner (1993) in particular, with his concept of 'Multiple Intelligences', has been influential in establishing the notion that intelligence is not fixed, but can be looked upon as a set of abilities and skills that can be developed and improved. His seven intelligences group together particular abilities and skills, e.g.:

Linguistic/verbal	Ability of expression through language
Mathematical/logical	Ability to process analytically and procedurally
Visual/spatial	Ability to see and imagine in pictures
Musical	Ability in the organization of music and rhythm

Interpersonal	Ability to relate well to other people
Intrapersonal	Ability in reflective thinking and developing self-knowledge
Kinaesthetic	Ability in use of the body and physical movement

Gardner considers we may each be born with all the abilities, but that, according to our external influences, we will develop some fully and others hardly at all. So his theory offers yet another way of 'reframing' for young people their ideas about themselves and their abilities.

On the other hand, a 'reframe' can be as simple as the use of different words. Richard, for instance, never asks students how they got on with their *work*, he always asks 'How did you get on with your *learning*?' The reframe of work to learning encourages a shift in perception to something that *means* something different to a young person.

Reframing is also a good strategy to use with 'all or nothing' thinking. Like the example above 'I've never been any good at Maths'. What this young person is saying is that they've never at any time, at any place, anywhere in their lives had any experience of being good at Maths. Another example of 'all or nothing' thinking is in the use of 'always' as in 'I always make mistakes'. Being alert to 'never' and 'always' will mean you can challenge the 'all or nothing' thinking with a question. Helping young people think about an occasion of success – however small – will break down the global perception and reframe it to a more realistic understanding.

The mention of Einstein earlier, and his quote that you can't solve a problem with the same sort of thinking that created it, also points us to the fact that there are always different ways to think about things. The model of Neuro-Logical Levels developed by Robert Dilts (1990) gives us a framework for thinking about issues in different ways. As well as being different ways of thinking, the 'levels' also represent different aspects of our neurology – the different ways that we perceive, think and process information. So whereas the level of *Environment* will relate to information we passively receive from our sense organs, the level of *Behaviour* concerns the physical actions we take in interacting with our environment and the people around us. When we get to the level of *Identity*, this concerns our sense of self which can involve our whole nervous system. When a major change in life circumstances such as redundancy or bereavement is experienced, the threat to a person's sense of self can have such a powerful affect that it can make them physically ill.[4] On the other hand, if we make a positive change at the level of *Identity*, the change can transform our beliefs and behaviour, in fact the transformation can flow through all the other levels. If we think back to the example of smoking in Chapter 3: actions that try to stop people smoking don't always work because they try to address smoking at the level of a *Behaviour*. Whereas, particularly for adolescents, smoking is linked very closely to issues of *Identity*, and it is when we address issues at that deeper level of perception that real change can be made.

If we think again about that statement 'I've never been any good at Maths', we can use the levels to think about ways this can be reframed to help a young person think about the issue differently (see Fig. 14). As well as being an 'all or nothing' statement it is a statement that suggests a limiting belief; a belief perhaps developed from repeated failure that has hardened into a sense of identity experienced as 'I'm a stupid person at Maths'. Addressing inability at Maths by giving additional practice would be an approach at the level of *Behaviour*, and there could be a danger there. As Terry Mahony (2003: 10) advises, the danger of addressing the wrong level is that it treats the symptom, not the cause, and there is likely to be a re-occurence at a later date. The higher up the levels positive change can be made, the more likely the lower levels will be influenced. And the more a limiting belief is questioned, the weaker it becomes (Will Thomas 2005: 33).

Environment (*The Where and When*)	Do they have the right equipment to enable them to do Maths at school, e.g. pen, pencil, notebooks, ruler, compass, calculator? Are they in the right class/level for learning Maths?
Behaviour (*The What*)	'What part of Maths don't you find easy?' 'So you haven't been able to do this up to now. What could make it easy?' 'What's stopping you being good at Maths?' 'You say you've been no good at Maths because you always play up in class? What would happen if you didn't play up?' 'You say the teacher winds you up. What would happen if you didn't allow the teacher to wind you up?'
Capability (*The How*)	What wider abilities do they have that involves the use of elements of Maths? Does their part-time job involve dealing with cash and working out change? If they work in a hairdresser's, have they noticed how the stylist uses percentages to work out colourings? Can they recognize how elements of geometry occur in buildings and use that knowledge to understand schoolwork? If their job is stacking shelves or working in a baker's shop, do they realize how they 'know' elements of algebra in relation to the number of tins left in a carton, the number of pies left on a tray?
Beliefs and values (*The Why*)	'What evidence do you have for this belief that "I've never been any good at Maths"?' 'When did you first acquire this belief?' 'How did you first acquire this belief?' 'If you didn't have this belief, what would be different?' 'What else would need to be happening for this belief to be true?' 'What if you were to "act as if" you didn't have this belief? What would you be doing?'
Identity (*The Who*)	'That's good. It's a sign that you're an intelligent person that you can recognize for yourself the areas you need to increase your learning.'

Figure 14: Logical levels for reframing 'I've never been any good at Maths'

What you can see in the example at the *Identity* level is the potential for a real shift of perception. A strategy of reframing can indeed be as simple as Richard's example of changing 'work' to 'learning', or it can be a way of using words that puts a whole new frame around reality for a young person. Change at this level will engender a different belief, with a resultant positive rather than defeatist approach to tackling Maths.

> **Thinking Space 10**
>
> 'For centuries, the ancient Mayans had beautifully balanced prayer wheels. Yet they made their dogs pull loads on cross-sticked travois whose pointed ends dragged clumsily on the ground. They seemed unable to "think wheel" in any general way: wheels were prayer, period. Why didn't it occur to them to attach a small wheel to the dragging end of the travois? ... why did the people of the Olduvai Gorge spend thousands of years using digging sticks for digging up roots before adapting them as drills to poke holes into the dirt for planting seedlings? What makes slaves of us – our culturally shaped ways, Williams James's habit mechanisms, or the two working in hand-in-glove that constitutes the interaction of mind and culture?'
>
> Jerome Bruner 1996: 166

Reframing for relaxation

I thought of putting something about relaxation in Stage 1. After all, Creating Comfort, I thought, would be an appropriate time to be helping young people with relaxation. But my friend Anne D. said young people don't know how to relax. They often need help to reframe their physiology before they can reframe their mindset. She described how a young person may come to see her tense and edgy, how they may sit on the edge of the chair: their body language suggesting a troubled state of mind. Before Anne gets to the issue they want to talk about, she will suggest 'Let's just both lean back in our chairs for a moment', then perhaps 'You seem to be holding your shoulders rather tensely, see how far you can drop them down'. Then again perhaps 'What if you were to straighten your legs?', or 'Just rest your hands gently on your legs'. All the while she will be modelling the actions herself, 'Now take a deep breath in ... and out again'.

Notice that by leaning back in the chair the young person will probably have to look upwards. Since looking down could indicate emotional processing (see above), getting someone to look up is a very quick way of shifting them out of what may be negative feelings.

Notice also that none of the phrases are asking the young person to 'Just relax'. If young people don't know what it is to relax, there's no point in telling them to do so. All the while Anne's voice and language will be inducing a state of light trance. We all 'go into a trance', probably on a daily basis, it's just an altered state of awareness. It may be when we are watching television, when our conscious attention 'drifts away' when someone is talking in a monotone, when we allow ourselves to become absorbed in beautiful scenery, an inspiring piece of art. A light trance can be a very refreshing place to be, and it is also the place where our unconscious mind is open to learning without the distractions of the rationalization of the conscious mind. Remember from Chapter 5 that learning is not simply cognitive and rational.

So Anne's approach will be 'teaching' the young person to *experience* a relaxed state. In a gently modulated voice, her language will use techniques of trance induction; frequent pauses and phrases that can act as instructions to the unconscious mind, e.g.:

> 'And now that you've ... **let go of your legs** ... you'll be aware that they are feeling heavy.'
> 'And now ... as **the tension is gone from your shoulders** ... you can feel the tightness dropping away.'
> 'You notice the difference in your breathing ... with each breath you **breathe out your worries**.'

Once Anne notices the young person appears more comfortable she may use the moment to anchor the comfortable state. 'How does that feel now?' may be the next question. Then 'And have you ever felt like that before?'

This may bring up a memory of a time and place where the young person felt happy and contented. Anne will encourage them to visualize the moment so they can describe it in detail. It may be a time when they were with someone close to them, when they felt warm and cared for, or they may have a memory of a particular place they associate with a good feeling. 'And would it be good to know you could go there and feel like this any time you choose?'

As you saw in Chapter 5, young people can learn to associate a resourceful state with something they can see, hear or hold. We can also use parts of our own bodies to act as the stimulus, which is Anne's approach. Once she is sure the experience of relaxation is as profound and comfortable as it can be, she will tell the young person to touch the tips of their thumb and first finger together. 'There, now you know that whenever you need to feel this good again, you just have to do that and you will get the feeling.'

Of course it's important to ease the young person back from the experience of the relaxed state and help them switch back to their conscious awareness. Anne may shift her own position as an indicator, then say something like:

> 'Now ... what do you think of my new poster?'
> 'Did I hear rain just now?'

Then:

'What did you want to talk to me about?'

'Ah', you may well be saying to yourself 'but isn't this instruction. And didn't you say in Chapter 3 that coaching is not about instruction?' And I suppose you could be right. But I also said that coaching involves a high level of skills and sensory acuity. This 'instruction' is a far more subtle process than straightforward directions to the conscious mind – which could generate resistance – and it also takes place within a supportive relationship that has a basis of rapport. The overriding factor is the importance of relaxation for learning as suggested by Eric Jensen (2008: 50). He records a research study with two groups at Stanford University's School of Medicine, where the overall score on a memory test was 25 per cent higher for the group that received relaxation instruction.

The difference also in Anne's approach is that as well as engaging the unconscious mind, the 'instructions' are to the body. It's a recognition that the body learns as well as the mind; that actions and movement can play a powerful role in learning (Eric Jensen 2008:105). And sometimes the quickest way to reframe thinking is to reframe the physiology first.

Themes of the CARE model – Stage 2

Language

Questioning is a key skill in coaching, and Stage 2 has illustrated the range of ways questions can be used to switch focus from problems to solutions, and to change ways of thinking about learning.

Generally, open questions will be better than closed questions, and an open question will be one that starts with What, Where, When, How, Who or Why. I usually suggest a little caution over using 'Why'. Without the support of an appropriately empathetic voice tone 'Why' can sound like interrogation or be a little value-laden, as in **Why** didn't you do your coursework?' It just needs a little thought to reframe a 'Why' question using one of the other options, e.g.:

'What happened that prevented you from doing your coursework?'

It may seem surprising, but precise grammatical correctness is not the most important feature in forming coaching questions. The more important feature is the message for the unconscious mind that can be wrapped up in the form of a question: particularly when you alter your tone of voice to place an emphasis on the message you want to convey. There was an earlier example of forming a compliment as a question, here's another example:

'What exactly were you doing when **you were being good at Maths**?'

Then again, you can make inferences in the form of questions. In this respect, an alternative response to a reported lack of coursework could be:

'Were you planning to do your coursework this evening, or will you be **doing it tomorrow**?'

Notice that this question is giving the illusion of choice, but the assumption embedded in the question is that the coursework is going to be done!

This is also an example of the point made in Chapter 4 about how we can take ways of speaking for granted until we start to analyse them; until we become aware of the subtle ways we can influence other people. When Anne was saying '.... let go of your legs,' it was an instruction to the unconscious mind. But rather than being a direct instruction, because it was wrapped up in the sentence 'And now that you've ... **let go of your legs** ... you'll be aware that they are feeling heavy', it became an *embedded command*. If you're still feeling sceptical about the ethics of this tactic, can you be sure you never use embedded commands yourself? Have you ever said to young people 'Don't **run along the corridor**'? In order for the brain to process that directive, it first has to form an image of what it's being asked **not** to do. So every time you ask someone **not** to do something you are giving an embedded command to do it! (Remember my instruction in Chapter 4 '**Don't** think about a blue elephant with pink spots'?)

This is a powerful strategy and plainly it needs to be used ethically and for the benefit of the young person. Instruction, for instance can always be stated in positive terms, such as 'Walk along the corridor'. Similarly, given careful thought, embedded commands in coaching language can influence positively and with integrity.

Well-being

As I mentioned at the beginning of this chapter, Stage 2 is the time when high challenge and high support peak together. Thus it is a stage of balancing well being with moving young people forward in their learning. Sometimes small failures can appear out of all proportion to their real importance, sometimes a young person will be living with unhappy and difficult life circumstances: there are many factors that can contribute to feeling demoralized and demotivated. At times like these, we may identify a need to inject a little impetus, to assist a young person to shift to a higher gear. Young people don't always recognize the resources they already have that can be used to advantage. It may be an attitude or an approach they've used in the past that brought success. It may have been a small success, but a success with which they associate positive feelings. Once you have enabled a young person to recognize the learning resource, you can talk them through the strategy in Fig. 15 to amplify the positive feelings. It then becomes a further resource they can use themselves when they need to lift their spirits and spur themselves forward.

Olympic Gold!

Ask the young person to stand up and imagine that lying on the floor in front of them is an Olympic Gold Medal.
It's a rather special Olympic Gold Medal.
It's pure gold and large enough to stand upon.
It's highly polished and it gleams so brightly that the rays shine upwards.

Now ask them to think about a time when they used their ability to learn effortlessly and effectively.
(You will probably have uncovered a time when they maximized their learning resources during your coaching conversations, and if necessary you can remind them.)
Ask them to imagine themselves back at that time.
What are they seeing, what are they hearing, what are they feeling that they felt at that time?
Get them to really re-live the time, place and feelings associated with maximizing their learning resources. Use your sensory acuity to judge they are fully re-living the experience.

Now ask them to take a deep breath and step into the centre of the Olympic Gold Medal.
As they stand there the brilliance of the gold intensifies the experience, as they re-live the moment, they can feel a glow from the feeling of doing something well.
As the feeling ebbs away, ask them to step back outside the Gold Medal.
Tell them that this is their learning resource, this is their Olympic Gold Medal, and it's available to use in the future.
When they need to, they can step back into their Olympic Gold Medal, re-live the experience and use their learning resource for what they want to achieve.

Figure 15: Olympic Gold

Goal setting

So far throughout this book there has been much to emphasize the positive. Goals need to be stated in positive terms I asserted in Chapter 4, a solution focus shifts thinking from problems to solutions, negativity can be reframed to a more positive viewpoint.

Alongside there has also been an emphasis on being realistic. While there is no doubt having goals enhances and sustains motivation, unless they are specific, realistic and at the right level of challenge, there is a danger they will not be achieved. Lack of achievement of goals can be demoralizing and demotivating: a potentially worse effect than not having goals at all.

So being effective in goal-setting may mean being realistic about potential obstacles. When obstacles appear, it is all too easy for young people to give up on a goal, see the obstacle as an issue too difficult to overcome and rationalize it as a reason not to achieve a goal.

It's better to think about obstacles in advance so they present no surprises, and Jack Canfield (2005: 57–9) gives a useful formula for doing this. He suggests obstacles come in three forms: *considerations*, *fears* and *road blocks*.

Say you're working with a young person on setting a goal for a certain level of academic achievement – a particular grade in a particular exam perhaps. The sort of thought that could pop into their head might be 'I'll have to work a lot harder' or 'I won't have time to watch television/go out with my friends/play computer games', etc.

These *considerations* are all the reasons why the young person may be thinking the goal will be impossible. They will be the unconscious obstacles in the way of achieving the goals. Using your skilled questioning to surface the *considerations* will mean they can be brought out into the open, confronted and dealt with, e.g.:

> 'What things might distract you from achieving this goal?'
> 'What other things might you want to be doing instead of working towards this goal?'
> 'What else?'

On the other hand, *fears* are feelings, and for adolescents these may become major obstacles to achieving goals. You might be helping a young person to build their self-confidence by working on a goal to be the first to speak the next time they're involved in group discussions. Thinking about it may raise a fear of making a fool of themselves in front of their peers, a fear of being laughed at, being rejected. Young people may need reassurance that such fears are not unusual; everyone experiences fear to some degree when taking up a new challenge. Fear can often be the spur that heightens performance.

Finally, Canfield (2005: 58) describes *road blocks* as external circumstances. For our purposes, these could be that a young person does not have access to necessary financial resources, may experience opposition from certain adults, may have commitments as a family carer. This may be the area where, as a coach, you recognize a need to draw on other resources – other professionals, or any part of the community and agency network that forms a network of support around a young person (see Chapter 4).

Sometimes the route to the solution is not a direct one. The path may be littered with leaves to sweep aside, stones to pick up and cast away, even heavier boulders that need more than one person to shift. But if we keep our eyes on the solution, these can only be temporary obstacles to be dealt with along the way to the ultimate goal.

> **Reflection**
>
> Skill in questioning has been a major feature of *Raising Awareness*. It can be quite a shift from the usual 'teacher' formula of using 'questions to which the teacher knows the one right answer' to adopting a style of questioning that encourages young people to open up avenues in their own thinking.
>
> Another challenge in Stage 2 may emerge from reflection on your own thinking and learning style. It is comfortable to stick with your own learning preference, and make the assumption that students will learn the same way. The challenge lies in considering whether the reason a young person may be doing less well might be because your style of teaching and coaching reflects your own learning preference. It's a challenge also to resist using theories of learning styles to stereotype young people; rather to use them as a means of helping young people explore how different ways of learning may help them realize their potential. The heightened sensory acuity developed in Stage 1 will feed your curiosity about the fascinating differences in people in their ways of behaving, speaking, thinking and learning.
>
> Reframing has demonstrated that there are always different ways of looking at issues: finding solutions is more productive than wrestling with problems, changing words can change the way people think, changing language can influence young people to think of themselves in different, more positive ways. Reframing stimulates double loop learning and opens up more possibilities. Coaching itself is reframing a traditional way of teaching.

Stage 2 – Practice pointers

- Having a solutions focus builds on 'what works' for young people
- Solutions can evolve from the complex interaction of academic achievement, personal development and social and life skills
- Small steps will act towards a solution
- Questioning is a crucial skill in coaching
- A model of learning styles will give young people a language to understand their learning
- Multi-sensory integrated learning activities will encourage learning attributes that may be under-used
- Reframing can change ways of thinking and perceiving

- Reframing can challenge limiting beliefs
- Instruction in relaxation can assist learning
- Goal-setting can be made more effective by addressing obstacles.

Notes

[1] John Whitmore 2002:100.

[2] There was no physical reason for Zara not speaking. Neither do I believe her not speaking was evidence of a serious phobic condition such as selective mutism. The reason I say this is because after just a few weeks of gentle coaxing, she began to contribute to group discussions. By the end of the year, she was happy to go along with the rest of the group and even be interviewed for local radio.

[3] See Alistair Smith (1996) for examples of how schools have used different methods. Also Jacquie Turnbull (2007: 31–2) for a 'Unique thinking comfort-zone' questionnaire. For free VAK test, see www.businessballs.com/vaklearning stylestest.htm.

[4] I have given examples elsewhere of the powerful effect when there is a threat to professional identity (Jacquie Turnbull 2007:17-20)

7 Stage: 3 Re-awakening the Flow of Learning

Got to let the textbooks go and let some of the learners take the lead.

Edward Jones, Senior Advisor

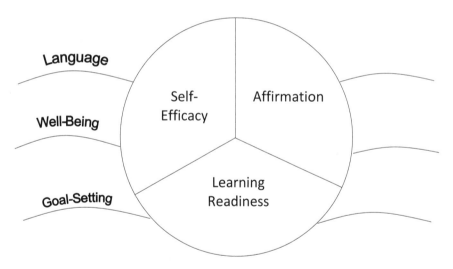

Figure 16: Key words for Stage 3

Following the challenge of raising awareness in Stage 2, in Stage 3 there can be a shift of balance towards young people taking more of the lead in their learning. We still have to keep in mind, of course, that the framework of the CARE model is not a linear progression, and at any time we may have to 'tweak the plates' to maintain progress towards our overall goal of developing independent learners. But to achieve this goal, by now the emphasis needs to shift to allow young people to experience more control over their thinking and learning experiences.

As you saw in Chapter 3, we are all born with an innate urge to explore and learn about our environment. Learning then was as natural as breathing; our ability to learn is the reason we have evolved into the cleverest creatures on the planet. Learning is not only natural, as Michael Brearley (2001: vi) reminds us, it can be magical as well: 'Learning is the single most potent feature of human motivation, growth and fulfilment'.

That 'magical' element of learning is something that social psychologist Mihaly Csikszentmihalyi (1991) has spent his life exploring. He has studied thousands of people from surgeons to rock climbers to understand how they sustain enjoyment from what they do. He describes it as 'flow': that feeling when we are so absorbed in an activity that we can become completely oblivious to our environment:

> In flow we feel totally involved, lost in a seemingly effortless performance. Para-doxically, we feel 100 per cent alive when we are so committed to the task at hand that we lose track of time, of our interests – even our own existence. Intense flow can happen anywhere: in making love, in listening to music, in playing a good game of squash or chess. But it also happens surprisingly often at work – as long as the job provides clear goals, immediate feedback, and a level of challenges matching our skills. When these conditions are present, we have a chance to experience work as 'good' – that is, as something that allows the full expression of what is best in us, something we experience as rewarding and enjoyable.
>
> Howard Gardner et al. 2001: 5

Sadly, we have to concede that many young people will not have had the experience of being in 'flow': social factors may have led to them developing 'failure identities', they may lack the motivation to achieve through seeing 'schoolwork' as irrelevant. On the learning coach training course, the trainers adopted the term 'The Zone' to describe the flow experience; a term they thought young people might be more able to relate to. It was the source of some amusement when one delegate – a youth worker – related that one young man could relate 'flow' to the feeling he experienced when he was nicking cars! Which is a point that Gardner et al. make: feelings of 'flow' do not always signal that a person is performing 'good work'. Nevertheless, the more important point is that the feeling can be recognized by a young person, which is a starting point for attempting to replicate it in more worthy activities.

Self-efficacy

Self-efficacy, 'personal mastery' and 'agency' are all terms that relate to the ability to be in control of one's life, having the capability to achieve valued goals and prevent undesirable outcomes. Unsurprisingly, a strong determinant of self-efficacy will be beliefs: Albert Bandura's (1992) research has been consistent in showing that efficacy beliefs have a significant influence on motivation and attainment.

As you saw in Chapter 2, Carol Dweck's research revealed different responses to learning challenges that related to different beliefs about intelligence. With the *Helpless Pattern* young people would take a difficulty as an indicator of personal adequacy, would give up far too quickly and become anxious. Failure would then become a self-fulfilling prophecy. On the other hand, young people displaying a *Master-Orientated Pattern* welcomed the opportunity to confront obstacles and had an optimistic belief in their ability to overcome them. So self-efficacy, or 'mastery', is not related to level of intelligence: rather motivation, emotional state and actions will be based more on what young people *believe* than on reality (see Chapter 4).

You will have noticed that the importance of beliefs has been a feature throughout this book: the beliefs that underpin the CARE model were outlined first before moving on to describe the practice. Then in Chapter 6 you saw how change at the levels of *Identity* and *Beliefs* had the potential for a shift in perception that would affect *Behaviour*, and how questioning a limiting belief such as 'I've never been any good at Maths' could weaken it and reframe it more realistically.

One of the other features of a strong sense of self-efficacy you will notice from Fig. 17 is that it fosters interest and 'deep engrossment in activities'. You may think this phrase suggests a similar experience to that described by Csikszentmihalyi as 'flow'; so we can see a relationship between a level of efficacy and the potential to attain the rewarding experience Csikszentmihalyi describes.

So as well as addressing limiting beliefs, are there other ways we can we help young people develop self-efficacy and thereby experience the 'magical' element of 'flow'? Albert Bandura believes self-efficacy is learned, so there is every reason to believe that in coaching we can assist young people towards this experience.

If we look at how Bandura (1995: 3–5) sees the *sources* of self-efficacy, we can identify how in coaching we may be able to help young people develop in this direction. He identifies four sources:

- *Mastery experiences* The experience of success is the most effective way of creating a strong sense of efficacy. These will not be easy successes that bring quick results – this expectation only leads to people becoming easily discouraged by failure. Rather the experience of some setbacks can serve the purpose of teaching that success usually requires some effort. Showing resilience in the face of difficulties is a necessary part of young people becoming convinced that they have what it takes to succeed.

- *Social modelling* When people see others like themselves persevere to succeed it instils a belief that they too can succeed if they persevere in a similar fashion.

- *Social persuasion* People can be spurred to greater effort, and can sustain efforts towards achieving a goal when they are persuaded verbally that they possess the capabilities to attain it.

- *Physiological and emotional states* Stress reactions, tension and mood will affect people's judgement of their personal efficacy. It is not the strength of emotional and stress reactions that is important, rather how people perceive them. Negative reactions can be interpreted as vulnerability and reduced performance, whereas a positive mood can enhance self-efficacy.

People who have a low sense of efficacy in given domains shy away from difficult tasks, which they view as personal threats. They have low aspirations and weak commitment to the goals they choose to pursue. When faced with difficult tasks, they dwell on their personal deficiencies, the obstacles they will encounter, and all kinds of adverse outcomes rather than concentrate on how to perform successfully. They slacken their efforts and give up quickly in the face of difficulties. They are slow to recover their sense of efficacy following failure or setbacks. Because they view insufficient performance as deficient aptitude, it does not require much failure for them to lose faith in their capabilities. They fall easy victim to stress and depression.

In contrast, a strong sense of efficacy enhances human accomplishment and personal well-being in many ways. People with high assurance in their capabilities in given domains approach difficult tasks as challenges to be mastered rather than as threats to be avoided. Such an efficacious outlook fosters intrinsic interest and deep engrossment in activities. These people set themselves challenging goals and maintain strong commitment to them. They heighten and sustain their efforts in the face of difficulties. They quickly recover their sense of efficacy after failures or setbacks. They attribute failure to insufficient effort or to deficient knowledge and skills that are acquirable. They approach threatening situations with assurance that they can exercise control over them. Such an efficacious outlook produces personal accomplishments, reduces stress, and lowers vulnerability to depression.

Albert Bandura 1995:11

Figure 17: Albert Bandura text

Stage 3 is a point at which we can review how features of the previous stages may already be contributing as sources of self-efficacy, and develop further strategies to enhance young people's belief in their capability to manage themselves and achieve goals.

Mastery experiences

As Bandura says, things that are achieved easily will not necessarily serve as experiences to develop self-efficacy. Developing resilience in the face of setbacks and frustrations is the more important element. It's the principle that applies in the many sorts of outward bound and physical activities designed to challenge young people, not only physically, but emotionally as well.

Assisting young people towards a mastery orientation can have a two-fold approach. Firstly, as in the example above, it can be providing young people with challenging experiences where they can achieve mastery. They may not be as physically stretching as outward bound activities, but in my experience one of the most effective in confidence building is when young people are put in a position of having to mentor or 'teach' their peers or young children. Appendix 2 gives an example of how a school has integrated many opportunities for mastery experiences by means of mentoring, counselling and leadership of younger pupils.

On the other hand, it might be thought a risky strategy to take young people who would normally 'play up' in a school environment, and place them in a primary classroom with the expectation that they are going to lead younger children in learning. Yet the rewards are usually worth the risk. There can be so many elements to the experience. It can generate a sense of responsibility when young people are faced with a group of children much smaller than themselves, all gazing up at them in expectation. It can help them recognize their own knowledge and abilities when seen in relation to the less developed abilities of much younger children. It is not a particularly risky strategy in relation to setting young people up to fail, because younger children will usually be very accepting and admiring of a teenager. Faced with the responsibility, the experience usually draws the best out of young people.

The subject of their 'teaching' is really the less important factor – it can be about a particular interest of theirs or what it will be like when the children go to high school. The more important outcome is that de-briefing on the experience can help even the most diffident young person recognize the resources of knowledge and skill they can draw upon when required.

Thinking Space 11
Quote from a teacher talking about students teaching a class: '*The key principles which appeared most clearly here were that involvement and excitement occurred when learning was self-directed and initiated by personal choice of the student*'.
Carl Rogers and Jerome Freiberg 1994:87

The second approach is helping young people identify things they have already learned to do, to draw out the features they can replicate elsewhere. I wouldn't want to suggest that the young man in the example above who was nicking cars should be encouraged to repeat that activity to gain experience in mastery! But if he was good at it, he could be encouraged to deconstruct the elements of skill and knowledge to gain an understanding of his capability to overcome obstacles.

Young people may not yet have recognized that the skills they develop in part-time jobs or leisure activities can be attributes they can productively transfer to other areas of achievement. Once we have learned something, it is difficult to return to a state of 'not knowing': we operate in a state of 'unconscious competence' which is one reason why it is difficult for professionals like teachers to describe what they do. Once an activity has been thoroughly 'learned' we tend to function intuitively, as with driving a car, riding a bicycle or touch typing. I never learned how to cook from my mother because every time I asked her how much of a particular ingredient to use, she always said, 'Oh – you *know*'. Well of course I didn't 'know', that's why I was asking, and she was unable to tell me because she had become so practised that she handled the ingredients as if by instinct.

There will be things that young people have learned, masteries they have experienced, where they have forgotten how they first learned. They also may not fully appreciate how many different components there are to the learning. I'm not really talking about the recording of Key Skills or Competences here, although these formal processes have a role. Rather, the unpacking of a mastery experience can be used in coaching to illustrate the full extent of learning achievements, as in the example of David.

David had not been a high achiever academically, and he lacked confidence in that area, but he was a very good footballer. The day before I met with the coaching group he had scored what proved to be the winning goal for the school team, and I picked up on this when we were having a discussion about the different ways we learned. 'Take David', I said to the group, 'what different sorts of learning did he have to use to score that goal yesterday? He gained the ball to start with by tackling another player, so he would have to know how to use just the right amount of force, the angle and speed to do that safely. Then, at the same time as retaining control of the ball at his feet, he had to look up and judge the distance to the goal. He would be using his knowledge to assess whether any wind speed would affect the flight of the ball, and whether it needed a curving or a straight trajectory. In the same instant, he would be assessing the position of the goalkeeper and the other players, and predicting the way they would be likely to move once he kicked the ball. Then using just the correct amount of muscle power, and at the same time maintaining his balance, he kicked the ball so that it arched over the head of the defenders, past the goalkeeper, into the back of the net. 'Now', I added emphatically, '*that's* what I call intelligent behaviour.' Finally, addressing a question directly to David I asked, 'Tell us David, did you always score every time you took a shot at goal?' Of course David had to say he didn't, there had been many, many times when he'd kicked for goal and not suc-ceeded, but of course that hadn't meant he gave up trying. And naturally it had taken a great deal of practice to achieve his level of expertise.

If nothing else, this was articulating for David his degree of mastery, and helping him to think about how he could apply the features of this experience in other domains – particularly in relation to the need for resilience in persevering. For the rest of the group, it was a useful metaphor around which to focus a discussion on how other activities – even those more mundane than scoring a goal – also combined a range of elements that would have had to be 'learned', but which they had come to take for granted. You may want to think of an illustration of your own – an activity that you know a young person has learned to do – from which they can 'model' the process to see how the elements can be replicated in other areas. The coaching questions below are some that can be used to model the process and tease out the elements:

I'm interested to know how you learned to do that.
I've never done that, how do you do it?
Take me step by step through how you do that?
What learning did you have to do to be able to do that?
What do you have to think about when you're doing that?
What does it feel like when you're doing that?
What is it important to pay attention to when you're doing that?
What are you aware of when you are doing that?
What is that an example of?

Social modelling

We all know of people who inspire us; who provide us with aspirational role models of behaviour and achievement. Some may be famous examples whose sayings you feature in your peripheral posters. They may provide models of perseverance, like Einstein, or Thomas Edison, who is reputed to have tested 1,000 filaments before finding the right one to create the electric light bulb. Or they may help us recognize the source of self-esteem, like Eleanor Roosevelt, who said 'Remember, no-one can make you feel inferior without your consent'. Or they may be people who have overcome extreme disability to provide inspiration for others, like Helen Keller.

While famous people such as these can provide examples we can aspire to, Bandura (1995: 3) believes that the impact of social modelling on our own beliefs is much stronger when the model is someone like ourselves. The greater we perceive a similarity, the more we will be persuaded by the model's successes or failures. So in addition to famous examples, we can be alert to opportunities to highlight for young people the mastery attributes demonstrated by their peers. As in the example of David above: there can be a sense of identification with a fellow student struggling with academic work, yet also the recognition that with the application of practice and persistence, he is also someone who has achieved mastery on the field of football.

Plainly young people relate more easily to their peer group and can be strongly influenced by them. The peer mentoring project described in Appendix 2 originally came into being because the teachers recognized that young people preferred to talk to a fellow student about issues such as bullying rather to than an adult. Being alert to features of self-efficacy in young people provides the opportunity to exploit them as social models for the benefit of other students.

So it was with Michael. He had left school without any qualifications and little ambition. It was when he worked as a volunteer in a special school that he began to form the idea that this was an area in which he would like to work. He also recognized that without any qualifications, he would be unlikely even to be considered for paid employment. So he took the decision to return to school and complete his education, and this was where I first met him. 'Miss, I'm dyslexic', was his form of introduction when he first appeared in my class. 'I'd rather call you Michael' was my response. (Have you ever thought about why, if someone has a physical complaint, say measles, we wouldn't dream of calling them 'measlic', yet when it's something that relates to mental or cognitive functioning we label them 'it' rather than 'having it'?)

Unfortunately Michael had been given labels throughout his education. At his primary school the headteacher had labelled him 'stupid' and sat him in the corridor most of the time. By the time a more enlightened head arrived and recognized his needs, he'd fallen too far behind in his development to have the confidence to attempt any formal qualifications. But the voluntary work had proved such an inspiration that he bravely came back to school to pick up where he'd let off.

Michael was great to have in the class. Because he was so evidently intent on overcoming previous disadvantage to work towards a goal he had set himself, he implicitly became a role model for the rest of the group. Michael's 'story' became a metaphor for modelling resilience.

Social persuasion

Bandura (1995: 4) considers it is more difficult to instil high beliefs of personal efficacy by social persuasion than to undermine them. Indeed it can be a big shift to take the first step in recognizing the subtle ways we influence and embed commands with the language we use, and that these can frequently be negative rather than positive. Eric Jensen (2008:107) writes that because 99 per cent of all learning is *non-conscious* – something that we are not consciously paying attention to – everything will suggest something to our complex minds, and thus we cannot *not* suggest.

So far in the CARE model I've tried to give an indication of the subtle inferences we convey in language. The effect of 'but', 'if',' 'can't and 'try' in Stage 1 for instance, and how changing the words will change the suggestion. In Stage 2, Richard's reframing 'work' to 'learning' and recognizing the influence of embedded commands have been other examples of the power of suggestion.

It's not just through the language we use that we exert social persuasion of course. The whole environment for learning and coaching will play a part in social persuasion. The inspirational sayings for peripheral learning in Fig. 12 will be playing their role in this. One of these that I've found usually attracts a great deal of interest is:

There's no Failure, only Feedback.

It's a powerful reframe, and of course as well as the non-conscious influences of the language we use, our whole approach in giving formal feedback to young people opens up the potential to 'nourish' or 'punish' (see Fig. 19). As you will see in the section on Affirmation below, formal feedback provides a further opportunity to encourage beliefs of personal efficacy.

There's a very important implication if we want our feedback to act as social persuasion towards developing self-efficacy. At first glance it may cut across assumptions that lie deep within our education and culture. It is illustrated in the findings of Carol Dweck's research and her concepts of a *Helpless Pattern* and a *Mastery-Orientated Pattern*, which describe the behaviours that stem from a belief that intelligence is a fixed trait, or a belief that intelligence can be increased by their students' own efforts. Of significance in the research was the finding that giving praise that told children they were smart or wonderful when they succeeded, made them vulnerable to a 'helpless' response later when they didn't succeed:

> it is not a good idea to try to encourage the achievement of underachieving groups by praising their intelligence when they succeed – even though it may be very tempting to try to boost their faith in themselves this way. Instead, our results suggest that when students succeed, attention and approval should be directed at their efforts or their strategies. This teaches them the importance of effort and strategies as a means to success and keeps them focused on effort and strategies as a means of overcoming failures.
>
> Carol Dweck 2000: 121

It may feel natural to us that we want to give young people praise to make them feel good about themselves and to boost their self-esteem. Dweck explains that she is not suggesting we gloss over students' unusual or exceptional achievements. Rather she is suggesting

> that it may be extremely important for these students that we keep the emphasis on seeking challenges, applying effort, and searching for strategies... This way, when they later hit obstacles, they will not feel they have toppled from the ranks of the intelligent. Instead, they will know how to cope.
>
> Carol Dweck 2000: 123

Plainly, the *process* of giving feedback, and the *focus* we take, can play a part in building resilience, and we'll return to that in the section on Affirmation below.

Physiological and emotional states

As Bandura explains, beliefs about efficacy can be affected by feelings of stress and negative emotions, as young people can interpret these responses as an inability to cope. Yet since Daniel Goleman assures us that emotional intelligence can be learned (see Chapter 2), we have an opportunity in coaching to help young people learn to understand and handle emotions as part of developing self-efficacy.

A big learning for adolescents will be reframing a belief that their emotional reactions are something beyond their control. Part of this can be an understanding of the two routes that channel emotional responses. As you saw in Chapter 2, firstly, our physiology has evolved to enable us to make quick emotional reactions when needed: the *amygdala*, part of our primitive brain, will kick in with an emotional response much faster than our rational thinking mind. The second is a slower route in which our thoughts play a key role in deciding what emotions will be experienced.

This will be the route where we cognitively 'decide' that exams are events to feel stressed about, or facing an audience is something to feel embarrassed about.

One way of thinking about the complex interaction of physical, mental and emotional responses that can lead to feelings of stress is to think about it in terms of a *stressor-response chain*.[1] This can help young people see that there are a range of opportunities to intercede to reduce the build up of stress and negative emotions (see Fig. 18). It also helps us to see how the CARE model can provide a framework of interventions as options to use in coaching.

Stressor-Response Chain	Intervention Point	Coaching Strategy
The event or situation that causes stress or negative emotions	Change the event or situation	Create a learning environment to reduce stress and induce a resourceful state (Stage 1)
How they 'see' it	Reframe the thoughts to think about it differently	Question limiting beliefs to weaken them. Reframe limiting beliefs to more realistic/positive ways of thinking about things (Stage 2)
How they 'feel' about it	Change the feelings	Use metaphors to talk about feelings (Stage 1: Well-being theme) Facilitate understanding of the physiological basis of emotional reactions (Stage 3)
The changes they notice in their bodies	Release the tension	Coach in relaxation techniques (Stage 2)
The Action response	Choose a different action response that makes use of the energy	Coach in assertiveness skills and effective time management to enable young people to take more control (Stage 4)

Figure 18: What to do to handle stress and change negative emotions

Affirmation

It may have seemed strange to read of Carol Dweck's research and her advice that it's not a good idea to praise the intelligence of children and young people when they succeed. At first glance this would seem in conflict with Geoff Petty (2004:70) writing that one of the commonest faults of novice and poor teachers is that they are not positive enough. But when you look a bit further, their points are not in conflict at all.

Dweck is advising that praise should be for students' *efforts*, and they should be encouraged towards building resilience by persevering to find effective strategies. Petty (2004: 65) is also saying that praise should be directed at the 'product', the work achieved and also how work has been approached, the *process*.

While the role of a teacher or coach is of course influential in relation to affirmation, if you think of the point about social modelling above, the role of fellow students in providing affirmation through the means of feedback can also be highly effective. By sharing with young people an understanding that the focus needs to be on the behaviour, not the person, that the purpose is to affirm the worth of their fellow student and identify what they can do to further their learning, the feedback can indeed be *Nourishment*. By making judgements and attempting to boost the worth of the giver, the process at the very least will give little encouragement or incentive, at worse can be de-motivating, and becomes more like *Punishment* (see Fig. 19). Learning to give feedback can be a learning process where there is as much learning for the giver as for the receiver. The Principles are guidelines that can be used to help young people support each other with nourishment rather than punishment.

Nourishment		Punishment	
Deals with the behaviour, not the person	*The arguments don't all relate to the question.* *Holding the wrench at a different angle would give a better grip.* *The delivery of your presentation was particularly good.*	Deals with the person, not the behaviour	*You don't appear to have read the question.* *You look clumsy the way you're holding the wrench.* *You were great.*
Describes the behaviour	*The first paragraph is not as strong as the rest of the essay.* *You have used the right method here.* *Aiming to keep your voice tone up would improve your presentation.*	Makes a judgement on behaviour	*You can do better than that.* *That's good.* *Mumbling is no good for a presentation.*
Is specific and in straightforward language	*Have a look at the length of sentences to see if making any of them shorter would improve the reading.* *Keep up the stirring until the sauce thickens.* *When you stand up straight you appear more confident to the audience.*	Is vague and in general language	*The overall grammar and articulation of the argument should be improved.* *The ingredients need to coagulate to avoid curdling.* *Overall appearance is important when giving a presentation.*

Focuses on behaviours a young person can control	*Where do you think you might put paragraphs that would help the reader?* *Keep your pencil well sharpened so the lines won't be too thick.* *Taking deep breaths before you start your presentation will help you feel calm.*	Refers to behaviours outside the young person's control	*Your writing is quite difficult to read – perhaps that's because you're left-handed.* *You seem a bit heavy-handed in drawing the lines.* *Your hands were shaking during the presentation – it's a bit of a distraction to see that.*
Young person's needs are the focus	*Tell me what would be of most help to you.*	The coach's needs distort the feedback	*If I were you, I'd do it this way.*
Open about real feelings	*I'm a little uncertain about this subject – perhaps we could do some research about it*	Feelings are hidden or misrepresented	*You should know about this – why haven't you looked it up on the internet?*
Designed to affirm the worth of the young person	*You're working really hard.*	Designed to inflate the worth of the coach	*I had to work much harder than that when I was a student.*

Figure 19: Principles of giving feedback
Acknowledgement for the format to Stenhouse Consulting

A sharing of responsibility for affirmation can generate a culture of a community of learners. This has been identified by David Hargreaves (2005) as a key feature in schools and colleges that demonstrate effective practice in learning and learning to learn. As well as a passion for learning being central to the work of teachers and learners, classrooms are *learner-centred*: close attention is paid to the knowledge, skills and attitudes which the learner brings to the classroom. In this environment, classrooms are also *assessment-centred*, both formative and summative assessment become tools for learning, and students evaluate themselves and one another in ways that contribute to understanding. There is a clear recognition that students do not learn in isolation, and also that the giving of feedback involves developing skills in interpersonal relations:

> Students are encouraged to help and support one another and to collaborate in a spirit of intellectual camaraderie. They work in groups with attention paid to listening skills, body language, techniques of respectful disagreement techniques, (sic) etc. The ethos is characterised by mutual respect and the development of the self-management needed for resilience in learning, and it culminates in the creation of independent, reflective learners for life.
>
> David Hargreaves 2005:17

The Feedback Sandwich

You'll note from the quote above that the aspects of active listening and body language are important elements in giving feedback. These elements were introduced in Stage 1 and, along with building rapport, they maintain their crucial importance in relation to feedback. They are the skills needed to ensure the recipient is in a resourceful state if the feedback is to be valued and used to improve learning. It's also useful to have a framework for giving feedback, to ensure the principles are applied, and the advice of writers such as Dweck and Petty are put into practice. Using the *Feedback Sandwich*[2] as a metaphor can help in this respect:

Top Layer	Refer to something specific that you genuinely believe has been well done *'That comment you started your presentation with really caught our interest. I thought that was a good choice.'*
Filling	What can you point to that the young person can do to improve, that is relevant and can make it even better? *'You identified the points well. By giving a little more information to describe each point you will show that you have a good grasp of the subject.'* N.B. Too much filling is difficult to swallow Too spicy and indigestible a filling can cause upset Reasonable bites can be swallowed and digested
Bottom Layer	Give a general positive comment *'Overall, I thought you presented the topic in a way that kept our interest throughout.'*

Learning readiness

As you saw in Chapter 4, there are several perspectives to take account of when considering learning readiness. There are the theories of stages of cognitive development, the fact that young people experience brain-growth spurts at specific ages and that the timings will differ for boys and girls. There is the issue of whether a young person has experienced a stimulating environment to encourage a growth in neural connections, or whether they have had limited social and emotional experience. A key challenge for a teacher/coach will be taking account of all the variables and getting the level of challenge right for each student. Acknowledging these considerations, and taking account of the fact that every young person will be different, I want to keep the focus on how a coaching approach may potentially influence learning readiness. Throughout the process of the CARE model, we have been seeking to create for young people a state of 'relaxed alertness' which researchers see as the optimal state for learning (Gordon Dryden and Jeannette Vos 2001: 135). However, some young people face situations in their schooling that serve to turn them away from learning rather than prepare them for it (see Thinking Space 14).

Thinking Space 14

Jane had been a keen student who had plenty of encouragement and support at home, and who had worked hard to achieve good results in her GCSEs. She looked forward to starting studying for A-levels with anticipation, excited at the prospect that it was the next step along her chosen path to university. First day back at school after the summer break and Ann was surprised that Jane returned home in a particularly grumpy mood. She hadn't expected that; Jane had been looking forward to starting the new course of study and had set off cheerfully enough that morning. Having a chat over dinner, Ann was able to get to the bottom of it. The day had started with a 'pep talk' to the new sixth formers from the school head. But rather than matching Jane's mood of cheerful anticipation, the tone was rather more serious. You've got a very hard year ahead of you, you've got to be prepared for a great deal of hard work if you're not going to fail, was the line that was being taken. All delivered in a stern tone, with heavy emphasis on the seriousness of their situation. And the final dampener to any youthful enthusiasm was, 'If you think you've worked hard up to now, it's nothing like you've got ahead of you!'

This was a head teacher who plainly thought a stick was a more efficient way of priming young people for learning than a carrot. But for Jane, and who knows how many others on that day, it merely served to crush her enthusiasm and curb her motivation. Maybe this was the approach that had worked for this particular head, but there was no account taken that young people could be different.

Just as being alert to our own learning style is important to help us guard against favouring our own style in teaching / coaching, we also need an awareness of our own motivation for learning. Are you like Jane, does the prospect of a goal to be achieved energize you and help you to move *towards* it? Or would you be likely to respond to the head, and be motivated to move *away from* the possibility of failure? Rather than imposing our own pattern on young people, it's another aspect to be curious about. Isn't it *interesting* how people are different?

Looking for leverage

With a solutions focus, we have seen that small actions can count towards solutions (see Chapter 6). It is surprising – and even exciting – when we discover that some small steps can generate big change.

It's similar to when you're feeling stressed and under pressure and a small, apparently trivial incident can make you flip and lose your temper. And you will no doubt have experienced emotional outbursts from some young people just because another looked at them the wrong way. The good news is that the principle also works in reverse: desirable changes can happen with little effort. Generating change is not about piling on more pressure, rather it can be surprisingly easy when you can identify a point of *leverage*. It's knowing where and how to intervene so that a small effort can get a huge result (Joseph O'Connor and Ian McDermott 1997: 21).

It is indeed a principle that appears to work with all living 'systems' – whether individuals, groups, schools or even whole societies. Malcolm Gladwell (2000) calls it the 'Tipping Point', and he explores fascinating examples of social epidemics that appear to start with small incidents – little things that make a big difference. The fall of the Berlin Wall would be one illustration. There had been a history of political and economic reasons behind it, but the actual event was quick and dramatic (O'Connor and McDermott 1997:19).

Can we make the principle work for us in 'tipping' young people towards learning readiness? Fundamentally, Gladwell (2000: 257) thinks the theory of Tipping Points requires that we reframe the way we think about the world. Well, there's been quite a bit about reframing throughout this model, particularly in relation to limiting beliefs. Then there's also been an articulation of the values that underpin the CARE model (see Chapter 3), and they are beliefs that fit with what Malcolm Gladwell has articulated as an essential element of large-scale change:

> What must underlie successful epidemics, in the end, is a bedrock belief that change is possible, that people can radically transform their behaviour or beliefs in the face of the right kind of impetus.
>
> 2000:258

I remember Anne D. telling me that the parents of a young man had written to her to thank her for the help she had given their son. Apparently his approach to schoolwork had been completely transformed. When Anne chanced upon him in a corridor sometime later she stopped to chat and to say she had been pleased to receive the letter. And she was interested, what was it that had caused the complete turn around in his attitude? The young man thought for a moment, then said 'When you told me I had a choice'.

Thinking Space 15

There is a park near my home and the road home takes me along the edge of a large open green space. I was walking this route home one day when I only half consciously registered that someone was jogging around the opposite side of the park. As I walked along, this person jogged nearer to my side and eventually came out of the gate into the road ahead of me. I was deep in thought and it was only when I heard 'Hello Miss' that I looked up to see a young woman had crossed the road to speak to me. I really had to do a double take before it registered who it was. 'Rhiannon!' my surprise was genuine. 'I didn't recognize you.'

It was about a year since Rhiannon had been in my class, and she had been one of the most trying students I had ever encountered. She was overweight, rude, lacked any incentive to work and, despite my best efforts, she couldn't even turn up to class with the basic requirements of a pen and paper, yet alone having done any study. The main problem was she really didn't want to be there; she had only stayed on at school at the insistence of her parents.

But this young lady in front of me bore little resemblance to the Rhiannon I remembered. She was slim, tanned and fit looking, slightly panting from the effort of her jogging. I couldn't help remarking on how well she looked. 'I've been getting fit, Miss', she explained, 'I've lost 3 stone.' Still feeling stunned at the transformation I asked what had brought it about. 'I saw a film about the army Miss, and I thought that looked good, so I've applied and I've been training ready to join.'

We had a nice chat, I wished her well, off she jogged and I carried on walking home. But she stayed in my thoughts a long while. I thought about how hard I had tried to motivate her, to try to stir a glimmer of interest in the subject we were studying. I even remembered that the girl sat next to her had commented one day 'You know Miss, you really **do** try to help us don't you?' But Rhiannon had looked on blankly, oblivious to my efforts to generate a spark of interest.

Yet now she was transformed. It had only taken a film about the army to inspire her to a degree of change that I would never have thought possible. I hadn't been able to find the leverage myself, but at least she'd found the key that re-awakened the flow for herself, and I was really pleased for her.

So tipping points can be something practical, like Rhiannon seeing a film about the army in Thinking Space 15. Or it can be something more symbolic, like the changed belief of the young man who Anne had been coaching. The most important thing as far as coaching for learning is concerned is finding what works, finding the key that will re-awaken the flow. Plainly, to do that will not always mean persevering in one direction. It may mean stopping doing what isn't working and trying something different. It means maintaining a belief that if someone is not ready for learning, or if change isn't happening, then it's for the coach to keep adjusting to the young person until the key can be found.

When Professor Tim Brighouse gave the Wales Education Lecture in 2005, he gave us a quote from a Victorian headteacher who was reflecting on his early career teaching in the streets of Gloucester. It reminds us that however much has changed, much stays the same. The main message is undeniable: locks are different, however valuable we may think our existing approaches are, we have to keep learning and adapting ourselves to find the right 'key' to unlock learning readiness for different young people:

> There I found the secret of St Augustine's golden key which, though it be of gold, is useless unless it fits the wards of the lock. And I found the wards I had to fit – the minds of those little street urchins – very queer and tortuous they were too. And I had to set about cutting and chipping myself into the shape of a wooden key which would have the one merit of a key – however common it might look – the merit of unlocking the minds and opening shut chambers of the heart.

Thinking Space 16

'In the end, Tipping Points are a reaffirmation of the potential for change and the power of intelligent action. Look at the world around you. It may seem like an immovable, implacable place. It is not. With the slightest push – in just the right place – it can be tipped.'

Malcolm Gladwell 2000: 259

Themes of the CARE model – Stage 3

Language

Throughout the CARE model there has been an emphasis that learning is not just a cognitive and rational exercise, rather we have to recognize the physiological, emotional and social influences. Many situations during schooling will be anxiety-provoking; part of coaching will be helping young people learn coping strategies so that anxiety doesn't overwhelm them and prevent them realizing their potential.

In Stage 2 there was the suggestion that part of 'Raising Awareness' could be awareness of how to relax. You'll remember that slowing breathing was a feature of the relaxation technique: quick breathing encourages arousal, whereas taking slow deep breaths will enable a young person to control feelings of anxiety.

Once a young person has experienced the feeling of relaxation, slowing their breathing can be another intervention strategy to prevent the build up of stress or anxiety (see Fig. 18). They can enhance the effect by saying a word to themselves as they breathe out. It could be 'relax', 'easy' or 'cool', but the best option is one they choose as meaningful to themselves.

Which leads us to the whole question of self-talk. In counselling, rational–emotive therapy in particular urges the need to challenge the beliefs and negative self-talk that can keep people locked into problems.[3] You've seen in the CARE model an emphasis on challenging limiting beliefs and reframing 'all or nothing' thinking such as 'I've never been any good at Maths'. Gerard Egan (1994: 80) writes that self-talk can also often be 'disabling' because people get into the habit of *talking themselves out of* taking action. For young people that might be 'It's too hard, I can't do it, I'll never make it, there's too much to do'.

As we're moving towards empowering young people to be independent learners, as well as challenging negativity with our coaching questions, we can also enable them to recognize how their self-talk may be having a negative influence on their learning and development. We can coach them in an 'intervention' to *talk themselves into* a more positive frame of mind so. Negative self-talk in relation to exams, for instance, can have the disabling effect that Egan describes. Whether the source is a fear of failure, or a concern about lack of ability, the resultant self-talk can initiate avoidance or procrastination in preparing properly. Once you have surfaced the negative self-talk in coaching, and challenged its influence, young people will have a strategy to empower themselves to deal with potentially stressful situations. Fig. 20 outlines the process of converting flawed self-talk in relation to facing an examination.

Well-being

Earlier in this chapter there was mention of the role of social modelling in inspiring young people by their efforts and achievements. It was mentioned that Bandura (1995: 3) maintained that the impact of social modelling is greater when the model is someone like ourselves.

This is not the same as saying we should completely dismiss our own influence on young people, in relation to their well-being in general, and their approach to learning in particular. It may be as Bandura (1995: 4) says, that it is more difficult to instil high beliefs of personal efficacy in young people than to undermine them, but, on the other hand, we have also seen the view that everything will suggest something to our complex minds, and thus we cannot *not* influence (Eric Jensen 2008:107).

Perhaps the most powerful modelling role we can undertake is seeing ourselves as learners, which was demonstrated for me when I met Rachel, a teacher in a sixth-form college. Her enthusiasm and excitement for learning was contagious, but it hadn't always been that way. Rachel had been teaching for 10 years when she felt she

Steps	Coaching Approach
Surface the self-talk	Elicit *exactly* what the young person is saying to themselves about a forthcoming exam. Encourage them to ask themselves: *'What am I saying to myself?'* *'What am I thinking about the exam?'* *'What am I feeling about the exam?'* *'What is the worst that could happen?'* *'Am I afraid of what other people will think of me if I fail?'*
Challenge the self-talk	Encourage them to challenge the limiting beliefs. Demonstrate how to check for exaggerations and assumptions: *'What's the evidence for that?'* *'Never? Never ever?'* *'Will other people judge you as a person just on the result of an exam?'*
Convert the flawed self-talk	Do a reality check. Retain all the learning points: *'I can see why I'm feeling anxious – I really haven't done enough revision yet.'* Use scaling to assess the importance of the exam: *'On a scale of 1 to 10, in relation to the worst thing that could ever happen to me, this exam rates about ...'* Where the self-talk is flawed, replace it with sound dialogue: *'The floor is not going to open up and swallow me.'* *'I can do deep breathing to ease anxiety.'* *'As long as I know I've done my revision I can only do my best.'* *'I'm still a worthwhile person whatever the result of the exam.'*
Practise the realistic self-talk	Encourage the young person to practise the realistic self-talk out loud. They can do this for themselves as many times as they need to feel comfortable with it.
Acknowledge the feelings	Help the young person to understand that there will still be feelings associated with the experience. The aim is to change negative and unproductive feelings to something more manageable, not to eliminate feelings altogether. It is perfectly natural to have an element of nervousness or apprehension, these can even heighten performance. The aim is to break free from the disabling effects of negative self-talk, and to adopt realistic thoughts and feelings in order to maximize potential.

Fig. 20 Changing negative self-talk to counter examination stress
Adapted from Back and Back 1991: 81

wanted to start learning again, so she embarked upon a Master's degree. Now she felt revitalized by the experience, 'I've found a love of learning I missed out on in the past. I didn't appreciate then how lucky I was to be learning'. Because Rachel shares her enjoyment of her course of study with her students it has become a mutual learning experience: 'It made me appreciate what my students do on a daily basis, and I gained the respect of my students by talking about my own action research. We have a mutual respect in working towards deadlines, and they tell me off if I miss my deadlines!'

Plainly Rachel is open and engaging with her students, and is unabashed at placing herself on an equal footing as a learner. Her approach reminded me again of how being learners ourselves is integral to finding the key to unlock learning readiness in young people. As well as the quote earlier from Professor Tim Brighouse,[4] at the same event he reminded us that in addition to the intellectual and cognitive domains, outstandingly successful teachers are exceptionally strong in what we now call emotional intelligence. Thus, in their emphasis on student well-being, the features of the approach of outstandingly successful teachers is nearer coaching for learning than instruction in that they:

- **Build confidence** by thinking of the comfort of their pupils
- **Strengthen pupils' feeling of growing competence** by remarks and tasks subtly directed to the present and next level of learning
- **Are optimistic about the future** – 'Nobody in our class fails, everyone succeeds'
- **Make young people identify with learning** and the fun of learning by their language and the use of a wide variety of tasks
- **Ensure that learning is a group activity**
- **Make it plain to young people that learning is a co-operative activity** by engendering a collective spirit, that includes the teacher, to extend young people's cognitive horizons to increase their likelihood of becoming confident autonomous learners
- **Are creative about the curriculum** – always tinkering and adjusting the curriculum to appeal to different young people
- **Are learners themselves**.

Thinking Space 17

'Traditional teaching, no matter how disguised, is based essentially on the mug-and-jug theory. Traditional teachers might ask, "How can I make the mug hold still while I fill it from the jug with these facts that the curriculum planners and I regard as valuable?" But your attitude as a facilitator has almost entirely to do with climate: How can I create a psychological climate in which the child will feel free to be curious, will feel free to make mistakes, will feel free to learn from the environment, from fellow students, from me, from experience? How can I help him or her recapture the excitement of learning that was natural in infancy?'

Carl Rogers and Jerome Freiberg 1994:170

Goal setting

Even in the most limited learning settings, it is probably true to say that much more use is made of visual materials than may have been in the past. There has been considerable emphasis throughout the CARE model on the impact on non-conscious learning of the physical environment generally and peripheral posters in particular. In relation to conveying information, Eric Jensen poses the question of whether the best way is through discussion, reading material or computers, and refers to research that suggests that concrete vivid images are the most influential:

> Neuroscientists theorize that this is because (1) the brain has an attentional bias for high contrast and novelty; (2) 90 per cent of the brain's sensory input is from visual sources; and (3) the brain has an immediate and primitive response to symbols, icons, and other simple images.
>
> Jensen 2008: 56

So Jensen concludes that visuals are an important key to remembering content; where teaching/coaching relies upon direct instruction only, recall drops very quickly, but with the addition of peripherals, 'effortless, subject-specific, longer-lasting recall is generated' (2008: 57).

As well as use of external images, Jensen also suggests that students can be challenged to generate evocative images through visualization. One of the most famous examples of the use of visualization in creative thought was Albert Enstein. As you saw in Stage 2, he claimed that his ground-breaking scientific discoveries started with visual images – such as visualizing himself riding on a beam of light – before he moved to convert the understanding gained into scientific formulae.

As mentioned in Chapter 4, to be achievable goals need to be specific and measurable. Even so, there can also be reasons why the momentum towards achieving a goal is not sustained. When outcomes are not reached, it can lead to disillusionment with the whole process of goal setting.

However, if we draw together other aspects of the CARE model, we can discover how the achievement of goals can be supported by factors other than being specific in identifying goals. After all, we have seen that learning is not just cognitive and rational, there are emotional and social elements as well. Earlier in this chapter there was mention that 99 per cent of all learning is non-conscious, so that everything will suggest something to our complex minds. So if we now add in the brain's capacity to respond to symbols, icons and imagery, we can use the potential power of visualization to enhance the setting of goals.

Mighty oaks from tiny acorns grow.

You will no doubt be familiar with this proverb, and it is also a powerful metaphor for achieving results. Using the acorn metaphor can help young people explore goal-setting more deeply and fully than just setting simple targets. A fully grown oak tree may look mighty, but it's actually the acorn that's more impressive. Without the acorn, the oak would never exist, and the acorn has had to overcome many obstacles on the path to becoming an oak.

The metaphor can help us think about the requirements of successful goal fulfilment. For instance, it wouldn't make much sense to plant an oak tree in the desert and expect it to survive without any help. And if you planted an acorn tonight it would be unrealistic to look out of the window and expect it to be grown to an oak tree the next day.

Perhaps the most important use of the ACORN metaphor will be in devising a route to large – possibly life-changing – goals. People can often set such goals without checking the likely overall effect of achieving them. When this happens, they can often find that the goal wasn't what they really wanted after all. While we wouldn't want to restrict young people from aiming high, at the same time many can be attracted to pipe-dreams, fantasies and unrealistic and unachievable results. Using the ACORN model in coaching is a way of doing a reality check on a goal, and harnessing the power of visualization to establish the goal in the unconscious mind. (Don't underestimate the power of this. Some years ago I used this method to create a long-term goal for myself of publishing a book. Seven years later, in 2007, I achieved it. It wasn't that I drove myself forward in a single-minded fashion, consciously thinking about my goal every step of the way. In fact most of the time I was so busy I didn't really think about it at all. Rather it was as though, having thoroughly worked through the idea to find it was right for me, the idea became so firmly planted in my unconscious mind that I was moved towards it almost despite myself. It became a process whereby a lot of things came together that moved me towards the goal. But importantly, if I hadn't set the long-term goal, I wouldn't have been able to recognize events as being relevant to my goal, and I may not have kept up the overall direction.)

Step 1 Act as if	Use your rapport building skills to ensure the young person is in a relaxed comfortable state. Ask them to think about a long-term goal they would like to achieve. You are going to ask them to 'act as if' they have already achieved the goal, so get them to state in positive accurate words what the goal is. (Remember, no negatives like 'I'm not stressed any more' 'or 'I haven't failed the exams' because the brain cannot think about *not* wanting something without first thinking about the very thing you don't want! Say what they want, not what they don't want.) Now ask them to visualize the situation they are in when they have achieved the goal. *What are you seeing?*

	What are you hearing? *What are you feeling?* Explore this until you are sure they are fully 'acting as if' they were in the situation of having achieved the goal.
Step 2 **Check**	Do a reality check on the goal. *Having achieved your goal, how does it affect you?* *How else does it affect you … ?* *And what does that mean for you?* *What are the effects on other people, family, friends …?* *What other effects could there be?*
Step 3 **Ownership**	After answering all these questions, is the goal something they still want? Use your sensory acuity to check that the young person still appears committed to the goal. Ask them: *After truthfully asking the questions, do you feel 100 per cent committed to the goal?* *Are you ready to begin and maintain the actions that will be needed to achieve the goal?* If they are unable to congruently answer 'Yes' to these, go back to **Act as if** and reassess the goal. It may need to be a different goal altogether.
Step 4 **Resources**	*What resources to you already have?* This could be the learning they have already achieved, the people they can call upon for support, the time they can allocate to the goal. What resources can they acquire, and from where and whom? What learning will they need to progress themselves towards the goal, are there other people who can help them with this? *Do you need any new resources in terms of skills or behaviours?* Will they need to improve skills such as time management? Will they need to improve their confidence in social situations?
Step 5 **Now do it!**	Write out a detailed action plan and *take the first step now!*

Figure 21: ACORN – powerful steps in goal-setting[5]

Reflection

The work of a professional in any sphere is such a complex activity that it plainly involves more than the acquisition of skills and knowledge. Just as learning is more than a cognitive and rational exercise, but also involves emotional and social elements, so improvements to our working practices must involve personal as well as professional development.

The theorists cited in this chapter have been explicit in this respect: both the need to have strong self-efficacy to be able to create mastery experiences for young people, and the view that outstandingly successful teachers are strong in emotional intelligence have been featured.

These aspects are important areas of learning about ourselves. Our strongest capacity for influence will be the extent to which we can role model the attributes we are seeking to develop in young people. An open and enthusiastic attitude to learning, seeing learning as a lifelong activity, is a basic element if we are to go any way in enthusing young people for learning.

Since the theorists are unanimous that both self-efficacy and emotional intelligence can be learned, we can use the guidelines in Stage 3 in our own personal development. We can learn to recognize how we can intervene and limit the effects of negative stress. We may seek out a valued colleague to act as our own coach and give us feedback that will provide personal support and insight to improve our efforts. We can identify a range of individuals who display different attributes we aspire to, and seek to model their attitudes and behaviour to enhance our own personal development. By re-awakening the flow of learning for ourselves we stimulate our interest and enthusiasm and have the potential to ignite similar attitudes for young people.

Stage 3 – Practice pointers

- Self-efficacy is the ability to be in control of one's life, able to achieve valued goals and prevent undesirable outcomes
- Beliefs about self-efficacy have a significant influence on motivation and attainment
- Self-efficacy can be encouraged by providing mastery experiences, social modelling, social persuasion and influencing physiological and emotional states
- Intervention at different points can be used to prevent the build-up of negative stress
- Feedback needs to ensure nourishment rather than being used to punish
- The principle of 'leverage' means that desirable changes can happen with little effort
- The influence of negative self-talk can be challenged and reframed
- Visualization is a powerful learning method and can be used to enhance the setting of goals
- Outstandingly successful professionals are learners themselves.

Notes

1 The outline of the stressor-response chain taken from the Open University's Handling Stress pack for group work for dealing with stress.
2 Acknowledgement to Stenhouse Consulting for permission to use the Feedback Sandwich format from their training materials.
3 See Ellis and Dryden 1987 for the practice of rational–emotive therapy.
4 Extracts from the 2005 Wales Education Lecture delivered by Professor Tim Brighouse by permission of the General Teaching Council for Wales.
5 Acknowledgements to Stenhouse Consulting for permission to use their original model, which is also featured in Jacquie Turnbull 2007: 88–90.

8

Stage 4 – Empowerment

'Empowerment [...], is not something you give me or I give you; we co-construct it between us by the actions each of us takes.'

Paul Jackson and Mark McKergow 2007:10

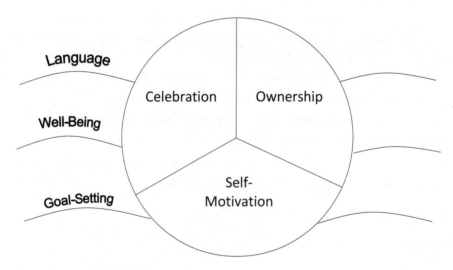

Figure 22: Key words for Stage 4

The stance throughout this model has been that learning is not just a cognitive and rational exercise, but also has to take account of social and emotional factors. Similarly, we need to look upon our own professional development as having an intimate relationship with our personal development. You have seen in the last chapter that the eminent theorists confirm this as an undeniable factor. In relation to teaching, Bandura (1995: 20) sees a strong relationship between efficacy beliefs and both the general approach a teacher will adopt, and the type of instructional activities they are likely to favour. He cites a wide range of research that concludes not only will teachers with a low sense of self-efficacy be likely to adopt a 'custodial' orientation and rely on negative sanctions to get young people to study, but they can also be left feeling overwhelmed by disruptive and non-achieving students. Rather than managing the stresses by directing their efforts at resolving problems, they may adopt a pattern of avoidance or escapist coping, which can contribute to burnout.

Similarly, we've seen the view expressed that highly successful teachers are strong in emotional intelligence; which enables them to manage a potentially stressful occupation and maintain a confidence and optimism in the potential of their students.

If we think back to how I have been defining a model of coaching, the approach has been twofold. Firstly, to develop a framework, an overarching philosophy that can be applied in a range of working practices with young people, including teaching. Secondly, to identify a skill set that will enhance existing practices of developing learning for young people. It is in relation to this second aspect that personal development for a coach becomes important. Coaching is not only a highly skilled enterprise, it is one that operates within a set of beliefs and values that may challenge those of traditional schooling, which in many cases remains remarkably resistant to change, despite our constantly developing knowledge about how people learn. It is in relation to both expertise and attitude that strength in self-efficacy and emotional intelligence assume importance, and this becomes evident when we move to think about empowerment.

Empowerment for young people means achieving our long-term aim for coaching of helping them develop as autonomous self-motivated learners. What it does *not* mean is 'power over' young people; rather for those of us involved in coaching, empowerment means developing the personal attributes that will enable us to construct an egalitarian relationship with young people, develop a high level of skills and maintain our own physical and emotional stability to work in a complex and changing environment.

Thinking Space 18

'Raising aspirations and working in the difficult and shifting sands of "potential" is not only about supporting working class children to get good grades and go to university (although it may be this too). It is not purely instrumental, or driven by attainment outcomes. The work of learning mentors is person-centred: it is about supporting and guiding children and young people to move in the direction of personal growth.'

Leora Cruddas 2005: 78

Self-motivation

For both young person and coach, a prime feature of empowerment will be self-motivation, the ability to move ourselves in achievable steps to the next level of performance (Will Thomas and Alistair Smith 2004: 28). Eric Jensen (2008:119) claims that 'the unmotivated learner' is a myth; there is no such thing. Indeed, as you saw in Stage 3, we are all born with an innate urge to explore and learn. So rather than learners being unmotivated, Jensen reminds us there are 'temporary unmotivated states in which learners are either reinforced and supported, or neglected and labelled'.

There is of course a difference between strategies that attempt to motivate learners externally (extrinsic motivation), and motivation that springs from within learners themselves (intrinsic motivation). As you saw in Chapter 1, a claim of *behaviourism* was that people would exhibit required behaviours in response to rewards, and a common feature of schooling has been the use of inducements in the form of praise, stickers, prizes and positive feedback on completed work. You also saw in Thinking Space 14 an attempt to stimulate motivation by generating anxiety, and threats of an unwelcome outcome can also be used as a misguided strategy for generating motivation.

Such strategies – particularly in relation to giving rewards – may of course be successful initially. However, two features need to be acknowledged. Firstly, the more rewards are used, the more the effects become weaker, leaving learners wanting bigger and better rewards. Secondly, if rewards are successful, all they really do is produce the required behaviour. If the intended purpose of using a reward system is to stimulate intrinsic motivation, Eric Jensen (2008: 121–2) points out that in fact it can actually prevent it. Because a reward system is only directed at producing certain predictable behaviours, there is rarely an incentive to be creative. Learners may respond to rewards, but it is more about working the system than learning. Rewards alone will certainly not assist a young person to access the magical 'flow' of learning described in Stage 3.

Plainly, we have to acknowledge that for young people who have grown up in a culture of low expectations, and who may have acquired 'failure identities' throughout their schooling, eliciting self-motivation will be quite a challenge. Clearly also, for such young people, reward systems may be a necessary strategy to even keep them engaged in the process of education. But if we are really serious about our long-term aim of establishing a basis for life-long learning, then encouraging self-motivation becomes another of the balancing acts of coaching.

The balance, as you can see in Fig. 23, is between too little challenge and inspiration, resulting in boredom and apathy; and too much challenge being

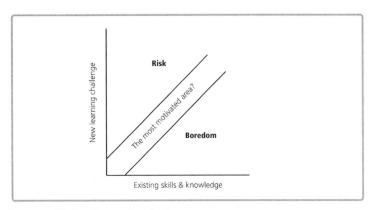

Figure 23: Risk, boredom and motivation

Permission received from Continuum to reproduce Fig. 7.8 as it appears on page 198 of *Reflective Teaching* by Andrew Pollard, published by Continuum 2008

experienced as risky and leading to fear and anxiety. The most motivated area lies somewhere in between, the area where a young person is balanced at the optimal position for an open and receptive attitude to learning; the 'zone' in which they experience their potential for excitement, curiosity and self-motivation.

So as Jensen (2008: 124) has suggested, although some learners will respond to rewards in the short term, the danger is that systems of rewards will actually establish dependence upon external factors and thus prevent the development of creativity and the ability to tackle complex problems. Intrinsic motivation is more important '... in order to get learners to be creative and have greater subject interest, high self-esteem, and the ability to be reflective ...'. Plainly, these factors have a crucial relevance for lifelong learning, and are necessary components of empowerment. Jensen goes on to identify a list of strategies for eliciting intrinsic motivation; while none of them cost anything – in that no rewards or bribes are necessary – they do involve more initial thought and preparation to create a climate of intrinsic motivation.

If we look back over the CARE model we can see how most of the strategies Jensen identifies map across to the Stages. We can see that in the process of a coaching approach we have implicitly been preparing the ground for intrinsic motivation rather than relying on external inducements. Stage 1, for instance, concentrated on establishing a trusting relationship, creating an emotionally safe and stimulating environment for learning, and stressed the importance of managing emotional 'state'. The emotional element has not always featured strongly in schooling, but it is a crucial factor in motivation. The human will is not directly tied to the human intellect, as James Flaherty (2005: 121) reminds us. Rather, emotion fits between the two: great coaches – such as in sport – have always known this and have spoken directly and sometimes exclusively to the emotions.

Stage 2 added in the need to manage physiological state, and to have an awareness of differences in learning, so that learners could become motivated by recognizing how their particular inclinations could be strengths rather than deficiencies. Then in Stage 3 we saw the benefit of sharing success stories, finding social models that could model learning, and using feedback to both support and stimulate further learning. As well as being particular practices that match the strategies Jensen identifies, the approach to goal setting has been to endeavour to make goals so compelling that they draw young people towards them. Overall, the whole philosophy of coaching as I have perceived it has been a driver towards intrinsic motivation – underpinned by a belief that people have all the resources they need, that they can develop and grow in a trusting relationship, and with the benefit of a stimulating environment and learning experiences to ignite their natural curiosity.

Thinking Space 19

The findings of this study correspond with what many parents and teachers have learned from frustrating personal experiences: Students often do not adopt the high academic aspirations imposed upon them. Clearly, a determinant of student aspirations is their belief in their academic efficacy. Efforts to foster academic achievement need to do more than simply set demanding standards for students. They need to structure academic experiences in a way that enhances students' sense of academic efficacy as well.

Barry Zimmerman et al. 1992: 673

Ownership

As you saw in Chapter 4, ownership involves much more than a handing over of tasks for students to complete single-handed. In just the same way that goals are much more likely to be achieved when they have been created and are 'owned' by young people rather than imposed upon them, empowering young people as learners can mean giving up 'power' and control to promote ownership of their own learning.

Promoting ownership by young people is part of a wider movement that has included a recognition of the need to take account of the student 'voice'. In the UK the setting up of student councils has been a formal mechanism for acknowledging this need, but in addition, the DfES in England is acknowledging that 'reflective schools' go further – 'They are engaging pupils actively in shaping learning and teaching' (2006: 21). There are others of course who feel the movement has not gone far enough; for many teacher educators, for instance, teaching *methods* are still central. Anita Woolfolk Hoy (2000: 264) would prefer to prepare teachers to focus more on learning than on method, claiming that if you understand how students learn and you understand the subject, you can invent teaching methods.

Thinking Space 20

'It is likely that most people are capable of better learning than they currently demonstrate, and that improvement in learning is possible, individually and socially desirable, and indeed necessary. Only minor improvements in learning will come about through a search for new styles of teaching within the present style of teacher control. Substantial improvement depends on a fundamental shift from teacher to student in responsibility for, and control of learning.'

J. R. Baird 1986: 2

There has been a similar emphasis taken in this book in relation to coaching, but that aside, if young people are really to take ownership of their own learning, there are certain skill sets we can encourage that will empower them in this direction.

Skill set no. 1 – Time Awareness

I have resisted the phrase 'Time Management' in this sub-heading. Time itself is not something that is within our gift to 'manage'. Throughout their schooling, young people will have had their time managed for them: their school days will have been divided up and delineated by school bells and formal timetables. Nothing much can be done about that given the management needs of state education. Yet to take ownership of their own learning, young people will have to have some sense of control over their own affairs. Goal-setting has been a theme throughout the CARE model, and there are of course other skills that can be learned in relation to generating feelings of being in control. Developing the ability to organize their activities within a time frame is the first of two key skill sets I think are important to identify for a stage of empowerment.

On a day-to-day basis, we all have an equal share of time, yet there are incredible differences in how we make use of our allocation. My mother always said 'If you want something done, ask a busy person', and indeed it does seem that some people will always find time to do something extra despite already leading very full lives. Rather than managing time itself, what these busy people are able to do is manage *themselves* to cope with their allocation. Of course you can take a mechanistic approach: young people will probably be familiar with homework diaries and the like, and they can aid our efficiency. But *effectiveness* is qualitatively different from efficiency and involves far more than the use of particular time management aids. Being aware of how we individually experience time is a first step towards learning the skills.

Overall, it's helpful to have an action plan: something to work through with young people to demonstrate that productive use of time is not something that 'just happens', neither is deficiency in that area due to some personal inadequacy. Rather it is something that anyone can achieve with a co-ordinated approach. A simple step-by-step approach could run something like this:

Step 1   Personal experience of time

Step 2   Planning

Step 3   Addressing procrastination

Step 4   Review

Then the four steps can be broken down into different activities to build a sense of control in relation to time:

Step 1: Personal experience of time

'Just a Minute'
You can engage young people in thinking about their relationship with time with a simple exercise which can be run with one young person or a group divided into pairs. One person acts as timer, and the other has to sit quietly until they think a minute has passed, then they tell the timer they think the minute is up. No counting or looking at a watch or clock of course! It can be a fun exercise with a group if the timers write down the actual timing when their partners tell them they think a minute is up so the range of different estimates in the group can be seen – you can get anything from half a minute to a minute and a half.

The serious point of this is that it's a starting point to discuss how time is experienced in different ways. There may be occasions – perhaps during a school day – when time seems to drag. At other times, it may seem to fly. And if young people have experienced being in the 'flow' of complete absorption in an activity, they may also recognize these are moments when they can lose all sense of time.

'Action Research'
Reviewing how time is actually spent can be a really enlightening experience. However young people may *think* they spend their time, the chances are an analysis of how time is *actually* spent will produce some surprises. You could introduce this as a piece of action research that that will give them practice in skills that will be relevant for the workplace.

They need to decide first on a series of codes to identify different activities, e.g. R for reading/research, J for part-time job, S for socializing, TV for watching TV, etc. Then agree a period of time when they will record what they are doing – an average week usually gives a good sample. If they draw up a chart breaking down the days into half hour or one hour slots, they can then use the codes to record their activities.

Analysis in the form of a bar chart or pie chart will give them insight into the actual use of their time. In relation to the time they spend in formal education or training settings, it's useful to think about whether they are involved in active learning, or something else – such as a distractor activity or day-dreaming. If it's the latter, it's worth posing a question about what might happen to change that – and I'll return to that issue later in the second skill.

That aside, it's often the case that they find they have more time to give to learning than they realized. It's also important to stress that this is not an exercise to schedule in as much 'work' activity as possible: leisure is just as important and one aim of this exercise is to help them achieve a work / life balance that will stand them in good stead for the future. The whole ethos of the CARE model has been about balance and the needs of the whole person. Discussion can range around how important to them different activities are: there will be some social and leisure activities that it will be important to maintain for their overall health and well-being. If there's a temptation to mark up some activities as W for waste of time, you could point out that young people need to have time to enjoy being 'young'. Even older people need a bit of fun and even 'silliness'! This exercise shouldn't be used to instil a feeling of guilt that time is 'wasted'. That's just one line of thought this piece of research can trigger and can be part of on-going review at Step 4.

Step 2: Planning

One of the things that can emerge from the research can be a recognition of the particular times when they work at their best. Research is beginning to show that adolescents may work best in the afternoons – not a fact that fits well with having to comply with a school timetable!

But from this exercise they may be able to pick out times when they feel most motivated and energized, and similarly, that there are other times when their energy dips and they find it hard to concentrate. For myself, I know that early mornings are best for anything that needs serious thought, and as I always get a post-lunch energy dip I fill in that time with routine tasks that don't need much thought until my energy picks up again. Struggling against body rhythms can be a drain on energy and counterproductive in the long term. Learning when to take a break for a drink of water or something to eat, or moving around, are essential short-term strategies.

You can also use the opportunity in coaching to help young people be aware of how they can take best advantage of the brain's capacity for learning. The brain needs 'downtime': regular breaks from active conscious learning that allow the unconscious mind to absorb new material or ideas. Also, as you saw earlier in Thinking Space 8, awareness may not be instant: it may need a period of unconscious processing to accommodate new concepts into a person's mental map.

In this respect, it can be the case that they don't always identify the difference between time for research and production time. Trying to conflate the two can lead to misjudging the time needed to complete an assignment, which can be anxiety-provoking. Generally speaking, for any piece of work, a longer timespan invested in the research and planning stage will mean less time spent in production, and this is another principle that can apply when planning learning.

This is all part of developing judgement in relation to the time needed to complete tasks. Young people may put off starting a piece of work because they think it is so large and will take them a great deal of time. On the other hand, they may delay starting because they think a piece of work will *not* take long; then when they do start they find it is taking much longer than they estimated and they are then up against a deadline.

> **Thinking Space 21**
> 'Procrastination is an inbuilt human defence against pain and stress, although an accumulation of tasks set aside can result in much greater stress.'
> David Clutterbuck 1998:61

Overall, the insights gained can help them construct their own schedule that will maximize their prime time potential while minimizing the effects of their least productive times. As always, language and terminology are important for the meanings they generate. I would steer away from the term 'timetable' – young people have had timetables imposed upon them throughout their school years. Since the schedule is something constructed by themselves and for themselves, a term such as 'personal life and learning time chart' may be more indicative of the overall aim of achieving a work/life balance.

Step 3: Addressing procrastination

We probably all play games with ourselves to find good reasons why we shouldn't get on with something important or undertake some serious learning. As William James is reputed to have said: 'Nothing is so fatiguing as the eternal hanging-on of an uncompleted task'.[1] Yet time without number I've heard students say 'I only start an essay at the last minute because I work best under pressure'. And because the outcome has usually been satisfactory, they've been able to convince themselves this is the best way of working. The reality is if mistakes are made because work is rushed, there's no time to correct them. And when the unforeseen happens – as it frequently does – it can create unnecessary stress.

Leaving things until the last minute means the motivation has come from the externally imposed deadline, rather than an internal motivation to do their best work. Part of taking control for themselves can be using a 'Game Plan' that helps them recognize the excuses and delaying tactics and counter them with prompts for action. Using this in coaching can help young people open up the range of options they have (see Fig. 24). Starting may be the hardest thing to do but it is the most important. It's helpful to remember that, in engineering terms, moving friction is greater than starting friction, so it's important to start somewhere and get going!

Excuse	Response
I don't like doing this	Find which part of it you *do* like doing to get you started. Reframe self-talk from 'I don't like this' to tell yourself which part you *do* like. Give yourself a time frame to work at it – and decide on a reward to give yourself when you've finished – ring a friend for a chat, play a computer game, etc. Visualize the reward you are going to give yourself when you've finished to get you started.
It's so big I don't know where to start	Use the 'salami' approach and slice it up. Start on a small part, not necessarily the beginning, but start somewhere. Even better, do the worst first and get it over with.
I don't know how to do it	What help do you need? Who do you need to ask? What's stopping you asking for the help you need?
I need more information before I start	Where will you find it? What's stopping you finding it now?
I've got too much to do	How important is it in relation to the things you have to do? How urgent is it in relation to the things you have to do? Can you afford to put it off? How are you likely to feel if you put it off? Will putting it off mean you'll have to rush to finish it and don't have the chance to do your best work?

Figure 24: Procrastination game plan [2]

Step 4 – Review

The first crucial difference between a timetable and a 'personal life and learning time chart' is that the latter is something owned by a young person. The second difference is that, while a timetable will dictate fixed points, a time chart will be a living document that is open to change as goals evolve and a young person learns more about themselves.

A time chart will of course start with a framework of fixed commitments that provide a core. Around that, it will be for the young person to arrange their activities and learning to best advantage. It can be a learning tool in itself: what at first thought may seem a good arrangement, may not work out in practice. A coaching discussion can be used to reflect on the reasons why this might happen, leading to a deeper understanding of what works.

A time chart is a useful, if not essential, tool for ensuring goals are achieved. Plainly, it will be comparatively easy to schedule achievement of short-term targets. But it is in thinking about long-term goals that a time chart really comes into its own. If you've used the ACORN method in Chapter 7 as a strategy for visualizing a long-term goal, then a time chart can be the means of stimulating purposeful action towards its achievement.

Thus a review of a time chart during a coaching discussion can help define the difference between those things that are urgent and need to be done, and how the important steps towards long-term goals and development can also be factored in. It is very easy to fill time with 'busywork', reacting to short-term deadlines and dealing with things that seem urgent. As Anita Woolfolk Hoy (2000: 268) puts it in a telling phrase, we can all be seduced away from real productivity by 'the dazzle of doing and the press of the practical'. Defining the difference between *urgent* and *important* may involve a recognition that producing work to deadlines and completing tasks may not necessarily equate to significant learning, as Andrew Pollard (2008: 288) reminds us:

> 'Active learning', as opposed to just 'busy work', is a qualitative category not just a quantitative one. 'Active learning' is linked to further factors such as motivation, stimulus and concentration.

This is a quote that sums up the essential difference between a mechanistic activity of acquiring a set of tools and skills, and a more fundamental approach where a change in behaviour is underpinned by a change in thinking and motivation.

Skill set no. 2 – Assertiveness

Along with time 'management', assertiveness is the other set of skills that facilitates a sense of ownership and being in control, and consequently provides a protection against the build-up of negative stress.

In a similar way to acquiring the skills of time 'management', the practice of assertive behaviour can be approached in two ways. There are behavioural techniques that can be learned and practised and they may improve effectiveness in the short term. This would be similar to using a time management tool or aid. But also in a similar way, adopting certain techniques alone may not necessarily bring about fundamental change, if they are not underpinned by a change in understanding and awareness.

Nowadays, the idea of 'being assertive' may appear rather dated. But it's useful as a way of defining effective from non-effective behaviours. Its significance becomes relevant when we think of the concepts we have identified in this book as being important to empowerment. They are concepts that have relevance both for young people and for those of us who are involved in their education. Self-efficacy and emotional intelligence for instance – assertiveness can be a behaviour that demonstrates strengths in these elements in practice. The further aspect that underpins assertive behaviour is good self esteem, and we can see how this is revealed if we try to define assertiveness against other behaviours.

Think back to Zara in Thinking Space 9. She had been a silent member of class throughout her schooling. She always sat head bowed, hoping she wouldn't be noticed. When there was no option but for her to speak, her voice was so quiet it was almost a whisper. She frequently stumbled over her words, and she blushed to the roots of her hair. Zara was an extreme demonstration of *submissive* behaviour.

On the other hand, you will no doubt have met up with young people whose behaviour is quite the opposite. For me it was Christina. You always knew when Christina was in the room, and the class was totally different when she was absent. Her voice was always loud, she didn't seem to be able to access any quieter register. But it was more than that, it was her general domineering manner with the other students. And even with me, I have to say. I remember once trying to remonstrate with her over some misdemeanour, and she lost her temper in an instant, and flounced out of the room, slamming the door as she went. Christina provides an illustration of *aggressive* behaviour.

Then there was David, who always appeared agreeable and compliant and never disagreed with anyone in group discussions. When I asked him how his work was progressing, and whether he needed any help, he always assured me everything was fine. Yet I always had a sense that he wasn't really being straight with me. The frustrating part was I was usually proved right when it came to him producing work; I often felt it was deliberate that he submitted half-hearted attempts at an assignment. When we planned activities in a group, he was the one who would agree with everyone at the time, but then grumble to his particular friend about what had been decided. It was very difficult to feel able to trust David: his behaviour could be categorized as *passive aggressive*.

These three have certain things in common. Submissive, aggressive and passive aggressive behaviours all stem from a basis of low self-esteem. They are a way of coping with perceived threats from other people and situations. Although the behaviours may appear to bring satisfactory short-term results, the long-term effects can be harmful to personal health, to relationships and to prospects for employment.

For young people favouring these behaviours, the underpinning lack of confidence and the lack of interpersonal skills mean they are not well placed to develop an empowered approach to their own learning and development.

Assertive behaviour on the other hand is indicative of good self esteem. It signals someone who is mature enough to be able to communicate in a straightforward manner, to express their own feelings and opinions without putting down the feelings and opinions of others and to be able to stand up for their own rights while respecting the rights of others.

Yet because young people are already negotiating a difficult physical, emotional and social transitional stage you may be questioning whether assertive behaviour can be learned at this stage? The way I look at it is this. If part of assertiveness is being aware of feelings and being able to express them in a direct manner, then this relates to emotional intelligence. If being assertive means being able to feel in control, and approach threatening situations with assurance, then the behaviours must be underpinned by a strong sense of self-efficacy. Therefore, coaching in assertive behaviour will be one way young people can be enabled to acquire the attributes to develop self-empowerment.

Assertiveness – how it looks and feels

A useful exercise with young people is to think of illustrations of different behaviours – such as those I've given above for submissiveness, aggression and passive aggression – and to tease out how we are able to identify them. What do these behaviours look like? And sound like? In order words, what are the body language factors people using these behaviours tend to exhibit?

It's likely you would come up with something like the following:

Submissive: Shoulders may be bent, head bowed. Difficulty in making eye contact. Voice would be quiet, perhaps hesitant. Worried facial expression. Overall impression of being a 'pushover'.

Aggressive: Tense and rigid body posture. May be staring in a threatening manner. Frowning or grimacing. Voice loud, may be shouting. Overall impression of being out of control.

Passive aggressive: Not as tense, yet not appearing completely at ease. Eye contact may look 'shifty'. False smile. Voice tone uneven with tendency to sound 'whingeing'. Overall impression of distrust.

It's not surprising that we can recognize behaviours in this way. As you saw in Chapter 5, body language was the first language we learned, and we interpret meanings from other people's body language. Significantly, psychologists claim 93 per cent of what makes us effective communicators is due to body language factors rather than the content of what we say.

So if we can identify other behaviours in this way, what does assertiveness look like? As with the other behaviours, you can then help young people to think of someone they consider a model for assertive behaviour in order to think about how it looks. This might suggest something like:

> Standing upright, yet relaxed. Direct eye contact, without staring. Responding to other people in a genuine manner. Voice tone even. Overall impression of congruence and trustworthiness.

My stance throughout the book has been that techniques alone will not necessarily bring about shifts in attitudes and understanding, and this applies whether you are thinking about coaching, teaching or learning. However, there is one aspect where experience has demonstrated a quick and easy way of changing thinking.

My understanding of our human condition is that there is no cut-off line between our body and brain. There is no magical barrier round about our neck that separates brain from body, thinking from doing. We are immensely complex integrated systems where change in one part affects another – as in the now well-established link between emotional distress and the suppression of the immune system.

Thinking Space 22

'Learning is not all in our heads: it's a mind-body experience. How you feel and how they feel is important. It influences every single learning experience.'

Eric Jenson 2008:110

We can take advantage of this by appreciating that the link between brain and body is not a one-way system. Our brains may affect our physical behaviour, but the reverse can also be true. What we do with our body can affect how we think and feel. If a young person is feeling miserable or emotional, the quickest way to help them lift themselves out of it is to get them to look up at something above their heads. How does that work? Because when people are looking down, they are likely to be processing kinaesthetically, and accessing emotions; when they are looking upwards, they are likely to be processing visually so their internal experience will shift (see Chapter 6, and notice also how the way we use language reflects this, e.g. feeling down, feeling low, lifting spirits, looking on the bright side).

So having identified what assertive behaviour 'looks' like, we can coach young people in adopting the physical appearance. Using a social model is a useful tactic here. Even when I was in my thirties, I was still quite shy on social occasions when there were a lot of people I didn't know. I would tend to creep into a room almost hoping people wouldn't notice me. Then I used my friend Gwen as a social model. I noticed that she walked confidently into a room, walked straight up to a group of people, smiled, introduced herself and asked them how they were enjoying the event. I've modelled the approach ever since, and never been rebuffed; people respond if you offer your name first and show an interest in them.

Young people may have many situations to feel nervous about – interviews, presentations, exams. Coaching them to adopt the physical demeanour of confidence, and anchoring it, means they can adopt it when they need to. As with Anne's strategy for encouraging relaxation (see Chapter 6) you can coach them into adopting an upright balanced posture, practising making eye contact and eliminating any distracting gestures and fidgeting. In other words 'acting as if' they really felt confident.

When I'm approaching situations where I might need to be assertive, I sometimes tell myself I going to slip on my 'confidence coat'. When young people are able to do this on a regular basis, two things will happen. Firstly, they may notice people respond differently towards them when they are giving off an aura of self-assurance. Of course, we're not talking about *over*-confidence, which would be likely to get a different response. It may be a fine line between the two, and coaching would help young people define the difference. Secondly, because they are physically 'acting as if' they really were confident, the inner self-assurance will develop – the brain will get the message the body is sending!

Assertiveness – relating to others 1

As you've seen above, assertiveness is being able to communicate in a straightforward manner, being able to express feelings and opinions while at the same time respecting the opinions and feelings of other people.

Working with other people is a key skill for young people to acquire. The ability to work as a member of a team will enhance their employment potential. Being able to communicate and share ideas with a range of different people will not only assist their formal learning, it will enrich their social and intellectual development.

Plainly, the ability to listen is not only important for assertiveness, it is crucial for learning in general. The relevance of active listening for coaching has already been stressed (see Chapter 5). And since active listening appears to be something we don't do naturally, but has to be learned, it is also an important learning point for young people. Practice in listening can therefore feature in group coaching with great effect – and not a little fun! (See Fig. 25.)

Have the group divide into smaller groups of 3: 1 speaker, 1 listener, 1 observer.

Round 1: Instruct the groups that the speakers are to talk for 2 minutes on something of interest to them.
Listeners are to listen: they must demonstrate they are listening but *without speaking*.
Observers watch and notice what they notice.
Time them for 2 minutes.

Discuss in plenary: Did the speakers think the listeners were listening? How did they know that?
How did the listeners feel not being allowed to speak?
What did the observers notice? How were the listeners demonstrating listening?
(e.g. head nods, interested facial expressions, leaning forward, open body posture, smiling appropriately)

Round 2: Rotate the roles. Person who is speaker this time talks for 2 minutes on something of interest to them.
Listeners to listen. They are allowed to speak, but *only to demonstrate they are listening*.
Observers watch and notice what they notice.

Discuss in plenary: Did the speakers think the listeners were listening?
How did they know that?
What did the observers notice? What sort of things did the listeners say to show they were listening?
(e.g. mmm, *uh-huh. I see, go on ..., what happened next*?)

Round 3: Rotate the roles.
(This time brief the listeners outside the room that you want them to listen actively using the skills already identified. But they are only to do this for a minute, then they are to do something to show they are distracted and not listening attentively, e.g. look at their watch, fidget, move their position, look out of the window.)
Speaker told this time to talk about something that is important to them.
Observers notice what happens when the listener becomes distracted.

Discuss in plenary: What did it feel like to be interrupted / not listened to?
What did the observers notice when this happened?
(e.g. speakers lost the flow of what they were saying, may even have dried up completely, may have felt cross/annoyed/belittled.)

Figure 25: Active listening practice

As I've recorded elsewhere (Jacquie Turnbull 2007: 119), the interesting thing about this exercise is the *strength* of the comments you are likely to receive after the final round. The examples I've given of feedback from professional delegates in training have included:

- I was stunned
- I felt as if what I was saying wasn't important
- I was annoyed
- It was like being slapped in the face
- I felt worthless
- I was angry.

Remember, these are not from a real-life situation, this was in the artificial environment of a training room. Yet in my experience you can have expressions of quite strong emotions that are really heartfelt – and *all the other person did was stop listening*.

Plainly, you need care de-briefing. Just make sure all the young people are still talking to each other when they leave and not taking away any hurt feelings – just taking the learning from what can be a powerful learning experience.

Assertiveness – relating to others 2

Active listening is one way of demonstrating respect for other people's feelings and opinions. The other side of the coin is helping young people express their own feelings and opinions in a clear and direct fashion. There are two activities where they can practise appropriate language: working in groups and giving feedback.

Assertiveness is an empowered position because of the underpinning beliefs: a belief in the right to hold an opinion, and to express it. It's empowering for others because of the accompanying belief that others also have a right to their opinion, and to express it. It's a mature position because of a belief that opinions are not necessarily right or wrong, they're just different, and that disagreement need not necessarily lead to conflict (Ken Back and Kate Back 1991: 52).

Particularly, in group discussions, young people can learn to define opinion from fact by using 'I' statements when expressing an opinion, e.g.:

> The way I see it is ...
> It seems to me that ...
> I've found that ...
> I see it rather differently ...
> It's my belief that ...
> It looks this way to me ...

Even when opinions are expressed clearly and 'owned' by an 'I' statement, others may disagree. Then it's useful to coach young people to avoid the negative influence of 'but' (see Chapter 5). Discussions that are peppered with 'Yes, I hear what you're saying, but ...' can become like a tennis match. One person expresses an opinion, the other person bats it back to them with a 'Yes ... but', the first person lobs it back with another ... and so on. A process which becomes totally ineffective as far as producing creative ideas or learning, because each stays in their own entrenched position.

Notice also that 'I' statements are a feature of the Feedback Sandwich in Chapter 7. The Feedback Sandwich is a useful tool in relation to assessment for learning (AfL). AfL is now widely acknowledged as an effective strategy for raising academic attainment, and peer feedback is one approach whereby children and young people help each other to assess their learning. As with all things, the *process* of an activity generates learning as well as the product or outcome. Coaching young people how to give each other constructive feedback – using the Feedback Sandwich formula, and owning their opinions with 'I' statements – can be a learning process as much for the giver of the feedback as for the receiver.

Thinking Space 23

Rachel D. is the teacher in a sixth-form college mentioned in Stage 3. After teaching for 10 years she began to feel in a bit of a rut and felt she needed to start learning again. So she enrolled on a Masters degree, and found the whole experience not only re-energized her approach to learning, but revitalized her relationship with her students. As she put it, she felt 're-filled with new knowledge' and her enthusiasm spilled over into sharing her experience as a learner with her students.

Rachel felt that a mutual respect developed as a result of both teacher and students talking about their learning experiences. Quite apart from the improved relationship with her students, Rachel has recaptured a joy in learning for herself: 'I've found a love of learning I missed out on in the past. I didn't appreciate in the past how lucky I was to be learning ...'

Celebration

Sometimes a celebration will be an event, a festival, a ceremony. Other times we will celebrate a 'rite of passage', a changing from one state to another, as with a baptism, a bar mitzvah, a marriage. Another dictionary definition gives it as 'to do something enjoyable because of a feeling of pleasure at some achievement'.

That last definition allows us to see that celebration need not be something saved for the end of an experience. Celebration is also not the same as giving a reward. As we have seen, a reward is given by one person to another in order to elicit certain behaviour. A reward may engender some pleasure initially, but it is an experience where the giver is in control of the experience. A celebration, on the other hand, is more of a shared experience; a social pleasure-taking in acknowledging something that has been achieved.

Every time we give feedback we are celebrating small achievements. The formula I've described in Chapter 7 sandwiches something to work on for improvement between two positive achievements. Others may use 'Two stars and a wish' to highlight two things worthy of praise and one to aim for. Our genuine appreciation of small achievements can make them something to celebrate, and young people can model our attitude in giving feedback to celebrate similarly with their fellow students.

Each time you run an activity that requires young people to applaud each other you are creating an opportunity to celebrate. The reason the students enjoyed my spelling game (see Thinking Space 9) was probably not because of the nature of the task of spelling; it was more likely to be related to the celebratory applause for every student.

Sharing celebration with young people can also occur in quite subtle ways. Rachel in Thinking Space 23 has been so enthused by the re-awakening of her own learning that she has shared this with her students. By generating a mutual interest and respect, she has created an atmosphere that celebrates learning achievement.

Although celebration does not have to be reserved just for the end of something, at times of parting and moving on a celebration is a special way of marking closure. It's not just children and young people who like to be acknowledged. I've yet to meet the mature professional who doesn't respond when we hold our 'award' ceremony at the end of a training course. The 'awards' are not for a particular achievement: each delegate will write down a positive feature of another, and we create a small 'handing-over' ceremony where everyone gets a round of applause.

I used to do something similar with young people at the end of a school year. Everyone would have a sheet of paper stuck on their back, then we'd all have to write something on each one about how we'd perceived that person. Strictly positive comments only, and everyone had to be included. The protection of anonymity means that people can often write what they might not express otherwise. Then we'd take the papers off and read what people had written about us to the rest of the group. It's many years later, but I've still kept mine: I sometimes look at them and particularly treasure the ones that say I was a 'wicked' teacher and that I was 'safe'.

Of course there can be much grander celebrations. You'll see in Appendix 3 how Asha arranges a high status ceremony to acknowledge the achievement of young people who have been mentored. And you'll also read of the significant impact on one young man, far and above that which would have resulted from the academic achievement alone.

The impact of such ceremonies can stay with people for a lifetime. Even so, we shouldn't be blinded to the fact that the everyday, the ordinary, can provide causes for celebration. Mike was so concerned at the perception of one of his pupils that learning was a distressing experience (see Fig. 1) that he worked hard to establish an interactive and confident culture in his classroom. At the end of the trial period of his new approach, he checked again for any change in how his pupils now viewed learning. Fig. 26 shows a fairly typical response: learning was now experienced as a social activity: something that pupils engaged in with a smile on their faces. A cause for celebration indeed.

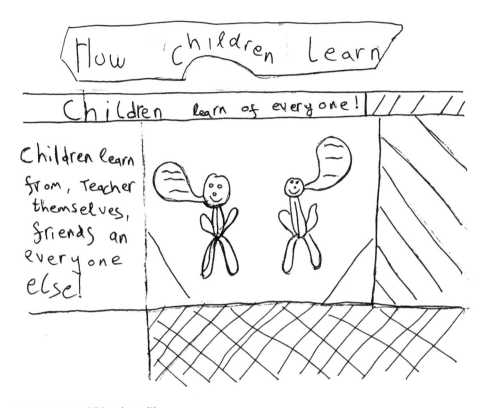

Figure 26: How children learn (2)

Themes of the CARE model – Stage 4

Language

I have placed a stress on skill in using language as an essential element in coaching throughout the CARE model. Language used skilfully can change the way people think; it can reframe their thinking to consider different options and open up choices.

At a stage of empowerment we can shift the emphasis to helping young people to recognize how they phrase their thoughts in language, and how these may be interpreted. As an example, David Clutterbuck (1998: 61) suggests a helpful use of a scaling tool in scrutinizing the commitment to learning goals, which I've adapted for use with young people. When a young person has set up a learning goal – mentally said 'Yes' to it – they can test the depth of their commitment by choosing the number that best represents 'The Meaning of Yes':

7	Yes:	I feel fully focused towards learning until I achieve the goal
6	Yes:	I feel a commitment to the learning I need to achieve the goal
5	Yes:	I am fairly excited about the goal
4	Yes:	I am willing to have a go
3	Yes:	The goal may be something worth pursuing
2	Yes:	The goal is quite interesting
1	Yes:	I'll go along with it
0	Yes:	But I can't really be bothered

You will see that once they have decided their level of motivation, it can open up discussion on possibilities for raising their commitment. If their commitment proves to be too low on the scale, it can prompt re-examination of the goal to check whether it was the right goal in the first place. It is an exercise they will be able to use for themselves in the future, not just to test their commitment to learning goals, but to test out the sort of language they are using to frame thoughts and ideas.

Well-being

When I outlined the stages of the CARE model in Chapter 4 I specified two things. Firstly, that solutions in coaching would need to take account of the complex interaction between academic achievement, personal development and social and life skills. Secondly that the stages did not progress in a linear manner, rather the process was more like balancing plates, moving back and forth between the stages.

At a stage of empowerment, it's useful to reflect on whether the process of a coaching intervention has been comprehensive in addressing these areas. The pressures towards academic achievement can often obscure other aspects of development in young people. We may need to remind ourselves that young people will not be able to learn if they are not in a positive emotional state. To empower young people we can help them recognize this so they will be able to 'balance the plates' for themselves in their future development.

Barrie Hopson and Patricia Hough (1976: 16–27) produced a comprehensive model of personal growth for young people under the headings of Sensing, Feeling, Thinking and Doing. As a person-centred approach, the CARE model has taken a similar holistic view of young people. Hopson and Hough's headings can be useful as a checklist for our own reflection on the coherence of the CARE model in practice. They can also be used by young people to reflect on the strategies they now have at their disposal for their own future development, and identify which aspects need continuing attention. Below are some examples they may identify as useful for the future:

Sensing	Relaxation techniques, anchoring, the Circle of Excellence, awareness of the physical environment for learning
Feeling	Expressing feelings directly, reframing limiting beliefs and feelings, awareness of the emotional element of learning
Thinking	Awareness of how language reflects and influences thinking, different styles of thinking
Doing	Recognizing the need for physical breaks when learning, active listening, social modelling

Goal setting

Throughout the CARE model we have had a primary goal of working towards realizing the potential of young people. We have been aiming to free them from limiting beliefs, enabling them to recognize the resources they already have, and empowering them with the skills, confidence and flexibility to deal with an unknown future where the only certainty will be a need for lifelong learning.

Empowerment of young people has meant giving up 'power over' them. If we have approached the practice of coaching for learning with an ultimate goal in mind of empowering young people as independent learners, then we will also have had in mind an ultimate goal of 'letting go'.

So the final overarching goal for us can be a check on whether we have been able to generate enthusiasm for learning in young people without making them dependent upon us as an expert with the answers. Have we been able to shift the emphasis in the relationship from being the controller of knowledge to the facilitator of learning? Have we been able to see them off on their life's path without some need of our own to cling on to the relationship? Have we had the balance right?

Reflection

I make no apologies for the frequent references back to earlier stages that you will have noticed in Stage 4. This reflects the approach at the outset that the stages were not to be viewed as progressing in a linear fashion, rather it would be a process of 'tweaking the plates' to ensure all the elements were being addressed as needed.

In addition to seeking the empowerment of young people as learners, Stage 4 encourages us to integrate our own empowerment as professionals. We can reflect on whether we have an intrinsic motivation to improve our practice, or whether we are reliant upon external factors to be able commit to our professional role with any enthusiasm. The techniques and attitudes of Time Awareness and Assertiveness are important to enable young people to be in control of their own learning, and they are

---

also relevant skills for our professional and personal development. Both are areas where a degree of skill is crucial to our self-management in general, and stress management in particular.

Stage 4 is also a time to consider whether we are creative enough in devising opportunities for celebration. By creating a climate of celebration we stimulate the emotional element of learning. By marking out achievements – however small – we can stimulate motivation. We can set a tone to generate a shared encouragement for learning achievements among young people and their peers, and ourselves.

Stage 4 – Practice pointers

- Intrinsic motivation stimulates creativity and high self-esteem
- The right level of challenge and support will stimulate intrinsic motivation
- Promoting ownership of learning involves more than handing over of tasks
- Giving up 'power' will promote empowerment
- Using time productively involves managing self rather than managing time itself
- Having an awareness of a personal experience of time is a first stage in using time productively
- A game plan for dealing with procrastination is an element of a time management strategy
- A time chart needs to be a living document that changes as goals evolve
- Assertiveness is more effective behaviour in the long term than submissiveness, aggression or passive aggression
- Adopting the body language of assertiveness can build confidence
- Active listening is a key skill for working with other people
- Celebration is a social acknowledgement of something achieved.

Notes

[1] *The Letters* on www.des.emory.edu/mfp/james.
[2] A version of Procrastination Game Plan also appears in Jacquie Turnbull 2007: 82–83.

9 Overview

Along with the recognition that we are preparing young people for a future none of us can comprehend, the movement to develop young people as independent learners has gained momentum. This book has been part of that surge towards the future, and I have been advocating that, as educators, we need to have an awareness that young people's cognitive, emotional and social development will all impact upon their ability to realize their potential as autonomous and creative learners. Despite the strength of the movement towards independent learning, doubtless there are some who still yearn for a simpler, more ordered life; one where they could concentrate on imparting their subject knowledge to compliant attentive groups of young people.

The movement also struggles within the structure of systems of state education designed for an earlier age. Generally learning still tends to be associated with particular buildings, with schedules of formal classes and timetabled curricula. In addition, the system of education in the UK mirrors the systems of all other countries in the world in sustaining a hierarchy of importance in relation to the subjects taught: English, Mathematics and Science, then the Humanities, then the Arts. Despite the introduction of Key Skills, of Diplomas and Baccalaureate, and a plethora of vocational learning opportunities, the superior status of the academic hierarchy retains its tenacious cultural influence.

And yet systems of state education originally came into being to serve the needs of industrialization. Before the nineteenth century, education was the domain of universities. Although state education began as a means to prepare the populace for the workplace, the system deferred to the needs of academia in relation to the curriculum. Despite the fact that the industrial age is past, and the future is yet unknown, the system still remains remarkably resistant to change. Is it an unrealistic aim to expect a system of state education to be capable of educating young people according to their individual talents, to encourage creativity and independence in learning to meet the needs of an unknown future?

Yet in one way, education has always played a role in preparing young people for contemporary life as well as work. Superficially, the role of schools in the distant past could be interpreted as merely schooling young people in the basics of the three Rs in preparation for work, and providing a wider subject base for those destined for higher education. Yet there would always have been a 'hidden curriculum' – all those ways that schools and teachers implicitly inculcated young people with the norms and values of society so they could take their place as adult citizens. The hierarchal structure of a teacher's employment, the formal relationships with pupils in 'subject' positions, the conditioning of a structured school day, drilling, learning as a class rather than as an individual would all have established the social requirements of the 'real' world. Even the fact that a hundred years ago female teachers were required to give up the role if they married, reflected the expectations of women's role in society.

Admittedly, also in the past there were other influences that cohered to support young people and convey a sense of societal uniformity. Structures of family life, the church, localized policing, the moral rhetoric of politicians would all have provided a framework of expectations for young people to anticipate their future role in society. With the potency of those influences significantly diluted, perhaps it is little wonder that educators complain that they are being required to fill in the gaps left by those influences and that the task of schooling young people in subject knowledge *and* preparing them emotionally and socially for adulthood is too large a task.

The role of education appears to have become more difficult and challenging because, not only is the future unknown, the world as we know it today is more complex, risky and precarious. Young people as a whole may have more material benefits than their predecessors, but those benefits themselves come at a cost. At a time when they are negotiating a stage of physical and emotional transition, young people are bombarded with a complexity of choices of how they should look, behave and aspire to be. The cult of 'celebrity' implies that people no longer have to be good at anything to attain recognition, anyone can be on television and that itself has become an aim for many.

We do, indeed, have different challenges as educators in the twenty-first century. But even allowing for the simpler role of schooling in the past, there would always have been teachers who would have seen it as their role to fulfil the wider 'moral purpose' of education. Everyone remembers a good teacher (or an adult who inspired and helped them) and the memorable features would not necessarily relate to the subject they taught. They might have been someone who had an enthusiasm for learning – you may not remember the content of the physics lesson or whatever, but you remember being captured by the enthusiasm. You may remember that they paid attention to you – that you couldn't escape unnoticed at the back of the class. You may remember that they appeared to see something in you that you hadn't recognized in yourself. With the benefit of hindsight, you may conclude that you would not have achieved, or taken the path that you did, or that you might have even dropped away from education, if it hadn't been for their particular and special interest. Even for those who do drop away from education, it may be that when they return to learning in later life, they are able to make a link with an educator who planted such a strong seed of love of learning that it proved ultimately irresistible.

So we have always had the seeds of our solution. Educators have always responded to the individual learning and development needs of children and young people. The influence of educators has always been like dropping a pebble into a pond – we never know the extent of the ripples or how many other people they may touch. We may live in more difficult and complex times than any previous generation, the future may be unpredictable, but at least our evolution has equipped us with the resources to respond to the new demands of educating young people. In Darwin's view, the species who survived were not the strongest or the fittest, but the most adaptable.

So what have been the themes in this book that I consider important as a way forward? How do we have to adapt to meet the needs of current and future generations? Firstly, seeing ourselves as learners is absolutely essential. If knowledge is likely to double every seven years as predicted, it's not just young people who will have to keep pace with change. We all need to be able to reflect on the knowledge we have and the skills we have acquired to check that they continue to be fit for purpose. The advantage of living in the information age is that we have access to a tremendous amount of research and knowledge to inform our practice. The disadvantage is that there is so much knowledge it can be difficult to find our way through without guidance. No one book could contain all the information you would need for coaching, and anyway it would be overtaken by developing knowledge in a very short time. My intention with this book has been to provide you with a series of signposts to other sources of knowledge that you can follow as your interest directs.

The second theme is that, although I have envisaged one use of coaching as part of the portfolio of a teacher's skills, it embodies a significant shift of emphasis from traditional pedagogy. It requires a particular set of beliefs and values and a skill set that is based around developing learning abilities rather than delivering subject knowledge. It follows therefore that coaching is a person-centred approach that does not restrict learning to a cognitive and rational activity, but acknowledges the influence of social and emotional elements.

The third theme is that I have tried to conceive of an overview, a framework to act as a guide, rather than a set of techniques that can be acquired and put into practice. A framework may give you a different perspective on your existing practice – because we already have the seeds of the solution in what we are already doing. And when new developments and ideas come along, it helps to be able to adapt them into a coherent model of practice that a framework can provide.

There is no better place to end a book such as this than with the words of a teacher reflecting upon the experience of following a professional development course:

> There is a big difference between changing the face of education in Wales and making a small step forward as a teacher in a classroom. Yet, as so many of us find ourselves here, we may be the place to start. The cutting edge, if you like, may not always be found in research papers and buried in streams of data, but in a place where the two very different worlds of research and classroom life meet. For myself, I have discovered new skills, new ideas and the knowledge and confidence to make and measure small changes. For my school, I have made a positive impact in the way children think about their own thinking, based on sound, up-to-date research. For education, I have developed the expertise of myself and other colleagues and contributed to a wider professional community. [1]

There has been a further element running throughout this book about balance, and perhaps it is the most important aspect of all. Balance has been mentioned several times in different contexts. But perhaps the most important element is getting the balance right between learning for academic and vocational outcomes and for personal growth and development for young people. I hope this book will help you address that balance and in doing so, make a contribution to your own personal and professional development.

Note

[1] Thanks to Rachel Mitchell of Hawthorn Primary School for allowing me to use her words. Rachel's reflection was included in the final report of the module 'Improving Practice through Action Research' run by Cardiff School of Education, University of Wales Institute, Cardiff, and I am grateful to Ann Hughes for permission to use it. The module is part of the pilot of the Chartered Teacher programme and thanks also to Hayden Llewellyn of the General Teaching Council for Wales for his helpful assistance.

Appendix 1

The Sorted Project – an alternative curriculum approach

Mandy works at a project run by a local authority in South Wales. As part of the Welsh Assembly Government's drive to reduce the number of young people classified as NEETs (Not in Education, Employment or Training), the project provides an 'alternative' curriculum for those who have either been excluded from school, or are at risk of exclusion. The young people are in the 14–16 years age group, and present a range of social, emotional and behavioural difficulties.

Mandy adopts a very practical approach to helping the young people have an experience of achievement. She is constantly searching for alternative qualifications that can be mapped across to provide an equivalent to traditional qualifications, such as GCSEs. For instance, within 6–8 weeks of starting on the project, young people will have achieved one Open College Network qualification which is mapped to Prince's Trust awards. When a parent interviewed for Mandy's research commented that life skills such as how to use money would be useful to learn, Mandy introduced an OCN Money Management award. She stresses that 'no learning is lost'. A portfolio approach suits the young people and means that they can record their learning in a variety of ways. She aims to encourage a sense of achievement by finding qualifications that provide recognition of all aspects of learning, so that the young people can gain confidence as they gain qualifications.

Two themes are evident in Mandy's style of working. The first is flexibility in approaching learning outcomes. Due to their varied emotional and behavioural difficulties, the young people do not always arrive at the project focused and ready to learn. When this happens, Mandy has no hesitation in scrapping her lesson plan, no matter how carefully prepared. But that's not the same as saying time is wasted. As Mandy puts it 'I know what I want them to achieve, it's just some days I have to go about it in a different way'.

The second theme is that Mandy seems to have found a balance between high support and high challenge. While she persistently boosts the self-esteem of the young people, she also doesn't give up in her expectations that they will persist with their learning. She provides support when it's needed, but also knows when to step back; 'I prop them up with scaffolding, then I gradually take it away'.

When Mandy carried out evaluative research on the project for her Master's degree, one theme emerged prominently. While the young people had been unable to form good relationships with school staff, they consistently commented on how being treated 'more like an adult' made the project a more enjoyable prospect for them. Parents and other workers involved with the young people also reported improvements in behaviour and motivation. Mandy has found that the findings of her research have supported themes already identified by policy bodies: if pupils with behavioural difficulties are not to be disadvantaged, there needs to be greater understanding of social, emotional and behavioural difficulties, and the correct setting and surroundings are vital if positive outcomes are to be achieved.

Appendix 2

Developing emotional literacy through peer mentoring and counselling in a Welsh-medium secondary school

I first met Siriol and Karen at a conference for teachers showcasing their initiatives as a means of sharing good practice. Siriol's presentation had impact because she brought along a group of young people to talk about their roles as peer mentors and counsellors. The audience were both captivated by the young people's sincerity and commitment to their roles, and impressed at the high profile given to the pastoral element of school life.

If I had any doubts that a caring ethos really had been embedded in Ysgol Plasmawr, they would soon be dispelled when I visited the school some time later. You'll be aware that when you visit a new school, you can gain a sense of the pervading ethos as soon as you cross the threshold. The politeness and responsiveness of students when I asked directions; the copious displays indicating that school life extended outside the building, both locally and globally; the environment of offices softened by comfy armchairs, colourful throws and noticeboards bulging with 'thank-you' cards – from clues such as these you gain a sense of the life of a school.

But none of this comes about by accident, and I wanted to know in particular how the school's focus on developing emotional literacy had begun. The school is only 10 years old, and Siriol recalled how a number of things had come together when the original senior management team were debating the sort of school they wanted to create. The headteacher at that time had used a questionnaire to tease out issues of student well-being. One of the questions was about bullying: 'Who would you be most likely to tell if you were being bullied?' students were asked. The vast majority opted for 'A friend'. Around the same time, Siriol went on a course on motivational interviewing where Karen was the trainer and things clicked together. If young people would prefer to talk to a friend about issues such as bullying, why didn't they train young people in the skills of motivational interviewing to enable them to be peer mentors and counsellors?

One of my questions had been whether the whole staff 'bought in' to this initiative, and the importance placed on pastoral support in general? Gaining wholesale support can be a challenge, and two strategies were directed towards its achievement. Firstly, when Karen was brought in to impart her skills of motivational interviewing, she first trained the staff. She was a skilled enough trainer to be able to adjust her approach to counter any resistance as it arose. Secondly, there is now a structure of staff support that ensures the momentum is carried forward: a 20-minute pastoral meeting for staff to discuss individual young people, and a voluntary pastoral care committee where staff look at ways to improve pastoral care overall.

As for the young people themselves, Karen has been delighted at their receptiveness to the training. Overall, they didn't demonstrate the entrenched viewpoints sometimes found in adults, but had an openness and acceptance of difference in other young people. Following training, they take up their roles as either peer mentors focusing on academic mentoring, or peer counsellors providing emotional support for issues such as bullying. Both the training and the roles are seen as enhancing emotional literacy through the development leadership skills. Year 9 mentors can meet up with younger pupils through the school's system of vertical registration, and they also offer help at breaks and lunchtimes. Similarly peer counsellors make themselves available during breaks.

Given the strong emphasis on the pastoral element, my second question was whether there was any evidence that this support impacted upon education attainment? Always a difficult question to answer, and perhaps the very difficulty of establishing any link is the reason many schools do not place the same emphasis on pastoral support as Ysgol Plasmawr. Siriol pointed first to the social mix of the school: 30 per cent of their intake being drawn from areas of social deprivation. Yet examination results appeared to be better than could be expected according to value-added criteria, with 73 per cent of pupils achieving A*–C at GCSE. Also of significance was the fact that the school had the lowest exclusion rate in the county. Karen also had a view from her own experience of the young people. Anecdotally, she thought that following counselling many who had not been expected to attend, had been able to turn up and sit examinations. But for both of them it was not all about achievement in examinations: by the time they left school, they were looking for young people to be more grounded human beings for having had emotional support, and better prepared as adults in society. And maybe, just maybe, there was the potential to break a cycle of deprivation for some young people.

Every initiative needs a driving force to sustain momentum and Siriol always has an eye to 'what next?' Work with families is being started: Karen will be running workshops for parents on communication with young people on issues such as substance abuse; strengthening families by bringing together parents and children in facilitated groups to improve communication. Other initiatives are continuing the theme of developing emotional literacy through leadership skills: the head chef of a local 4-star hotel is working with young people towards preparing a healthy meal for staff during British Food fortnight; junior sports leaders are coaching younger pupils, and also coaching in local primary schools; and then perhaps there could be a theme of incorporating global citizenship, and what about something to emphasize Welsh language and culture ...?

Overall, Ysgol Plasmawr seems to me to be an illustration of the potential of a broad 'educational' approach, as against the narrowness of 'schooling'. Siriol seemed saddened that so many teachers from other schools had commented to her that 'it could never happen in our school', to which one has to ask the question 'Why not?'

It seemed to me that there were certain features that had come together at Ysgol Plasmawr that ensured a high profile for pastoral support. First, there was an unpinning belief that young people will not succeed if they are not happy. Second, there was a member of the senior management team with the commitment to drive through initiatives to provide support together with emotional and social development for young people. Third, there was professional training so that staff and young people alike achieved a high standard of communication skills. A successful formula indeed, that may well be capable of being replicated elsewhere.

Appendix 3

REMA – Raising Ethnic Minority Achievement

Fitzalan High School's student profile is probably one of the most diverse in Wales: 63 per cent of students are drawn from minority groups, with 30 different nationalities featured. English is a second language for 56 per cent of pupils, and 20 different languages are represented on campus.

Within such a vibrant cultural mix there are of course groups with their own individual characteristics, and sometimes it needs the lens of statistical analysis to allow specific characteristics to emerge. So it was in this case; a research project highlighted a particular level of under-achievement among Somali students, a group with a large representation on Fitzalan campus. The Somali community has been established in Cardiff since the beginning of the twentieth century, and now comprises the largest Somali group in the UK.

Recognition of levels of under-achievement and accessing sources of funding to support projects is important, but it is just a first step. It is the individuals with the drive and commitment to provide the individual support who provide the 'difference that makes the difference'. Asha Ali is one such person at Fitzalan. She and the small group of other teachers involved in the REMA project target young people at risk of under-achievement at the end of Year 9, then mentor and support them through to their GCSEs. The young people are allocated a personal mentor who monitors their attendance as well as their progress. Asha and her colleagues meet with their mentees during assembly or PSE lessons, follow up any issues with particular subject teachers and also offer revision sessions out of school hours.

Two things recently came together that Asha feels has sharpened their approach and made their mentoring more effective. Attending an assertive mentoring course revealed how other schools had raised achievement by analysing statistical data in order to target young people more precisely. At the same time, Fitzalan improved their own database, so that there was now the facility to set targets based on a young person's potential, together with the level they should be working at. Asha is able to share this objective evidence with the young people and use it as a basis for goal-setting to raise their achievement.

Interestingly, the enhanced statistical tracking revealed something else. A member of the senior management team spotted that, when comparing like with like, the young people being mentored by the REMA mentors appeared to be making greater strides in improving their performance. There was objective evidence of year-on-year improvement in academic achievement. So the value of the enhanced support is being more widely acknowledged within the school.

As ever, I was interested in the value to the young people aside from their improving academic performance. One of the most pleasing aspects of the mentoring work is the high status given to celebrating achievement. An annual award ceremony provides the opportunity to celebrate all achievements, and attracted attendance by the First Minster of the Welsh Assembly and the local Member of Parliament among other notables. Asha recalls one young man's response to the event: 'It's the first time I've felt proud to be Somali'.

There has been added value for Asha also: she was able use her enthusiasm for the value of mentoring to progress her own professional development. For her Master's degree thesis she analysed the previous five years of records, demonstrating that young people being targeted consistently improved their performance. One hundred and twenty of the young people were asked to complete a questionnaire on the experience, and their views were followed up to improve the project, such as the valuable suggestion that they would have liked parents to be more involved.

There were plenty of comments about how the project had helped with school work and revision, e.g.:

- It helped me understand my work if I never understood it first time
- ... always had someone to support you when you found a subject difficult and was able to improve in a certain area by extra work
- I had help with coursework and also a lot of revision time was provided by REMA. I didn't realize revision could be so fun!

Aside from improving work practices, there were also many comments on how the young people felt their confidence improve overall:

- It boosted my self-confidence and enabled me to revise efficiently
- It made some major differences in some aspects such as exam technique, confidence, self-esteem and the ability to confront problems confidentially
- It made me realize I had more potential and knowledge than I realized.

This increase in confidence was very often linked to a wider appreciation of future potential options generated by goal-setting:

- We always talked about positive goals and worked hard on them (trying to achieve them)
- Gave me more confidence to achieve my goals
- Make me aware that the sky is the limit and my future is in my hands (and also it helped people to think positively about their ethnicity).

So in addition to the statistical analysis that demonstrated how the young people being mentored by Asha and her colleagues were consistently improving their academic performance, the young people involved were evidently gaining in self-awareness, motivation and confidence. There was also a strong sense of realism about the project: young people were not being encouraged towards unrealistic expectations, but were being supported and encouraged to achieve their own maximum potential. Perhaps this final quote summarizes this 'empowerment' ethos:

- ... made me realize that everyone needs help no matter how 'smart' or 'unsmart' you are and that asking for help when you need it is the 'smartest' thing to do.

Appendix 4

Changing teaching times

Gary moved from teaching some years ago to work as a senior executive. From time to time he has been asked what gave him the greatest satisfaction in his professional career. Each time he came back to his time teaching in a sixth form college, and, in particular, the deep sense of achievement he felt when a parent described the impact he had on their daughter. Even though she had the backing of a supportive family, this young person had not achieved as expected and had to repeat her fifth year. As a result, her self-esteem suffered, and she had a limited view of her abilities and potential.

It was some time later that Gary became aware that his teaching had a positive effect on the young person. Something about his teaching had 'switched the light on for her': she became enthusiastic about learning and willing to undertake extra research. Her confidence improved and she became a well-prepared communicator. Although her parents identified that it was Gary's input that was 'the difference that made the difference', there was a knock-on effect as her work in other subjects improved, and she was able to get good A-level grades to set her on the path to study international politics and history at university – perhaps an outcome that couldn't have been anticipated from her 'failure' to make the grade in a previous year.

As always, I was intrigued to find out what specific strategy Gary used to 're-awaken the flow' for this young person. Gary found trying to put his finger on it quite a challenge; it was a long time ago after all, and in those days there was less emphasis on reflection to reveal the specifics of teaching practice. One thing he was sure about was that he had an underlying belief in her potential; he never regarded her as lacking ability, just short on confidence.

But talking it through, certain things emerged about his approach. He had been aware of the importance of showing positive regard, and not being critical of individual efforts. He had tried to build her self-confidence by encouraging her to answer discussion points; making her feel she had a contribution to make for others in the group. Yet it was also interesting that for most of our conversation, Gary kept returning to aspects of *subject teaching* that he felt were important: being confident and enthusiastic about subject matter, structuring a lesson to stimulate a sense of learner security, having a continuity of purpose.

I was reminded of Rhys Griffith's reflection on his teaching in the 1970s (see Chapter 2) and how with hindsight he could recognize that in those days he and his colleagues were training pupils to pass exams so they could get jobs. Gary's memories also indicate a more dominant focus on subject knowledge. He admitted he'd had a general understanding of what motivated students and certain conceptual ideas of how people learn, yet he also had to admit that, as knowledge about learning and motivation has developed, there would be different challenges nowadays – in an environment where there is more emphasis on learning than teaching – to be able to recognize and adapt to learning and motivational styles.

Yet we can still see the basis of a 'coaching' model in Gary's reminiscences about his teaching. Plainly, he was a good teacher and you don't discard good practice just to take up a new style of intervention. Rather you evolve by building on the best parts of what has gone before. In Gary's example, he had an underpinning belief in the potential of his students, he was enthusiastic (maybe for his subject, but you can translate that to enthusiasm for learning as enthusiasm is infectious), he paid attention to individual needs as well as group and whole-class teaching, he had behavioural expectations, he sought interesting angles to engage the interest of his students, and he saw the need for young people to be able to visualize outcomes. All things that effective teachers do, and principles that can migrate into a developing model of practice that has a primary focus on facilitation of learning, rather than conveyor of subject knowledge. Overall, all we would expect from good coaching practice.

Appendix 5

The learning coaches of Wales

The educational policies of Welsh Assembly Government have been framed around a vision of making Wales a 'Learning Country', where all young people can have the best start in life, and where learning will be an everyday part of life and work in which the interests of learners come first.[1]

Part of the overall Learning Country policy has been a commitment to transforming provision for young people aged 14–19. The intention of Learning Pathways 14–19 is to encourage more young people to achieve their potential so they are better equipped for the world of work and become better informed and more active citizens. The policy comprises six key elements which are intended to achieve a balance of learning experiences with the support and guidance young people will need to achieve their potential:

- Individual Learning Pathways to meet the needs of each learner
- Wider choice and flexibility of programmes and ways of learning
- A Learning Core which runs from 14 through to 19 wherever young people are learning
- Learning Coach support
- Access to personal support
- Impartial careers advice and guidance.[2]

The introduction of Learning Coach support was anticipated to be one of the biggest changes to existing educational practice. Originally viewed as a *concept*, the suggested job description was deliberately broad-based in order to reflect the potential diversity of learning coaches working in schools, colleges, workplaces or youth clubs. Nevertheless, it was anticipated that two key interests would underpin their work:

1. helping 14–19 year-olds develop appropriate study skills
2. facilitating their choice between the options to be more widely available as the Learning Pathways policy was rolled out.

Having been involved in the early consultation process to define the role of a Learning Coach, and then in the writing and delivery of two of the training modules, I had a keen interest in seeing what the final report had to say about how the new role and training had been received across Wales. The first thing that struck me from the account of the first cohort trained was the indications that many of the people drawn to work as Learning Coaches had perhaps enhanced the perception beyond the original narrow concept of imparting skills and knowledge by the skills and attributes they had brought to the role.[3]

To start with, there is the identification of a much broader defining characteristic of the Learning Coach as 'anogaeth' – encouragement. Then there were the findings of the external evaluation of the first year of training. Some teething troubles had been experienced in delivery and support which perhaps was only to be expected given the time frame in which the training had been rolled out to nearly 300 participants across Wales. Apart from these minor difficulties, the evaluation found the status of the Learning Coach was proving popular and should continue. And, of course, of particular interest from my own perspective was the suggestion that future recruitment of coaches should value a core set of social and emotional skills to enable them to work with young people, other professionals and, in some cases, young people's families.

The significance of this has been reflected in the CARE model. I have emphasized a view of learning that is not just cognitive and rational, but social and emotional as well, and reflected the views of eminent theorists that effective teachers and coaches need to be strong in emotional intelligence and self-efficacy.

The broader characteristics of a Learning Coach could also be discerned in some of the reasons given by individuals for taking up the training. The report gives one as:

'... to help as many children as possible to reach their goal in life and be happy, because I work with a lot of children who are unhappy – just to make them smile' (p. 7)

A similar theme could be detected when I looked back on the assignments submitted by Learning Coaches during their training. One had written:

'On reflection, when working with J and the other students I have learnt that you need to get to know the student and build a trusting relationship before anything else.'

There was evidence for another theme that I later incorporated into the CARE model. Learning Coaches could be seen to be taking the perspective of the whole person, enabling young people to draw on their wider experience to support the requirements of their schooling. As another had written:

'Although H came across as confident with his peers, he did at times show a lack of self-esteem. We discussed this as his exams got closer. We looked at visualisation techniques which he could use during exams. I asked him to visualise as he would when he had his football training. This was something he had done with football. He was pleased he was able to transfer his skills. He was also keen to use his favourite footballer as a visual technique during his exams for motivation.'

The breakdown of the first cohort of 299 people who put themselves forward to train as Learning Coaches shows that the major location for coaching support is the school or college. Of the occupational backgrounds of the individuals, the majority were teachers, followed by similar numbers from the youth service and people involved in advice and guidance, and the final category were drawn from private training.

You will have seen that one of the ways I have envisaged that the CARE model might be used is as an *intervention* to complement the work of a teacher. So the majority interest from teachers is significant. In fact, at one school in Wales all the form tutors are taking training as Learning Coaches to enhance their ability to give personal support to the students in their form group. In other areas Learning Coach intervention has been targeted at particular populations: the dominant themes recognized are underachievement, specific learning needs, discipline difficulties, peer group problems, internal and external truanting, and catching up on missed classes and coursework. Coaches can work with learners who may be experiencing difficulties and who have been referred for special help; and they can also work with those young people who are more invisible, in one coach's phrase 'part of the wall-paper' of an educational institution. The wisdom of the original broad-based job description can be seen in the creative and flexible use of trained Learning Coaches.

An encouraging aspect of the report is the account of Learning Coaches who had expressed a marked interest in their own further training and professional development. For some, coaching experiences had acted either as a catalyst or a stepping stone to further career progression.

Overall, the 'balancing act' I have conceived in the CARE model is reflected in the approach of Learning Coaches in Wales. Coaches are demonstrating a balance in the support they provide in terms of offering very practical 'hints and tips' while also developing the longer-term empowerment of young people through building up their confidence and learning insights. For those of us working in education in Wales, a small country with a relatively poor showing in international statistics, yet struggling to achieve a vision of a Learning Country, the report brings a message to inspire further efforts:

> Raymond Williams noted that being truly radical means making hope possible rather than despair convincing. The Learning Coaches give hope during a time when education and training statistics alongside international skills audits might otherwise cause despair.
>
> Danny Saunders 2008: 41

Notes

[1] *The Learning Country* published by the National Assembly for Wales 2001.

[2] *Learning Pathways 14-19 Guidance* published by the National Assembly for Wales 2004: v.

[3] 'The Learning Coaches of Wales: Summary Document': Professor Danny Saunders and Welsh Assembly Government May 2008.

References

Abbott, J. and Ryan, T. (2000) *The Unfinished Revolution: Learning, Human Behaviour, Community and Political Paradox*. Stafford: Network Educational Press Ltd.

Adey, P. and Shayer, M. (1994) *Really Raising Standards: Cognitive Intervention and Academic Achievement*. London: Routledge.

Ajmal, Y. (2006) Solution Focused Mediation in Schools, pp. 3–6. *Solution News* Vol. 2 Issue 1 April 2006.

Argyris, C. and Schon, D. (1996) *Organizational Learning II: Theory, Method and Practice*. Reading, MA: Addison-Wesley Publishing Co.

Asthana, A. (2007) 'Bosses give school reform a failure mark', *The Observer* 12 August 2007.

Back, K. and Back, K. (1991) *Assertiveness at Work*, 2nd edn. Maidenhead, Berks: McGraw-Hill Book Co.

Baird, J. R. (1986) 'Improving learning through enhanced metacognition: a classroom study', *European Journal of Science Education* 8(3): 262–82.

Bandura, A. (1992) 'Exercise of personal agency through the self-efficacy mechanism', in Schwarzer, R. (ed.) *Self-efficacy: Thought Control of Action*, pp. 3–38. Washington, DC: Hemisphere.

Bandura, A. (ed.) (1995) *Self-Efficacy in Changing Societies*. Cambridge: Cambridge University Press.

Bartlett, S., Burton, D. and Peim, N. (2001) *Introduction to Education Studies*. London: Paul Chapman Publishing.

Bennett, N. (1997) 'Analysing management for personal development: theory and practice', in Kydd, L., Crawford, M. and Riches, C. *Professional Development for Educational Management*. Buckingham: Open University Press.

Berko, J. (1958) 'The child's learning of English morphology', *Word* 14: 150–77.

Brearley, M. (2001) *Emotional Intelligence in the Classroom*. Carmarthen: Crown House Publishing Ltd.

Brighouse, T. (2005) *Teachers: A Comprehensive Success*; The Wales Education Lecture. Cardiff: General Teaching Council for Wales.

Brockbank, A. and McGill, I. (2006) *Facilitating Reflective Learning through Mentoring & Coaching*. London: Kogan Page.

Bruner, J. (1966) *The Culture of Education*. Cambridge, MA: Harvard University Press.

Canfield, J. (2005) *The Success Principles: How to Get from where You Are to where You Want to Be*. London: Element.

Case, J. and Gunstone, R. (2002) 'Metacognitive development as a shift in approach to learning: an in-depth study', *Studies in Higher Education* 27(4): 459–70.

Chomsky, N. (1957) *Syntactic Structures*. The Hague: Mouton.

Claxton, G. (1996) 'Integrated learning theory and the learning teacher', pp. 3–15, in Claxton, G., Atkinson, T., Osborn, M. and Wallace, M. *Liberating the Learner: Lessons for Professional Development in Education*. London: Routledge.

Claxton, G. (1999) *Wise-Up: The Challenge of Lifelong Learning*. London: Bloomsbury.

Claxton, G. (2000) 'The anatomy of intuition', in Atkinson, T. and Claxton, G. (eds) *The Intuitive Practitioner: On the Value of not always Knowing what One is Doing*. Buckingham: Open University Press.

Clutterbuck, D. (1998) *Learning Alliances: Tapping into Talent*. London: Institute of Personnel and Development.

Coffield, F., Moseley, D., Hall, E. and Ecclestone, K. (2004) *Learning Styles and Pedagogy in Post-16 Learning: A Systematic and Critical Review*. London: Learning & Skills Research Centre.

Cruddas, L. (2005) *Learning Mentors in Schools: Policy and Practice*. Stoke on Trent: Trentham Books.

Csikszentmihalyi, M. (1997) *Finding Flow: The Psychology of Engagement with Everyday Life*. New York: Basic Books.

Davies, J. (2008) 'What my old pals Shaun and Warren have done is amazing', *Western Mail* 23 February 2008.

Davison, L., Bryan, T. and Griffiths, R. (1999) 'Reflecting students learning styles', *Active Learning* 10, 10–13.

Daws, P. P. (1973) 'Mental health and education: counselling as prophylaxis', *British Journal of Guidance and Counselling* 1: 2–10.

Dennison, P. E. and Dennison, G. E. (1994) *Brain Gym, Teachers Education*, Revised edn. Venture, CA: Edu-Kinesthetics, Inc.

Department for Education and Skills (2006) *2020 Vision: Report of the Teaching and Learning 2020 Review Group*. London: DfES.

Dilts, R. (1990) *Changing Belief Systems with NLP*. Capitola, CA: Meta Publications.

Downs, S. (1995) *Learning at Work: Effective Strategies for Making Things Happen*. London: Kogan Page Ltd.

Dryden, G. and Vos, J. (2001) *The Learning Revolution: To Change the Way the World Learns*. Stafford: Network Educational Press Ltd.

Dweck, C. (2000) *Self-Theories: Their Role in Motivation, Personality and Development*. Florence, KY: Taylor & Francis.

Egan, G. (1994) *The Skilled Helper: A Problem-management Approach to Helping*, 5th edn. Pacific Grove, CA: Brooks/Cole Publishing Co.

Ellis, A. and Dryden, W. (1987) *The Practice of Rational-emotive Therapy*. New York: Springer.

Entwistle, N. and Tait, H. (1990) 'Approaches to learning, evaluations of teaching, and preferences for contrasting academic environments', *Higher Education* 19: 169–94.

Eraut, M. (2000) 'Non-formal learning and tacit knowledge in professional work', *British Journal of Educational Psychology* 70: 113–36.

Erikson, E. H. (1959) 'Identity and the life cycle: selected papers', *Psychological Issue Monograph Series*, 1 (No. 1). New York: International Universities Press.

Evans, A. (2003) 'Creating connections across new learning systems in the UK's National Mentoring Pilot Project', in Kochan, F. K. and Pascarelli, J. T. (eds) *Global Perspectives on Mentoring: Transforming Contexts, Communities and Cultures*. Greenwich, Connecticut: Information Age Publishing.

Fairclough, N. (1989) *Language and Power*. Harlow: Longman Group UK, Ltd.

Fairclough, N. (1992) *Discourse and Social Change*. Cambridge: Polity Press.

Fisher, R. (2005) *Teaching Children to Learn*. Cheltenham: Nelson Thornes Ltd.

Flaherty, J. (2005) *Coaching: Evoking Excellence in Others*, 2nd edn. Burlington, MA: Elsevier Butterworth-Heinemann.

Fleming, I. and Taylor, A. J. D. (2003) *Coaching Pocketbook*. Arlesford, Hants: Management Pocketbooks Ltd.

Fletcher, M. (2000) *Teaching for Success: The BRAIN-friendly Revolution in Action*! Folkestone: English Experience.

Flynn, J. R. (1987) 'Massive IQ gains in 14 nations: what IQ tests really measure', *Psychological Bulletin* 101: 171–91.

Flynn, J. R. (2007) *What is intelligence? Beyond the Flynn Effect*. Cambridge: Cambridge University Press.

Fontana, D. (1995) *Psychology for Teachers*, 3rd edn. New York: Palgrave.

Fullan, M. (2003) *The Moral Imperative of School Leadership*. Thousand Oaks, California: Corwin Press.

Furman, B. (1998) *It's Never Too Late to Have a Happy Childhood: From Adversity to Resilience*. London: BT Press.

Gardner, H. (1993) *Frames of Mind*, 2nd edn. London: Fontana.

Gardner, H., Csikszentmihalyi, M. and Damon, W. (2001) *Good Work: When Excellence and Ethics Meet*. New York: Basic Books.

Gibbons, M. (2004) 'Foreword' to Leadbetter, C. *Learning about Personalisation: How can We Put the Learner at the Heart of the Education System?* Nottingham: DfES Publications.

Gladwell, M. (2000) *The Tipping Point: How Little Things Can Make a Big Difference*. London: Abacus.

Glaser, R. (1999) 'Expert knowledge and processes of thinking', in McCormick, R. and Paechter, C. *Learning and Knowledge*. London: Paul Chapman Publishing.

Glasser, W. (1969) *Schools without failure*. New York: Harper Row.

Goldberg, M. C. (1997) *The Art of the Question: A Guide to Short-term Question-centred Therapy*. Hoboken, NJ: John Wiley & Sons Inc.

Goleman, D. (1996) *Emotional Intelligence: Why It can Matter more than IQ*. London: Bloomsbury Publishing plc.

Goleman, D. (1999) *Working with Emotional Intelligence*. London: Bloomsbury Publishing plc.

Griffith, R. (1998) *Educational Citizenship and Independent Learning*. London: Jessica Kingsley Publishers Ltd.

Hacker, D. J. (1998) 'Definitions and empirical foundations', pp. 1–23, in Hacker, D. J., Dunlosky, J. and Graesser, A. C. (eds) *Metacognition in Educational Theory and Practice*. Mahwah, NJ: Lawrence Erlbaum Associates Publishers.

Hannaford, C. (1995) *Smart Moves, Why Learning is not All in Your Head*. Arlington, VA: Great Ocean Publishers.

Hannaford, C. (1997) *The Dominance Factor: How Knowing your Dominant Eye, Ear, Brain, Hand & Foot can Improve your Learning*. Salt Lake City, Utah: Great River Books.

Hare, K. and Reynolds, L. (2004) *The Trainer's Toolkit: Bringing Brain-Friendly Learning to Life*. Carmarthen, Wales: Crown House Publishing Ltd.

Hargreaves, D. (2005) *About Learning: Report of the Learning Working Group*. London: Demos.

Havighurst, R. J. (1972) *Development Tasks and Education*. New York: C. McKay.

Havighurst, R. J. (1979) *Developmental Tasks and Education*, 4th edn. New York: D. McKay.

Hook, P., McPhail, I. and Vass, A. (2006) *Coaching & Reflecting Pocketbook*. Alresford, Hants: Teachers' Pocketbooks.

Hopson, B. and Hough, B. (1976) 'The need for personal and social education in secondary schools and further education', *British Journal of Guidance and Counselling* 11, pp.16–27.

Horne, T. and Wootton, S. (2007) *Teach Yourself: Training Your Brain*. London: Hodder Education.

Hughes, M. (2004) *Coaching in Schools*. Cheltenham: Education Training and Support.

Hughes, M. (2006) *And the Main Thing is LEARNING*. Cheltenham: Education Training and Support.

Hyman, P. 'Back to basics: the simple lessons I learnt about good schooling', pp. 26–7 *The Observer* 24 June 2007.

Jackson, P. Z. and McKergow, M. (2007) *The Solution Focus: Making Coaching & Change SIMPLE*. London: Nicholas Brealey International.

Jensen, E. (2008) *Brain-based Learning: The New Paradigm of Teaching*, 2nd edn. Thousand Oaks, CA: Corwin Press.

Klenowski, V. (2002) Developing Portfolios for Learning and Assessment: Processes and Principles. London: Routledge Falmer.

Kline, N. (1999) *Time to Think: Listening to Ignite the Human Mind*. London: Ward Lock

Knight, S. (1993) *NHP at Work: The difference that makes a difference at work*. London: Nicolas Brealey Publishing Ltd.

Knights, A. and Poppleton, A. (2007) *Research Insight: Coaching in Organisations*. London: CIPD. www.cipd.co.uk accessed 20 October 2007.

Korzybski, A. (1933) *Science and Sanity*, 4th edn. Lakeville, CT: International Non-Aristotelian Library Publishing.

Laborde, G. Z. (1998) *Influencing with Integrity: Management Skills for Communication and Negotiation*. Carmarthen: Crown House Publishing.

Landau, M. 'Deciphering the adolescent brain', *The Harvard University Gazette*. www.waldorflibrary.org/articles/adolesce2.pdf accessed 27 June 2008.

Larrivee, B. (2000) 'Transforming teaching practice: becoming the critically reflective teacher', *Reflective Practice* 1(3): 293–307.

Leadbetter, C. (2004) *Learning about Personalisation: How can We put the Learner at the Heart of the Education System?* Nottingham: DfES in partnership with DEMOS.

LeDoux, J. (1998) *The Emotional Brain*. London: Phoenix.

McDermott, I. (2007) 'Coaching secrets of real change', *Resource* 12 June 2007.

McDermott, I. and O'Connor, J. (1996) *NLP and Health*. London: Thorsons.

Mahony, T. (2003) *Words Work! How to Change Your Language to Improve Behaviour in Your Classroom*. Carmarthen: Brown House Publishing Ltd.

Mehrabian, A. (1971) *Silent Messages*. Belmont, CA: Wadsworth.

Morgan, G. (1997) *Images of Organization*. Thousand Oaks, CA: Sage Publications Inc.

Morgan, G. (1997) *Imagination: New Mindsets for Seeing, Organizing and Managing*. Thousand Oaks, CA: Sage Publications Inc.

Murray, B. (1998) 'Research reveals potential cause of youthful impulsiveness', *American Psychological Association Monitor* 29(8) August 1998, www.apa.org/monitor/aug98/youth.html, accessed 6 May 2007.

National Assembly for Wales (2001) *The Learning Country: A Paving Document*.

National Assembly for Wales (2004) *Learning Pathways 14–19 Guidance Circular No. 37/2004*

Nelson-Jones, R. (1992) *The Theory and Practice of Counselling Psychology*. London: Cassell Educational Ltd.

Norman, S. (2003) *Transforming Learning: Introducing SEAL Approaches*. London: Saffire Press.

O'Connor, J. and McDermott, I. (1997) *The Art of Systems Thinking: Essential Skills for Creativity and Problem solving*. London: Thorsons.

Paris, S. G. and Winograd, P. (1990) 'How metacognition can promote academic learning and instruction', pp.15–51, in Fly Jones, B. and Idol, L. (eds) *Dimensions of Thinking and Cognitive Instruction*. NJ: Lawrence Erlbaum.

Petty, G. (2004) *Teaching Today*, 3rd edn. Cheltenham: Nelson Thornes Ltd.

Pinker, S. (2002) *The Blank Slate: The Modern Denial of Human Nature*. London: Penguin Books.

Pinker, S. (2007) *The Stuff of Thought*. London: Allen Lane.

Pollard, A. (2008) *Reflective Teaching*, 3rd edn. London: Continuum International Publishing Group.

Reynolds, D. (2007) 'Why more of us are learning to love the advantages of the Welsh Bacc', *Western Mail* 27 September 2007.

Reynolds, D. (2008) 'Education must get up to speed to meet needs of a changing world', *Western Mail* 15 May 2008.

Riches, C. (1997) 'Communication in education management', pp. 165–74 in Crawford, M., Kydd, L. and Riches, C. (eds) *Leadership and Teams in Educational Management*. Buckingham: Open University Press.

Riddell, M. (2007) 'Be brave, Mr. Brown, in the classroom', *The Observer* 15 July 2007.

Rogers, C. and Freiberg, J. (1994) *Freedom to Learn*, 3rd edn. Upper Saddle River, NJ: Prentice Hall.

Ryan, J. A. (2007) 'Raising achievement with adolescents in secondary education – the school counsellors' perspective', *British Educational Research Journal* 33(4): 551–63.

Saunders, D. and Welsh Assembly Government (2008) *The Learning Coaches of Wales: Summary Document*. Welsh Assembly Government.

Scanlon, M. (2008) 'Evaluation of an alternative education provision for disengaged adolescents', unpublished Masters degree dissertation, University of Wales, Newport.

Senge, P. (1990) *The Fifth Discipline: The Art & Practice of the Learning Organization*. London: Century Business.

Shayer, M. (2003) 'Not just Piaget: not just Vygotsky, and certainly not Vygotsky as *alternative* to Piaget', *Learning and Instruction* 13: 465–85.

Smith, A. (1996) *Accelerated Learning in the Classroom*. Stafford: Network Educational Press.

Smith, M. K. (2002) 'Malcolm Knowles, informal adult education, self-direction and andragogy. The encyclopaedia of informal education', www.infed.org/thinkers/et-knowl.htm, accessed 8 August 2007.

Solomon, R. C. and Flores, F. (2001) *Building Trust: In Business, Politics, Relationships and Life*. New York: Oxford University Press Ltd.

Solomon, Y. and Rogers, C. (2001) 'Motivational patterns in disaffected school students: insights from pupil referral unit clients', *British Educational Research Journal* 27(3): 331–45.

Sternberg, R. J. (1997) *Thinking Styles*. Cambridge: Cambridge University Press.

Tarthang, Tulku (1977) *Gesture of Balance*. Berkeley, CA: Dharma Publishing.

Thies, A. P. (2003) 'Implications of neuroscience and neuropsychology for the Dunn and Dunn learning-style theory', in Dunn, R. and Griggs, S. (eds) *Synthesis of the Dunn and Dunn Learning Styles Model Research: Who, What, When, Where and so What – the Dunn and Dunn Learning Styles Model and its Theoretical Cornerstone*. New York: St John's University.

Thomas, W. (2005) *Coaching Solutions: Resource Book*. Stafford: Network Educational Press Ltd.

Thomas, W. and Smith, A. (2004) *Coaching Solutions: Practical Ways to Improve Performance in Education*. Stafford: Network Educational Press Ltd.

Tortoriello, T. R., Blatt, S. J. and DeWine, S. (1978) *Communications in the Organization: an Applied Approach*. New York: McGraw-Hill.

Turnbull, J. (2004) 'Educating for citizenship in Wales: challenges and opportunities', *The Welsh Journal of Education* 12(2): 65–82.

Turnbull, J. (2007) *9 Habits of Highly Effective Teachers*. London: Continuum International Publishing Group.

Turner, D. (2004) *Theory of Education*. London: Continuum.

UNESCO (1996) Learning: The Treasure Within. Report to UNESCO by the International Commission on Education for the 21st century. UNESCO Publishing.

Unicef (2006) *The State of the World's Children 2007: Executive Summary*.

van der Veer, R. and Valsiner, J. (1991) *Understanding Vygotsky: A Quest for Synthesis*. Oxford: Blackwell.

Vygotsky, L. (1978) *Mind in Society*. London: Harvard University Press.

Watson, J. B. and Rayner, R. (1920) 'Conditioned emotional reactions', *Journal of Experimental Psychology* 3: 1–14.

Watson, R. (1998) 'Rethinking readiness for learning' in Olson, D. R. and Torrance, N. (eds) *The Handbook of Education and Human Development*. Oxford: Blackwell Publishers Ltd.

Welsh Assembly Government (2008) *National Behaviour and Attendance Review* (NBAR) Report.

West-Burnham, J., Farrar, M. and Otero, G. (2007) *Schools and Communities:*

Working together to Transform Children's Lives. London: Network Continuum Education.

White, J. (1998) *Do Howard Gardner's Multiple Intelligences Add Up?* London: Institute of Education University of London.

White, S. (2006) *Intelligence, Destiny and Education: The Ideological Roots of Intelligence*. London: Routledge.

Whitmore, J. (2002) *Coaching for Performance: Growing People, Performance and Purpose*. London: Nicolas Brealey Publishing.

Wills, C. (1993) *The Runaway Brain: The Evolution of Human Uniqueness*. London: HarperCollins.

Wood, D. (1998) *How Children Think and Learn*, 2nd edn. Oxford: Blackwell Publishers Ltd.

Woolfolk Hoy, A. (2000) 'Educational psychology in teacher education', *Educational Psychologist* 35(4): 257–70.

Yandell, J. and Turvey, A. (2007) 'Standards or communities of practice? Competing models of workplace learning and development', *British Educational Research Journal* 33(4): 533–50.

Zemke, R. and Zemke, S. (1984) '30 Things we know for sure about adult learning', *Innovation Abstracts* VI(8): March 9.

Zimmerman, B. J., Bandura, A., and Martinez-Pons, M. (1992) 'Self-motivation for academic attainment: the role of self-efficacy beliefs and personal goal setting', *American Educational Research Journal* 29(3): 663–76.

Index

Hillary, Sir E. 95f.
Hopson, B. 174
Horne, T. 109, 111f.
Hough, P. 174
Howard's End 114
Hughes, M. 41, 45, 65, 84
humanistic model 16–17, 49

identity 43, 45, 128n
    as neuro-logical level 119–120, 131
impression management 31
incremental theory 27
instrumentality 28
integrity 87, 89, 101
intelligence 13, 35, 118, 137, 139
    and learning 21–22
    see also emotional intelligence
    see also multiple intelligences (MI)
interaction 14
interpersonal
    relations 141
    skills 34, 166
Intervention 11, 38, 40, 53, 55f., 56, 58, 62,

Jackson, P. Z. 6, 104, 106, 135, 137, 154
James, W. 162
Jensen, E. 108, 123, 137, 147, 150–151, 156,
    158, 167

Keller, H. 135
key skills 134, 177
Klenowski, V. 36n
Knight, S. 59, 60
Knights, A. 73n
Knowles, M. 46

labelling 34
Laborde, G. Z. 60, 80, 83f., 89
language
    skill 38
    as a theme of the CARE model 67–69,
        123–124, 146–147, 173–174
    verbal and non-verbal 14
Larrivee, B. 29, 30, 31, 59, 63
Leadbetter, C. 55, 69
leadership skills 184

learn how to learn 4, 26, 33, 141
learners
    for life 4
    independent 16, 129
    'lead' 58, 72f.
    needs of 4
learning 19–35, 130, 141
    active 164
    agreed vocabulary for 12
    and the brain 20–21
    and development 7
    and self-awareness 3
    and thinking 3
    as belief 27–28
    as change in behaviour 13
    as construction of meaning 14–16
    as emotional growth & development 16–17
    as metacognition 26–27, 107
    as reflection 29
    as stages of development 13–14
    barriers to 50, 51, 54
    capacity for 12
    controlled by the teacher 11
    different perspectives of 12
    four pillars of learning 33–34, 35, 36
    'identity' 4
    independent 12, 16, 26, 38, 42, 55–6, 65,
        66, 68, 70, 72f., 130, 147, 175, 177
    journey 3
    lifelong 9, 11, 157
    needs 5
    organization 30
    ownership of 15
    process of 102
    readiness 14, 64–65, 130f., 142–146,
        149
    relationship with 103
    social 31–33, 192
    styles 23–26, 35, 107, 127f., 143f., 190
        see also metacognition
        see also left brain/right brain
        see also visual, auditory, kinaesthetic
    theory 13, 17
    of young people 155
    see also personalized learning
    see also single and double loop learning

Rogers, Colin 8
Rogers, Will 95f.
Roosevelt, E. 95f., 135
Rose, C. 109
Rugby World Cup 78
Ryan, J. A. 54n, 109
Ryan, T. 6, 13, 20, 37

'salami' approach 163
Saunders, D. 18, 193, 194n
scaffolding 15, 181
Scanlon, M. 18, 181–182
Schon, D. 30
schooling 4–7, 19, 32, 68, 178
  and beliefs about intelligence 22
  state system of 16
  young people's experience of 143
  see also education – compared with
      schooling
self-actualization 16, 50
self-awareness 3, 12, 25, 59, 66, 188
self-belief 66, 78
self-confidence 189
self-control 23
self-esteem 45, 46, 90, 111f., 135, 138, 165,
    166, 176, 181, 192
self-efficacy 63–64, 72, 130f., 131–139, 152,
    155, 165, 192
self-motivation 66, 156–158
self-talk 147, 153, 163
Senge, P. 62–63
sensory acuity 83, 89, 101, 104, 114–116,
    123, 125f., 127f., 152f.,
Shakespeare, W. 3
Shayer, M. 14, 36n., 38, 58, 62, 65, 66, 73n,
    103
De Shazer, S. 101n
single and double loop learning 30–31
skills 4
  social 45, 56, 103
  social and emotional 192
  renaissance 4
  for work and life 4
  see also communication
  see also key skills
SMART 71

Smith, A. 20, 40, 92, 94, 101n, 128n,
    156
Smith, M. 54n
social modelling 132, 135–136, 140, 147,
    158, 168
social persuasion 132, 137–138
social roles 32
social skills *see* life skills
socio-economic disadvantage 11
Solomon, R. 61, 84, 85
Solomon, Y. 8
solution focus 7, 17, 44, 45, 54, 62, 63, 72,
    102f., 104–107, 118, 127, 143
Solution focused Brief Therapy 101n
Sorted Project 181–182
Sperry, R. 107
stability 17
state 61, 72, 83
  for coaching 93, 101
  emotional 101, 157
  for learning 61, 72f., 83
  management 61, 89–95
  physiological and emotional 132,
      138–139
  resourceful 61, 92, 93f., 122
Stenhouse Consulting 141, 153n
Sternberg, R. 24, 25, 26
stress 92, 95, 101, 153
stress management 176f.
stressor-response chain 139
student councils 158
study strategies 103

Tait, H. 25
teachers 26, 32, 40
teaching 19f.
  difference from coaching 37f., 40–42
  effective 25
  and learning as integrated processes 4
  styles 59
  traditional practice 14
teaching assistants 37
techniques 55
Teicher, M. 35
Ten Entitlements of Young People 69
Thinking 3